BESTSELLING
BOOK SERIES

Building Research Tools with Google™ For Dummies®

Cheat Sheet

Parts of Google

Google Part	URL	What It Is. . . .Where to Find Out More about It
Answers	http://answers.google.com	Name your own price to get questions answered by Google Answers researchers; browse thoughtful answers to questions for free. . . . See Chapter 6
Directory	http://directory.google.com	Google search tools running against information categorized and vetted by the Open Directory Project. . . . See Chapter 7
Google Desktop Search	http://desktop.google.com	Downloadable application that uses Google's tools to search the information on your desktop. . . . See Chapter 5
Google Scholar	http://scholar.google.com	Searches for scholarly literature. . . . See Chapter 1
Groups	http://groups.google.com	Lets you search Usenet groups for postings. . . . See Chapter 7
News Search	http://news.google.com	Lets you search for recent news items. . . . See Chapters 1 and 9

Selected Google Operators

See Chapters 4 and 5 for detailed explanations of how to use these operators.

Operator	What It Does	Example(s)
OR	Matches any term	*wireless device* OR *computer* returns pages with *wireless* and *device* or *computer*
+	Inclusion, includes words normally omitted	*Star Wars +I*
-	Exclusion, returns results that do not include the term	*virus - computer*
" "	Searches for entire phrase	*Hamlet "to be or not to be"*
*	Wildcard; matches any word	*"Do you know the way to" *￼*
~	Synonym, matches Web synonyms as well as the given term	*traffic ~data*
inanchor:	Term must appear in the anchor text of links to the page	*inanchor: deciduous*
intext:	Term must appear in text of a page	*intext:HTML, intitle:surf -inurl:internet*
intitle:	Term must appear in the page title	*intitle:1120, intitle:walmart -inurl:walmart*
inurl:	Term must appear in the URL	*inurl:CIA, intitle:Google -inurl:Google*
link:	Returns pages that link to a page	*link:www.researchbuzz.com*
phonebook:	Finds residential and business phone numbers	*phonebook: D Smith, NY*
site:	Restricts searches to a site or domain	*site:fbi.gov*

For Dummies: Bestselling Book Series for Beginners

Building Research Tools with Google™ For Dummies®

Cheat Sheet

Google Web APIs

API (Web method)	What It Does
doGetCachedPage	Returns a page from the Google cache
doGoogleSearch	Runs a query against the Google search engine
doSpellingSuggestion	Returns a spelling suggestion (if any)

doGoogleSearch Web API Arguments

Argument	What It Is Used for
key	Developer key.
query	Google search string (the most important parameter).
start	Zero-based integer value specifying the offset (where to start counting) when results are returned. To return results starting with the first result, this value should be 0.
maxResults	Number of results to return, integer value 1 through 10.
filter	Boolean (true or false) value that determines whether close results, and multiple results from the same Web site, are filtered out.
restrict	Usually left blank (with empty quotes, " "; can be used to restrict searchs to one of Google's four topics or to a country (see the API reference documentation for details).
safesearch	A Boolean (true or false) value that determines whether results will be filtered for adult content.
lr	Stands for *language restrict*; can be used to control the languages which are search result matches.
ie	Stands for *input encoding*; not used any more so all results are returned in UTF-8, and whatever you put in this argument is ignored, so you can just leave it blank with empty quotes (" ").
oe	Stands for *output encoding*; as with ie all results are returned in UTF-8, and this argument is ignored, so you can just leave it blank with empty quotes (" ").

Copyright © 2005 Wiley Publishing, Inc. All rights reserved.

Item 7809-X.

For more information about Wiley Publishing, call 1-800-762-2974.

For Dummies: Bestselling Book Series for Beginners

Building Research Tools with Google™

FOR DUMMIES®

by Harold Davis

WILEY

Wiley Publishing, Inc.

Building Research Tools with Google™ For Dummies®

Published by
Wiley Publishing, Inc.
111 River Street
Hoboken, NJ 07030-5774
www.wiley.com

Copyright © 2005 by Wiley Publishing, Inc., Indianapolis, Indiana

Published by Wiley Publishing, Inc., Indianapolis, Indiana

Published simultaneously in Canada

For general information on our other products and services, please contact our Customer Care Department within the U.S. at 800-762-2974, outside the U.S. at 317-572-3993, or fax 317-572-4002.

For technical support, please visit www.wiley.com/techsupport.

Wiley also publishes its books in a variety of electronic formats. Some content that appears in print may not be available in electronic books.

Library of Congress Control Number: 2005921594

ISBN-13: 978-0-7645-7809-0

ISBN-10: 0-7645-7809-X

Manufactured in the United States of America

10 9 8 7 6 5 4 3 2 1

1O/SR/QT/QV/IN

WILEY

About the Author

Harold Davis is a strategic technology consultant, hands-on computer programmer, and the author of more than 20 books.

In addition to his work as a writer, Harold has been a technology company executive, enterprise consultant, software developer, professional photographer, and a legal researcher.

He has earned a Bachelors Degree in Computer Science and Mathematics from New York University and a Juris Doctorate from Rutgers Law School, where he was an editor of the law review.

Harold lives with his wife, Phyllis Davis, who is also an author, and their three sons — Julian, Nicholas, and Mathew — in the hills of Berkeley, California. His three sons keep Harold pretty busy, but in his spare time he likes to garden, hike, and poke around the Internet looking for new and obscure research resources.

The address for Harold's personal Web site is www.bearhome.com. He is a co-founder of Braintique, a site that offers free Web content, located at www.braintique.com.

Dedication

For Mathew Gabriel Davis.

Author's Acknowledgments

Special thanks to Jeff Cogswell, Phyllis Davis, Nicole Haims, Melody Layne, and Matt Wagner, without whom this book would not have been possible.

Publisher's Acknowledgments

We're proud of this book; please send us your comments through our online registration form located at www.dummies.com/register/.

Some of the people who helped bring this book to market include the following:

Acquisitions, Editorial, and Media Development

Project Editor: Nicole Haims

Acquisitions Editor: Melody Layne

Technical Editor: Jeff Cogswell

Editorial Manager: Carol Sheehan

Media Development Manager: Laura VanWinkle

Media Development Supervisor: Richard Graves

Editorial Assistant: Amanda Foxworth

Cartoons: Rich Tennant (www.the5thwave.com)

Composition Services

Project Coordinator: Nancee Reeves

Layout and Graphics: Carl Byers, Andrea Dahl, Barry Offringa, Heather Ryan

Proofreaders: Leeann Harney, Jessica Kramer, Carl William Pierce, TECHBOOKS Production Services

Indexer: TECHBOOKS Production Services

Special Help
Karen Wickre, Senior Editor, Corporate Communications, Google, Inc.

Publishing and Editorial for Technology Dummies

Richard Swadley, Vice President and Executive Group Publisher

Andy Cummings, Vice President and Publisher

Mary Bednarek, Executive Acquisitions Director

Mary C. Corder, Editorial Director

Publishing for Consumer Dummies

Diane Graves Steele, Vice President and Publisher

Joyce Pepple, Acquisitions Director

Composition Services

Gerry Fahey, Vice President of Production Services

Debbie Stailey, Director of Composition Services

Contents at a Glance

Table of Contents

Introduction

1 can't think of any simple modifiers that describe Google.

I was going to say that Google is "a complex piece of software." Then I was going to describe it as "a research environment with many moving parts." And then finally I was going to use the phrase, "a way of life." Anyway, you probably already have a pretty good idea of what Google is, even if, like me, you don't find Google easy to describe simply.

However you might describe Google, no one doubts that it's a great tool for researchers. What you might not know is that significant resources are available within the Google family that few people know about. For one thing, Google provides access to its essential functionality with an XML-based SOAP Web service — called the Google APIs Web service, or simply the Google APIs.

About This Book

This book describes the different aspects of Google and provides the information you need to successfully

- ✔ Understand the various Google tools, and how they can help satisfy your research needs
- ✔ Use Google's custom search syntax to effectively find information
- ✔ Determine whether the information you need can be found through Google (and where to start looking for it if it cannot)
- ✔ Become a better researcher by learning tips, tricks, and techniques honed by top research professionals
- ✔ Learn how Google works, and what mechanisms it uses to respond to search queries
- ✔ Harness the power of the Google APIs to build your own research tools

If you want to understand how to become a better researcher, or how to use Google more effectively as a research tool, you've picked up the right book.

If you understand software development and are interested in writing applications that extend the functionality of Google using the Google Web APIs, this book has the information you need.

What You Shouldn't Read

I never tell anyone not to read anything (particularly if I've written it). Seriously, folks, this book is intended for a number of different kinds of readers, including

- People interested in using Google more effectively
- Those interested in research and the Internet
- Webmasters who want to better understand how Google works (perhaps so they know better how to organize their own Web sites)
- Researchers and reference librarians who would like to know how to better use the tools that Google makes available — and perhaps want to know how to best help others use those tools
- Programmers (or researchers with a programming background) who would like to use the Google Web APIs to extend and customize the functionality of Google, and create great research tools

Not of all of these readers (meaning you) have the same interests, needs, or background knowledge (although, of course, I hope every word I've written will be fascinating and enthralling to each and every one of you!). If you're not interested in a topic, just skip it.

I've written each chapter of this book so that it stands on its own. However, there are a few dependencies you should know about:

- Chapter 5, which explains advanced Google operators, probably won't make as much sense to you if you haven't already looked at Chapter 4, which covers the more basic Google operators.
- The case studies showing how to create applications with the Google APIs in Chapters 16–18 expect that you've at least had a look at the introductory materials explaining how the Google APIs Web service works in Chapters 13–15.

Also, if you're in a hurry, you can skip sidebars, which offer info that isn't crucial (but that is really interesting).

Foolish Assumptions

I assume that you are computer literate, that you know how to use your Web browser, and that you have fooled around a bit (or even a lot) with Google. I assume that you possess a deep curiosity about research, and that you have a general working knowledge of how things work on the Web.

Part IV of this book assumes that you already know basic programming. Specifically, I assume you know enough C# and Visual Studio .NET to understand how to use the Google Web APIs to create new search applications. Unfortunately, there's simply no space in this book to teach basic programming, object-oriented programming, or the .NET framework.

To best understand the code examples in this book, I assume that you can sight read C#, or at least quickly pick it up.

If you want to re-create and run the programs in this book, I assume that you have Visual Studio .NET up and running, and know your way around it.

You can use the Google APIs to create programs in any language that can work with SOAP-based Web services — and you'll find information to help you in the appendixes if you decide to work with either of two popular languages, Java or Visual Basic.

May I recommend some of my other books? If you've never programmed, and would like to learn how, I suggest picking up *Learn How to Program Using Any Web Browser* (2004, Apress).

If you have some programming under your belt, and want to understand C# better, please try my *Visual C# .Net Programming* (2002, Sybex).

A good source of information about Visual Basic .NET is my *Visual Basic .Net for Windows* (2003, Peachpit Press).

One of the best ways to learn about the Java language is to open up Sun Microsystems's New to Java site (Sun, after all, wrote the Java language). Its address is `http://java.sun.com/learning/new2java/`.

How This Book Is Organized

In the spirit of making the organizational concept behind this book more clear to you, my dear reader, here are brief descriptions of the parts of this book.

Part I: Getting Started with Google Research

This part explains the "who, what, where, when, and why" of Google and research on the Web. You can find out how and why Google is so useful and discover what kinds of information you can get out of Google. You'll also find out about lesser-known Google applications and functionalities that are useful to researchers.

Part II: Crafting Queries and Using the Google Research Tools

The chapters in Part II show you how to become a power Google user. Chapters 4 and 5 are concerned with using operators to construct effective queries. (You need to know this material later if you want to build applications that query Google.) The rest of Part II focuses on Google applications in addition to the plain-vanilla Web search.

Part III: Building Valuable Research Content

In this part, I help you make more effective use of the larger Web for your research forays. I explain the steps you need to take to become a more efficient researcher and show you in detail some of the underlying mechanisms of Google and the Web. You also learn some the best and most effective ways to present research results.

Part IV: Building Research Tools Using the Google APIs

Part IV explains what the Google APIs are and how to use them, and shows you how to obtain a Google developer key and download the Google software development kit (SDK). You learn how to work with the `GoogleSearch` WSDL file, and program with the Google APIs Web service. The information in this part shows you how to build your own custom advanced search forms, how to track keyword trends over time, and much more. You need to have a background in programming to get the most out of this part.

Part V: The Part of Tens

I've always thought that the Part of Tens is one of the most fun parts of any *For Dummies* book, and, keeping with tradition, I've tried to make this part as much fun and useful as possible. Chapter 19 shows you Google-centric research resources on the Web. Chapter 20 shows you research tools that have been written using the Google Web APIs. You can use these tools alone or simply admire (dare I say oogle, er, Google) them as examples of what can be done using the Google APIs when programmers apply a little imagination, creativity, and grit.

Part VI: Appendixes

The appendixes to this book provide information about what you get when you download the Google software development kit (SDK), and help with creating Google Web API applications using Java or Visual Basic.

Icons Used in This Book

The icons used in this book are meant to easily and quickly help you get to the information that is most important as you maneuver through this book.

The Tip icon decorates information that is quick, dirty, and useful — meaning you can follow the advice in the tip and get results right away!

I use the Remember icon when it's important to recall some underlying fact or concept but easy to forget it (perhaps because it was explained some pages back).

The Technical Stuff icon is used to designate deep "propeller head" information that you may want to skim over — or skip entirely. I only use this icon when info gets so technical that only the truly geeky will enjoy it. In Part IV, the software development information never really stops being technical.

The Warning icon is used to help save you from yourself and stop you from doing something really, really bad. There's not too much you can do with Google that's really bad — except perhaps finding someone else's material on the Web, and using it without permission. So the Warning icon isn't used that much in this book.

Conventions Used in This Book

I'm often asked, "Why be conventional?" Well, maybe, once or twice I've been asked that question. In the context of this book, the answer is: "for the sake of clarity."

Conventions are used for consistency, so that you'll know what you are looking at. There are a few conventions in this book:

- Web addresses, or URLs, are reproduced in a special font:

  `www.google.com`

- Google search phrases and operators, programming tags, elements,
  arrays, and filenames also use the special font, like this:

  Use the `related:` operator to find pages that are similar.

  The `txtDevKey` control stores the developer key.

- Search term examples are italicized, like this: *ambidextrous armadillo.*

- If I am telling you that you should enter a search term exactly as I have put
  it in the book, the term appears in **bold** (rather than italics), like this: Type
  AND between two search terms to have Google search for both terms.

- I use a special font for code, and some code listings appear offset from
  the rest of the text:

```
Google.GoogleSearchResult r = s.doGoogleSearch
    (txtDevKey.Text, txtKeywords.Text, 0, 1 , false, "",
     false, "", "", "");
```

Where to Go from Here

What am I, your mother? How can I tell you where to go from here? Like most
things in life, it's up to you. (But when you make up your mind where you're
going, be sure to bring a sweater.)

You certainly don't have to read this book in order, but if you're relatively
new to Google, start with Chapter 1. If you're a more advanced user, check
out Chapters 4 and 5 and move directly to Parts II and III. If you are a software
developer, for gosh darn's sake, proceed to Part IV and build an application
that uses the Google Web APIs. Building applications is what it means to be a
software developer, after all.

You don't have to retype by hand the source code explained in this book.
If you visit the special companion Web site I've set up for this book, `www.`
`braintique.com/research/`, you'll find all the source code for the examples in this book ready for you to download and play with. In addition, you'll
find the compiled applications from the book ready for you to try out, and
links to many of the online resources mentioned in the book.

Wherever you go and whatever you do, may your journey be a good one. And,
by the way, drop me a line from time to time and let me know how it's going.
I can't promise to answer every e-mail, but I would be glad to hear from you
at the special e-mail address I have set up for this book: `research_google@`
`bearhome.com`.

Part I
Getting Started with Google Research

The 5th Wave   By Rich Tennant

RESEARCH
SERVICE
.50¢ – Min

In this part. . .

Pity the researchers of yester-year! They had to trudge through rain and snow and cross barren deserts, vast forests, and forbidding mountains to their local library. After this incredible journey, all too often the information they needed was not available locally, and they had to start over — or worse yet, rely on inter-library loans!

In this part, I show you Google from the perspective of a researcher, explain how Google fits in with the rest of the Web, and introduce the topic of building tools that automate researching.

Chapter 1 explains the kinds of search terms you can use with Google, shows you the parts of Google, and explains how to install and use the wonderful Google Toolbar.

Chapter 2 shows you how to validate Web research results and explains search engine alternatives to Google that may be helpful for some kinds of research.

Chapter 3 explains how to deliver research results and tells you about various ways to create your own custom software to build research tools that use Google.

Chapter 1

Googling the World

. . . .

In This Chapter

▶ Searching with Google

▶ Searching with a number

▶ Using Google shortcuts

▶ The parts of Google

▶ Downloading and using the Google Toolbar

. . . .

*H*ow do you easily find information about anything (or anyone)? You "google" it (or them) using Google's Web search. For many (if not most) people, the Google Web search engine is the information gateway to the Web (and the world).

You probably know that it's easy to enter almost any words or names in the Google Web search engine and get useful search results back. But you may not know that you can also enter many specialized numbers into Google's Web search box — such as shipment tracking numbers, product codes, and more — and get useful results. In this chapter, I tell you about some of the specialized information you can request from Google, how to use Google shortcuts to get information about stocks and travel, and how to use Google's wonderful "secret" calculator.

Google is the world's biggest one-stop shopping mall for finding information on the Web. Most likely, you already know about — and have used — Google's Web search functions. But you may not know about some of the other "shops" that are part of the Google Web information mall. In this chapter, I list many of the hidden parts of Google — including Google Answers, Google Directory, Google News, and Google Scholar — and tell you where in this book you can find more information about each specific part of Google.

Last, but hardly least, the Google Toolbar is a wonderful add-on to Internet Explorer that makes using Google more efficient and fun. In this chapter, I show you how to download and install the Google Toolbar, and explain its features to you.

Searching the Web with Google

To open the Google Web search window, which is also Google's home page, enter the *URL* (Uniform Resource Locator), or Web address, www.google.com, in your Web browser (such as Microsoft Internet Explorer).

When the Google home page appears, you see the familiar, simple, uncluttered window shown in Figure 1-1.

Figure 1-1:
The familiar Google Web search form is a simple way to find out about almost anything.

To search the Web with Google, enter your search terms in the text box. Click the Google Search button. The results of Google's search — a list of pages and their associated Web links — opens in your Web browser (usually in an amazingly short amount of time). For more information about what you find on a Google results page, and how to make the most of it, see Chapter 4.

If you click the I'm Feeling Lucky button instead of the Google Search button, the first result (the result at the top of the list that the Google Web search would otherwise spit out) automatically opens in your browser. This option can save time (by skipping the Google results page with its links) — but, of course, is a time-waster if the first result does not have the information you're looking for.

The vast majority of searches that you conduct with Google aren't fancy. You have done dozens, hundreds, maybe even thousands of them already. You just enter some words in the Google search box, separating each word with spaces. For a great many uses, this kind of "keep it simple" Google search is good enough.

The words entered for a Google search are sometimes called *keywords* or *search terms*. All the words in a search together are called a *search phrase* or *query*.

Researchers often need to search with greater precision than a simple keyword search allows. In Chapters 4 and 5, I explain how to use Google's *query language,* which strings together Google *operators* with keywords, to craft powerful and precise searches.

Searching using Google's rules

Even with simple Google keyword searches, there are some basic rules Google follows that you need to know about to get more out of your searches:

- ✔ Google searches for all words (well, most words — see the next bullet) in a simple query. ***Example:*** *midwest blizzard* yields different results than *moscow blizzard.*

- ✔ Google ignores many common words — such as *and, for,* and *the* — also called *stop words* (see Chapter 4 for more information), and most punctuation. ***Example:*** A search for *to be or not to be* does not provide meaningful results (such as a link to Hamlet's famous soliloquy) because *to, be,* and *or* are all stop words. In effect, this search is the same as searching for the word *not.*

- ✔ Google finds results anywhere in a document, not just in its text (for example, within the HTML title of a page). ***Example:*** Search for *organic farm* and Sun Organic Farm appears near the top of the search results list because of its Web address (www.sunorganic.com) and title, Sun Organic Farm.

- ✔ Google cares about word order: The first word is the most important in a search, and so on, reading left to right. ***Example:*** Just switch the word order to *farm organic* and it's a whole new search.

- ✔ Google returns pages ordered by *PageRank,* a measure that Google uses to gauge a page's popularity (see Chapter 2 and Chapter 11 for more information about how PageRank is calculated). ***Example:*** Search for *music* and you won't be surprised to find MTV near the top of the result set, but you will be surprised if your garage band's Web page is. You're not famous . . . yet.

- ✔ Proximity matters: If the words in your search are close together in a result, that result will be returned before results where they are not close together. ***Example:*** The search *moscow birthday* leads to different results than *birthday moscow* (the results of the first search are centered around the city of Moscow and happen to have birthday in them, while the results of the second search are pages about birthdays — such as Michelangelo's — that for one reason or another happen to also include a reference to Moscow).

- ✔ Google is case-insensitive: Google does not care about capitalization. ***Example:*** *moscow* and *Moscow* are the same thing (er, place) to Google.

- ✔ Simple Google searches are limited to ten keywords.

✔ Google finds its results depending on words that occur in Web pages (and that match your search words), not by analyzing your search phrase for its meaning. See the section, "Searching for words, not meaning," for more information.

Searching for words, not meaning

When Google pursues simple searches, it looks for word occurrences, not meaning. Although this point is simple, it is probably both the most subtle and the most important for getting good search results. You need to think about how words are likely to be used in Web pages.

For example, a search for *hello world* in Google might seem likely to produce results pointing to pages with information about spiritualism, ecology, and kids' programs. But if you are a programmer, or have ever learned a programming language, you'll probably know that it's a common custom to write an introductory program that displays the phrase "Hello World." Most of the results for a *hello world* search link to pages about programming, programming languages, and learning to program.

If you want to search for information about introductory programming, the query *hello world* might be a good way to go about it because on real-world Web pages the word "hello" and the word "world" usually appear in proximity in pages about introductory programs.

Effectively searching

Your simple Google searches can be highly effective, but they will probably work better if you follow these suggestions:

✔ **Be specific:** Targeted keywords work better than more general keywords (so the more you learn about a topic, the more likely you are to create successively more effective searches). For example, if you are looking for information about environmental impact statements in Alameda County, California, a search for *environmental impact alameda county ca* gives you much better information than a search for *environment northern ca*.

✔ **Use both singular and plural forms of words:** To Google, singular and plural forms of words are different words. You may need to try both singular and plural forms in successive searches. For example, if you are interested in monks and medieval music, a search for *monk polyphony* yields different results than a search for *monks polyphony* (so you should run both searches for the most useful results). You can run both searches together by combining the single and plural forms, for example, *monk monks polyphony*.

✔ **Use distinctive and important keywords:** If you can think of an unusual word that will most likely appear on most pages with information you are interested in, then you are most of the way to an effective, but simple, Google search. For example, if you are looking for material with information about building software that customizes Google, the search term *google apis web service* probably works well — better than *program google.*

Refining your search

One of the biggest problems with Google searches is sifting through the large number of results that are often returned. Many of these results are not what you are looking for.

There are several easy ways to refine a simple Google search. These techniques yield essentially comparable results. You can

✔ Add words to an existing query

✔ Use Google's Search Within Results feature

To add words to an existing search, first run the initial query, for example, *hello world.*

As I explain earlier, in "Searching for words, not meaning," a search for the phrase *hello world* might be useful if you are looking for introductory information about programming languages. But that doesn't mean that you'll *only* end up with results about programming — so such a restriction might be very helpful, seeing as how the last time I did this search, Google yielded some 16 million results.

You can refine your search so that you only find material about programming languages. Scroll to the bottom of the first Google results page and you see the Google search box with the search words *hello world* already in it. You can add the terms *programming language* immediately after the original search terms and click the Search button (see Figure 1-2). A new, refined, results page displays.

Figure 1-2:
You can add terms to the terms of an existing search.

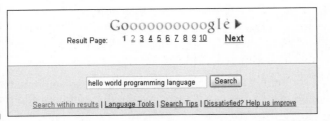

Goooooooooogle ▶

Result Page: 1 2 3 4 5 6 7 8 9 10   **Next**

| hello world programming language | Search |

Search within results | Language Tools | Search Tips | Dissatisfied? Help us improve

The Google search box, with the existing search terms already in it, also appears at the top of each search results page.

Alternatively, on a Google results page, you can click the <u>Search within results</u> link. This link appears at the bottom of each Google search results page (refer to Figure 1-2).

When you click the <u>Search within results</u> link, the Google Search Within Results window, shown in Figure 1-3, opens.

Figure 1-3: When you search within results, this window appears.

In the Search Within Results window, you can add the terms, such as *programming language,* that you want to use to refine your search. Google searches for the new term (in this case, *programming language*), but only within the results for the previous search *(hello world).*

Number searches

We live in a world in which things — and even people, eek! — are often identified by numbers. This makes it a gosh darn good thing that you can enter most of these numbers in Google and get meaningful results.

Google provides a shorthand way to search for a numerical range. For example, a search for *1066. . .1099* returns results for all numbers between 1066 and 1099. You can use numerical range matching if you are sure of most of a number, but not all of it; for example, if you know the first nine digits of a number, but not the last three digits.

You may be scratching your head at this point because you're not aware of all the meaningful results you can get when you enter numbers into the Google search box.

A "number" might be a mixed combination of numbers and letters used to identify something.

Some numbers you can search for include

- ✔ Airplane registration numbers
- ✔ Area codes
- ✔ FCC (Federal Communication Commission) call signs used as station identifiers; for example, the ham radio call sign KD7KH
- ✔ ISBN numbers, used to identify books; for example, 0-7645-7809-X
- ✔ Patent numbers; for example, 6285999
- ✔ Phone numbers, if you do a reverse phonebook lookup (providing the name and address associated with a number) (See Chapter 5 for more information about research that uses telephone information.)
- ✔ Product codes that are manufacturer specific
- ✔ Tracking numbers for shipments from Federal Express, United Parcel Service, and United States Postal Service
- ✔ UPCs (Universal Product Codes) used to identify a product
- ✔ VINs (Vehicle Identification Numbers)
- ✔ Zip codes
- ✔ Almost any kind of number used as an identifier

When you enter any of these types of identification numbers in Google, you may see a typical search results page with links that provide information using the number. Sometimes, however, you may see a special search results page — for example, if you search for a Federal Express shipping number, a page with a <u>Track FedEx package XXXXXXXXX</u> link appears. Clicking the link opens the Federal Express page used for tracking that package.

Google shortcuts

Google provides a number of helpful shortcuts that you can use to easily find a wide array of information. In this section, I tell you about three of these shortcut techniques. I show you how to use Google to

- ✔ Perform simple and complex calculations
- ✔ Find information about any publicly traded stock
- ✔ Get travel information

The Google calculator

The Google calculator does arithmetic for you, and also performs more complex calculations. You just have to use the syntax specified by Google — see `www.google.com/help/calculator.html` for complete information about using the calculator — and enter your expression for calculation.

For example, enter **42*12** in the Google box and click the Search button. The answer (504) appears on the results page, along with a link so that you can learn more about the calculator. Another link appears to search for the query *42 * 12,* just in case you really meant to search rather than to calculate.

Enter the expression **2*pi*26** into the Google search box and click the Search button. This expression evaluates to 163.362818 (which is the circumference of a circle with a radius of 26).

The Google calculator can do much more! Suppose you want to find the value of the famous mathematical expression $e\^(i\ pi)+1$. If you enter this expression in Google and click Search, you'll find that it evaluates to 0, as you can see in Figure 1-4.

To find out more about the expression shown in Figure 1-4, search Google for *Euler's Identity* or click the link that lets you search for more information about the expression $e\^(i\ pi)+1$.

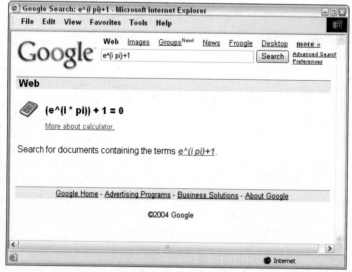

Figure 1-4:
The Google calculator can find the value of some pretty complicated expressions.

Finding out about stocks

To find out about a publicly traded stock, enter the word **stock**, followed by a colon, followed by the ticker symbol for the company (all without spaces) in the Google box and click Search. For example:

```
stock:goog
```

If you don't know the ticker symbol for a company, you can usually find it by searching for all (or part) of the company name, followed by the word *ticker,* for example:

```
Google ticker
```

When you use the `stock:` operator with a valid stock ticker symbol, the first link on the Google results page that appears is a <u>Stock quotes</u> link. Click this link to open a framed, tabbed page of financial and securities information. Tabs with information are provided by Yahoo! Finance, The Motley Fool, MSN MoneyCentral, and ClearStation.

Getting travel information

Finding travel information quickly is simple when you use the Google search box. Here are a couple of the travel shortcuts provided by Google:

- **Airport code:** Enter a three letter airport code followed by the word *airport* to find a great deal of information about the airport. For example, *oak airport* yields information about Metropolitan Oakland International Airport. The first link on the results page when you conduct this type of search is to the Federal Aviation Administration's travel conditions page, which provides local weather conditions for the airport.

- **Airline search:** If you enter the name of an airline, followed by a flight number — for example, *United 511* — the results include links to information about the flight status.

Getting local information

Google also provides some tools to help you find specific local information.

If you add a zip code (or city) after your other search terms, the first few results Google returns are local results within the zip code (or city) you specified. These local results are indicated with a little compass icon (see Figure 1-5). A compass icon appears at the top-left side of the search results page; click it if you want to see more local results.

Alternatively, you can use the Google Local service by visiting the URL `http://local.google.com`. Although it has been around a while, the Google Local service is still technically in beta, meaning it has not been "officially" launched yet.

With the Google Local page open, you can enter a local search term such as *chinese restaurant* and a location such as *10025* (you can enter the name of a city and state, or you can enter the zip code). Click the Search button. Google returns numerous local listings, along with a map showing locations and some other relevant local information (see Figure 1-6).

Figure 1-5: Local results are marked with a compass icon.

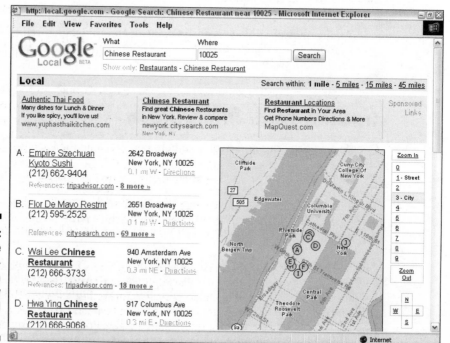

Figure 1-6: The Google Local service is a good way to get local information.

Mining Google for Information

Google has a lot more going on than meets the eye. The simple, elegant exterior of the Google search form is the visible tip of a vast submerged iceberg.

You can get beneath the Google surface with relative ease. For example, to open the Google Advanced Search, which is partially shown in Figure 1-7, simply click the Advanced Search link on the Google home page, or open the URL www.google.com/advanced_search in your browser.

I explain how to use the Google Advanced Search window, which is a great tool for refining your searches, in Chapter 4.

In addition to the Google Advanced Search window, here are some other hidden parts of Google that provide valuable information and/or tools for researchers:

- ✔ **Google Answers:** Google Answers is a service that allows users to name their own price to get research questions answered. Browsing questions and answers is free — and very informative — but you need a Google account to post a question. You can open Google Answers at www. answers.google.com. I explain how Google Answers works in Chapter 6.

- ✔ **Google Directory:** Google Directory uses the categorization scheme and sites selected by the Open Directory Project to find information that has been vetted by experts. The URL for Google Directory is http://directory.google.com; you can find out more about Google Directory in Chapter 7.

- ✔ **Google Groups:** Google Groups lets you search through millions of bulletin board posts made on every conceivable subject (Google Groups are the very same Usenet Groups that predate the Web, only with a new name). In its most recent version, Google has extended Google Groups, adding tools and group list management features that go beyond anything available through the old Usenet. You can find Google Groups at http://groups.google.com. I explain Google Groups in Chapter 7.

- ✔ **Google Images:** Google Images lets you search for pictures on the Web. This service has some surprising uses for researchers. You can open the Google Image Search at www.google.com/imghp?hl=en. For more information, see Chapter 8.

- ✔ **Google Language Tools:** Google Language Tools lets you choose a geographic area to search, translate text, and translate Web pages by providing a URL. You can also choose another language for the Google interface (such as the Search button) if English isn't your native language or if you just want to read everything in, say, Portuguese. You can open Google Language Tools at www.google.com/language_tools?hl=en to find out more about the translation tools provided in Chapter 13.

✔ **Google News:** Google News Search provides links to recent news items. If you have a Google account, you can set up automated search results on a topic and have the results e-mailed to you. You can open Google News at `http://news.google.com`. For more information, see Chapter 9.

✔ **Google Scholar:** Google Scholar lets you search for academic, peer-reviewed articles and citations. You can open Google Scholar at `http://scholar.google.com`. Google Scholar is currently in beta. I've included information about it here because scholarly materials are potentially extremely important to some kinds of research.

✔ **Google Video:** A pilot program that lets you search the transcripts of selected television shows displays the transcripts and still photographs. See `http://video.google.com` for more information.

In addition, Google has recently announced the digitization of major portions of research libraries including Harvard, the University of Michigan, Oxford, Stanford, and the New York Public Library. As this progresses, resources from the libraries will be available through Google.

Many parts of Google can be opened directly from the Google home page. Visit the Google Services page by clicking the <u>More</u> link on the Google home page. Links to all the items listed here appear on this page.

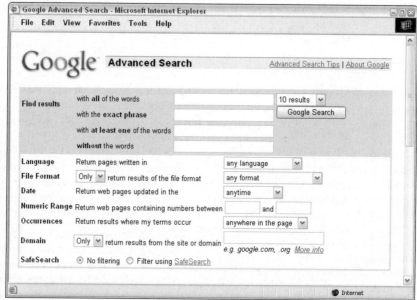

Figure 1-7:
The Google
Advanced
Search
window
lets you
refine your
searches.

Using Google Efficiently with the Google Toolbar

If you download and install the Google Toolbar, Google becomes part of Microsoft Internet Explorer. You can use the Google Toolbar to perform a Google Web search — no matter what Web page is currently open.

Understanding privacy and security issues

A couple of things about the way the Google Toolbar works raise some privacy and security concerns.

The privacy concern is primarily that the Google Toolbar sends anonymous information (such as the URLs of sites you visit as a result of your searches) back to Google headquarters. The purpose of this is to enable Google to provide you with information about a page such as its relative PageRank, Open Directory Project category, and more. This information is sent back to Google when you enable the advanced features during the Google Toolbar installation process. You'll know the advanced features are enabled if you see the PageRank icon as part of your Google Toolbar.

The security concern is primarily that the personal information you provide to the Google Toolbar to use for its AutoFill feature is potentially susceptible to misuse by unscrupulous Web sites. This is a real issue if you choose to provide credit card numbers for the AutoFill feature (I recommend that you do not). This information does not travel to Google — it is encrypted and protected with a password you choose on your own computer. However, an unscrupulous Web site could conceivably make use of hidden form fields to abuse the AutoFill feature and extract your credit card information.

Personally, I'm not too worried about the privacy issue, and suggest you make the most of the Google Toolbar by enabling the advanced features. However, if you do choose to use the AutoFill feature, and particularly if you provide sensitive information such as credit card numbers, you can monitor exactly what information is being passed to a Web site by holding down the Shift key when you click the AutoFill button.

To learn more about AutoFill security issues, look at the "Is AutoFill secure?" topic in Google Toolbar's Help section. To find this topic, open the Toolbar Help page (by choosing Help from the Toolbar's Google button menu, or opening www. google.com/support/toolbar in your browser). Next, click the Is AutoFill secure? link.

One other thing — the Google Toolbar automatically updates itself. On the whole, this is a very good thing because it means that you are always working with the most recent version of the software without the need for any intervention on your part. However, this feature does require that you trust the integrity of the Google software update process — something I think you can do.

If you're concerned about how Google handles and protects the information you provide, see http://toolbar.google.com/privacy. html, or click the Google button on the Toolbar and choose Help⇨Privacy Information.

The Google Toolbar also provides some very useful additional functionality — for example, it blocks pop-up windows. You can also get some information using the Google Toolbar that it is quite difficult to get in any other way. For example, the relative PageRank of a Web page appears on the Google Toolbar. (PageRank is explained in Chapter 2 and Chapter 11.) I use the Google Toolbar all the time, and once you try it I'm sure you will as well.

You can activate or deactivate the Google Toolbar in Internet Explorer by selecting or deselecting it from Internet Explorer's View⇨Toolbars menu or by right-clicking any toolbar and selecting or deselecting the Google Toolbar option in the context-sensitive menu that appears.

Downloading and installing the Google Toolbar

The Google Toolbar requires Microsoft Windows (Windows 95/98/ME/NT/ 2000/XP) and Microsoft Internet Explorer (version 5.0 or later).

To download and install the Google Toolbar, follow these steps:

1. **Visit** `http://toolbar.google.com`.

   The Google home page opens.

   From the Google home page you can click the More link to open the Google Services and Google Tools page. Click the Google Toolbar link (found towards the bottom of the page) to get to the Google Toolbar page.

2. **Click the Download Google Toolbar button.**

3. **When the File Download window opens, click the Run (or Open) button.**

   The Google Toolbar Installer opens.

4. **Click the Agree button to accept the Terms and Conditions agreement.**

5. **In the Choose Your Configuration panel of the installer, choose to enable advanced features or disable advanced features.**

   Essentially, the advanced features involved let Google show you information about Web pages you visit, such as their relative PageRank.

   In order to enable this feature, the Google Toolbar must gather and send anonymous information (the URLs of the sites you visit) back to Google, a fact that has raised some privacy concerns among the overly cautious. I recommend that you enable this feature (but see the sidebar "Understanding privacy and security issues" for more information).

6. **In the Your Final Instructions panel, choose a Google site to use for your searches and choose whether or not to use Google as the default browser search engine.**

   For example, if you are based in Greece, you might want to use the Greek version of Google, `google.com.gr`, for your searches rather than the default Google.com.

7. **Click the Next button to complete the installation process.**

Want the functionality of the Google Toolbar outside of a Web browser? Download the Google Deskbar from `http://deskbar.google.com/`. The Deskbar lets you search with Google right from your Windows taskbar.

Getting to know all the parts of the Google Toolbar

The Google Toolbar is extremely flexible, with many different configuration options possible depending on how you like to use Google. I urge you to download and install the toolbar right away, play with the options, and find out how you like best to use it.

See "Setting Google Toolbar options" to find out how to make as many changes as your heart desires.

One button on the toolbar is the AutoFill button. When you click the AutoFill button, personal information you have supplied is automatically filled into the appropriate fields in Web forms.

Figure 1-8 shows you the Google Toolbar in its default configuration, assuming that advanced features are enabled.

The most useful feature of the Google Toolbar is its ability to search the Web with any Web page open in your browser. To search the Web, enter your Google search query in the Search window and click the Search Web button.

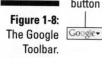

Figure 1-8:
The Google
Toolbar.

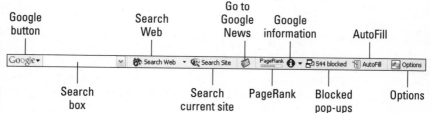

What if you don't run Internet Explorer?

If Internet Explorer is not your browser of choice, are you out of luck when it comes to the nifty features of the Google Toolbar? Google says that it is considering adding a toolbar for other browsers such as the Mozilla Project's popular Firefox and Netscape Navigator, but until Google makes good on this offer, you have to use other options to customize Google's functionality. Good news: That's not so hard to do!

If you download and install the Google Deskbar from `http://deskbar.google.com/` you can get much of the functionality of the Google Toolbar — but not, of course, in the context of a Web browser.

Here are some other options (in case you are not running Internet Explorer on Windows):

✔ If your browser of choice is Firefox — and a good choice it is! — you can download the Googlebar from `http://googlebar.mozdev.org/`. The Googlebar is a third-party product, not associated with Google, that emulates most of the functionality of the Google Toolbar, and it was built specifically for Firefox. You can run the Googlebar on any operating system supported by Firefox, including Windows, Linux, and the Mac OS.

✔ If you are using Netscape Navigator (either Mac or Windows), you can add Google Browser Buttons to your browser to pick up much of the functionality of the Google Toolbar. See `www.google.com/options/buttons.html` for more information and to get started with Google Browser Buttons. (This feature also works if you're using Internet Explorer on a Mac.)

✔ The Opera browser comes with many of the Google Toolbar features already built in. See `www.opera.com/features/` for more information about Opera's features.

✔ Many of the Google Toolbar features are already implemented in Apple's Safari browser for the Mac. See `www.apple.com/safari/` for more information.

The Google button

The Google button provides access to a wide variety of the parts of Google, including

✔ The Google home page

✔ Google Answers

✔ Google Groups

✔ Google Images

✔ Google Language Tools

✔ Google News

You can also use the Google button to open the Help information associated with the Google Toolbar.

The Search Web drop-down list

The Search Web drop-down list provides access to a number of Google features and parts, including (but not limited to) the following options:

- ✔ Search Current Site
- ✔ I'm Feeling Lucky (returns the single highest-ranked search result)
- ✔ Google Images
- ✔ Google Groups
- ✔ Dictionary

To use this button, type your search query in the search window, and then click the drop-down list arrow and choose the type of search you would like to perform.

The Google Information drop-down list

The Google Information drop-down list provides Google information and services related to a page, including

- ✔ The cached version of the page
- ✔ Similar pages (same as using the `related:` operator)
- ✔ Back links to a page (same as using the `link:` operator)
- ✔ Translation of a page into English

Setting Google Toolbar options

To change the appearance of Google Toolbar buttons, open the Google Toolbar Options dialog box, shown in Figure 1-9, by clicking the Options button on the Google Toolbar. Alternatively, you can choose Options from the Google drop-down menu.

The Options tab of the Toolbar Options dialog box lets you enable or disable the most important Google Toolbar features. The More tab of the dialog box lets you choose which buttons to display on the Toolbar. The AutoFill tab is used to supply personal information for use with the Google Toolbar's AutoFill feature, and to add credit card information, should you choose to do so.

Supplying personal information — particularly credit card numbers — for the use of the AutoFill feature poses a security risk. Please read the "Understanding privacy and security issues" sidebar before using this feature.

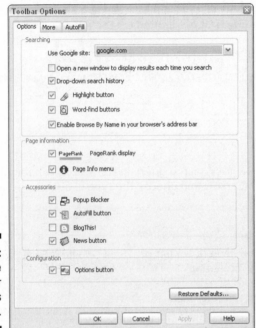

Figure 1-9:
The Google
Toolbar
Options
dialog box.

Chapter 2

Researching with Google and the Web

In This Chapter

▶ Evaluating the credibility of information on the Web

▶ Searching with engines other than Google

▶ Understanding search engine optimization

*R*esearchers are like others who use Google to find information, only a little more so! This chapter provides information you need to think like a researcher, including tips about how to

✔ Learn to carefully and thoroughly validate research results for accuracy.

✔ Cultivate understanding of the mechanisms that make Google function so that you can use Google better.

✔ Find sources for information (other search engines and information repositories) for those times when Google just doesn't provide the information you need.

In the world of software development, before you can automate a process by building a tool that performs the process, you need to be very clear about how to do the process manually. In the spirit of software development, this chapter helps you become a better researcher and points you to more resources about researching so that when the time comes, you will be able to build better research tools.

Validating Results on the Web

When you *validate* research results from a Google Web search, your goal is to determine the credibility of the information you've discovered.

Evaluating the credibility of a Web page, like any complex skill, is part art and part science.

The most important thing you can do when assessing credibility of information is start with a skeptical frame of mind.

Asking the following questions will help you decide if information you've found is, indeed, credible:

- ✔ Is the information published by a reputable source?

- ✔ Does the publisher of the page have a vested interest (particularly an undisclosed vested interest) in the subject of the information? For example, pollution statistics from a Web site called People For the Abolition of Automobiles might be skewed, just as pollution results presented by the MGGA (Manufacturers of Gas Guzzlers Association) may also be biased.

  Just because a source of information appears to have a bias doesn't mean that the information is useless. You just need to be aware of the bias as you compile search results so that you don't accept opinions as if they are facts.

- ✔ Is the Web page (and its parent site) internally consistent and put together carefully? Sites that are sloppy, and contain broken links and misspellings, are probably not good research sources. Ditto if the source contradicts itself or uses faulty logic.

- ✔ Does the page contain strident pop-up ads or adult material? This is not a good sign.

- ✔ Are purported "facts" on a page, particularly if they are seemingly unlikely, given attribution (via a hyperlink, or perhaps by referring to a book)?

- ✔ If the page contains information about when it was updated, is it fresh or stale?

Just because something appears in writing, or on a Web page, doesn't mean it is true. You can use the questions in this section as a starting place towards evaluating the information on a Web page, and you should always evaluate credibility carefully before giving any weight to the information on a Web page.

It's often revealing to take a fact or opinion offered on a Web site and use it as the basis for a Google search to see what others think of it.

Learning about Google

As a researcher, particularly one reading this book, you work with Google a lot. In life, it's good to know as much as you can about the technology (and people) you work with.

The best primary source for information about Google is the About Google page, `www.google.com/about.html`, which provides links to all sorts of information about Google.

The Google Blog, `www.google.com/googleblog/`, is a great place to keep up with current happenings at Google.

The Google Corporate Information site, `www.google.com/corporate/`, provides detailed information about Google the company.

Of course, you can always google Google by entering **google** as a search term in the Google Web search engine (this yields lots of interesting results).

Not directly about Google, but more about how users use Google (which may in the end come down to the same thing), is the Google Zeitgeist (or "spirit of the times" page), `www.google.com/press/zeitgeist.html`, which tracks how Google is used to search on an ad-hoc basis. (See Chapter 18 for more information about the Zeitgeist page and its relevancy for researchers.)

Google has indexed billions of Web pages. You can probably find support for almost any proposition, however outlandish it is, among these pages.

For more information about evaluating the credibility of Web sources, see Chapter 11.

Rumors fly quickly around cyberspace, and knowing whether the hot tip you saw on a Web site (or in an e-mail) is the real thing — or another digital folk legend isn't always easy. Be skeptical! One place I go to check out this kind of information is the Urban Legends Reference Pages, `www.snopes.com`. (And who says the legends have to be urban?)

Comparing Google with Other Search Engines

In my opinion, Google is the best search engine on the Web because it has the most efficient searching mechanism and the biggest reservoir of indexed Web pages. Right now, it is certainly the most popular Web search engine. But of course many other search engines are available, each of which may offer access to some kinds of information more easily than Google.

Keep on top of Web searching technology. There were hot Web search engines before Google, and Google may not be the last word in search technology.

Some search engines came before Google, and were already mature when Google was first unleashed only a few years. Others are newly minted, and have aspirations towards being the next Google.

It's obvious, but I sometimes get carried away by how wonderful Google is as a research tool, and forget that Google is not the Web. There are parts of the Web — the so-called *invisible Web* — that neither Google nor any other search engine can "see." For example, Webmasters can intentionally decline to have their pages indexed. And Google may not be able to return information from subscription-only Web sites. See Chapter 10 to learn more about finding research information that is not available through Google.

Primary source search engines

Table 2-1 shows some of the non-Google search engines available, with a comment indicating why the search engine might be of interest to a researcher (considering that you already have Google).

Table 2-1	Primary Source Search Engines (Other Than Google)	
Engine	**URL**	**Why It's Worth Trying**
AltaVista	www.altavista.com	AltaVista created the first index of the Web (in 1995), and at one point was the big kahuna of Web searching. Now owned by the pay-or-search-placement business Overture Services, AltaVista may still be worth a look — if only out of nostalgia.
Ask Jeeves	www.ask.com	Ask Jeeves specializes in natural language searches, so you can "ask" it a question and expect to get a (mostly) reasonable answer from its site index and paid listings. The extent of the natural language processing this site does is debatable. Mostly it takes questions and removes common words; then it performs a regular search. Ask Jeeves uses the Teoma database and index.

Engine	URL	Why It's Worth Trying
A9	www.a9.com	This search engine from Amazon makes keeping track of sites you've visited easy and lets you view thumbnails of Web pages (a useful feature). But it yields Google-like results because it uses Google to conduct basic searches. An interesting feature is that it combines Google search results with Amazon Search Inside the Book results, so if you think the information you are looking for might be in a book, this is a good search engine to try.
GigaBlast	www.gigablast.com	Founded a few years ago, GigaBlast claims to be able to index "up to 200 billion Web pages with the least amount of hardware possible." A very cool search engine.
HotBot	www.hotbot.com	One of the oldest search engines on the Web, HotBot is owned by Terra/Lycos. HotBot uses an index and database supplied by Inktomi by default. You can click a button and have HotBot alternatively use the index and database supplied by either Google or Ask Jeeves/Teoma. The ability to switch indexes and databases is a neat feature, but the native (Inktomi) search lacks depth and advanced functionality.
IceRocket	www.icerocket.com	IceRocket is a good place to find current Web content — as opposed to established Web sites. It specializes in blogs and RSS (Really Simple Syndication) feeds; it has a great index of cellphone camera pictures.
MSN Search	http://beta.search.msn.com/	MSN Search is gearing up to be a "Google-killer," although it currently has far fewer pages indexed than Google.

(continued)

Table 2-1 *(continued)*

Engine	URL	Why It's Worth Trying
Snap	www.snap.com	The premise behind Snap is that users care most about the ease of refining searches, and that search results are best improved using feedback from users about completed searches. In addition, Snap prides itself on its "transparency" — all financial transactions regarding referral and advertising fees are fully disclosed, often on the home page.
Teoma	www.teoma.com	Teoma claims to deliver more relevant research results using *site clustering* technology, which ranks a site based on the number of same-subject pages that reference it, not just its general popularity. Teoma is owned by Ask Jeeves, and supplies the Ask Jeeves database and index.
Yahoo!	www.yahoo.com	There's only one Yahoo! Because commercial entities have to pay an annual fee for a Yahoo! listing, search results (to generalize) tend to have a more "big business" feel than Google.

Meta-search engines

Another kind of search engine is the *meta-search* engine. Meta-search engines amalgamate, or aggregate, information from a variety of sources; in fact, they often combine information from a number of different Web search engines. A good resource for learning more about meta-search engines is the University of California, Berkeley, Meta-Search Engine page www.lib.berkeley.edu/ TeachingLib/Guides/Internet/MetaSearch.html.

As the saying in software development goes, "Garbage in, garbage out." Be careful: The quality of information in a meta-search engine depends on the information it derives from other search engines. Some meta-search engines include results from primary engines that rank placement according to fees paid. Web sites that have bought their ranking are usually not disclosed in any way by the meta-search engine, so you don't know which of your search results are essentially ranked via money paid (rather than via some objective measure of site popularity).

At one extreme, you can find highly professional meta-search engines designed for specialized kinds of research, such as Ex-Libris's MetaLib, which is aimed at libraries and librarians. (I describe MetaLib in Chapter 20.) These professional tools are objective (meaning they don't promote results on the basis of fees paid) but usually require a subscription or institutional affiliation for access.

Table 2-2 shows some of the more popular general-purpose meta-search engines (these meta-search engines are not specialized like MetaLib, and do not require a subscription).

Table 2-2		Meta-Search Engines
Engine	*URL*	*Why It Is Worth a Look*
Clusty	www.clusty.com	Originally created by Carnegie-Mellon University, this meta-search engine uses *clustering* technology (which ranks pages based on the number of pages within a given subject that link to it) and places results into logical categories.
Copernic	www.copernic.com	Copernic uses an *agent* technology to create customized meta searches. It targets over 90 different search engines for raw data. You tell Copernic which primary engines to monitor and what queries to ask, and Copernic can go on checking for information for you over time.
Dogpile and Metacrawler	www.dogpile.com; www.metacrawler.com	Dogpile aggregates information from a number of popular search engines and provides particularly good results of white and yellow page searches. But beware of paid content that isn't marked appropriately. Metacrawler, the InfoSpace search engine, uses the raw Dogpile information with phone info site Switchboard's white and yellow pages (see www.switchboard.com).

(continued)

Table 2-2 (continued)

Engine	URL	Why It Is Worth a Look
SurfWax	www.surfwax.com	SurfWax provides targeted tools using multiple information sources hitting specific areas, such as tools designed for legal searching and tools designed for searching within schools and universities.
Vivisimo	http://vivisimo.com	Vivisimo uses clustering technology to aggregate information from numerous less well-known search engine sources.

Getting a Quick Introduction to Google's Technology

Google uses a *Web crawler,* also called a *bot* or *spider,* to search the Web for Web pages. Google then stores copies of the Web pages in its servers and indexes the pages. When you enter search words in the Google Web search window, Google compares your search terms with its index, and returns results accordingly. That's the system in a nutshell.

Of course, it is a little more complex than that. Google search results are returned in the order of their *PageRank.* To put it simply, the more pages that link to a given Web page, the higher the PageRank of the Web page is likely to be.

Calculating PageRank is not quite as simple as I've made it sound here, and some of the details about how it is done are proprietary (which is the same thing as "secret," but takes five syllables).

You can find more information about how Google works, and about PageRank, in Chapter 11.

Introducing Search Engine Optimization

Search Engine Optimization (SEO) is the black magic, craft, or art (depending upon whom you ask) of writing or editing Web pages and sites so that they move up in search engine rankings and are returned at the top of a list of search results.

The history of Google

Google was incorporated in 1998 by two Stanford University computer science graduate students, Larry Page and Sergey Brin, who met in 1995. The pair was soon collaborating on the Stanford Digital Library project.

By early 1996, Page and Brin were working on a search engine named Backrub, which was named for its ability to analyze the *back links* pointing to a site. This linkage information is used to rank Web pages and sites.

In 1998, Andy Bechtolsheim, one of the founders of Sun Microsystems, provided the two's first substantive funding by writing a check for $100,000 made out to Google Inc. By the way, a google is a variant of the term *googol,* the number 1 followed by 100 zeros (10 000 000 000 000 000 000 000 000 000 000 000 000 000 000 000 000 000 000 000 000 000 000 000 000 000 000 000 000 000 000 000 000 000 000 000 000). To give you an idea of

how big this number is, it is much larger than the number of all the atoms in the universe! The term was coined by nine-year-old Milton Sirotta at the request of his uncle, mathematician Edward Kasner, in 1938. Page and Brin liked the name Google because it reflected their "mission to organize the immense, seemingly infinite, amount of information available on the Web."

By autumn of 1998, the beta version of Google was handling 10,000 searches a day. By mid-1999, Google had more than 500,000 searches per day, and had moved to quarters in Palo Alto dubbed the Googleplex.

By 2001, Google was hosting 100,000,000 search queries per day. By autumn of 2004, Google users were performing more than 200,000,000 searches every day using Google, and Google had completed an Initial Public Offering (IPO).

This is an important subject because if a Web page is not in the top search results, very few people can find it. Webmasters want to know about SEO to improve their rankings and increase traffic to their sites. On the other side of the aisle, researchers should understand the basics of SEO techniques to ascertain how they influence site ranking (and validity) within research results.

As a general rule, people don't look past the first three pages (or 30 listings) of search results.

The importance of optimizing search results is such that some SEO consultants are reportedly paid fees as high as $500 per hour. (This sounds like a good gig if you can get it! Anybody want to hire me?) However, Google claims that the whole subject of search engine optimization is entirely transparent, and that the only trick to it is publishing content on the Web that people find genuinely interesting and/or useful. You can find more information about Google's take on SEO on the Google Information for Webmasters site, www. google.com/webmasters/ (look for the <u>Guidelines</u>, <u>Fact & Fiction</u>, and <u>SEOs</u> topic links towards the bottom of the page).

Methinks Google doth protesteth overmuch. Some SEO techniques, such as the ones I explain in this section, do help with search result ranking in Google. However, it's clear that trying to get too cute often backfires. For example:

✔ **Bad meta tags:** In particular, adding irrelevant meta tags to pages (*meta tags* are descriptive HTML tags intended to be read by software such as the Google Web crawler and not by the humans visiting a Web page) isn't a very good idea — Google lowers the PageRanks of such pages.

For example, the common practice of including a popular movie star's name as a meta tag in a page having nothing to do with the star will likely lower (not raise) a page's ranking.

✔ **Link farms:** Trading links with other sites solely for the purpose of improving your rank will usually do more harm than good. If the sites are identified as *link farms* — sites that consist only of links and/or exist for the purpose of trading links — Google will "mark-down" your ranking.

Here are some "real" SEO techniques that improve the ranking of Web pages within Google's search results (and help researchers find the information they need):

✔ Good content that is of genuine interest goes a long way.

✔ Simple site designs are better than busy pages. Google cannot "read" images, and is not particularly fond of Flash, Java, or JavaScript, either. Text-based pages with plain formats and simple HTML are most successful.

✔ Pages with content that is often renewed tend to get more attention than pages that don't have anything new.

✔ Determine the most important keywords that are relevant to your content. You can make this determination by searching in Google with a variety of keywords and analyzing results, by creating a program using the Google APIs that tracks keywords (as I explain in Chapter 18), or by registering for the Google AdWords program (you can start at www. google.com/ads/index.html) and seeing how expensive different keywords are to advertisers. With keyword importance information in hand, add the most important keywords (but not too densely) to titles, headings, URLs, and image tags on each page.

✔ Cross-link within your Web pages.

✔ Create links from your pages out to relevant, popular Web pages (these links are called *outbound* links).

✔ Request that sites that have content related to your pages link to you (these links are called *inbound* links).

A good resource for learning about optimizing your site for Google is the Google FAQ at Webmaster World, www.searchengineworld.com/spiders/google_faq.htm.

It's really helpful to get an idea of how your Web pages and sites are viewed by a Web crawler such as the Google bot. The best way to do this is to open your Web page in a text-only browser. One text-only browser is Lynx. If you don't want to get into the hassle of downloading the source code for Lynx for the Windows platform and compiling it, the easiest way to see use Lynx to see what a Web page looks like when it is reduced to its text is to use Lynx Viewer, www.delorie.com/web/lynxview.html.

Figure 2-1 shows the home page for Braintique, www.braintique.com, in its text-only form on Lynx Viewer as a Web crawler would see it. In contrast, Figure 2-2 shows the same page in full living color in a normal Web browser as you'd see it every day on the Web.

Figure 2-1: The Braintique home page viewed as text only.

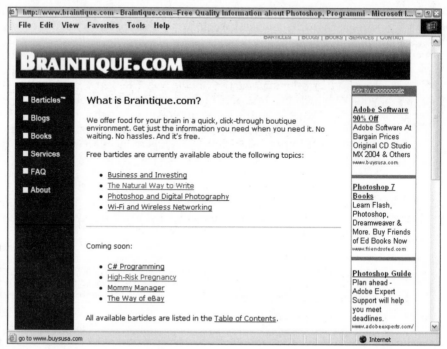

Chapter 3

Delivering and Automating Research Results

A research question can mean many things, depending on who is asking the question. In order to effectively answer research questions, you need to know your audience. By understanding who your research is for, you can narrow the research questions so that you can effectively provide pinpointed and elegant results. This chapter explains how to get started.

Research results don't do anyone any good if you keep them to yourself. This chapter explains many of the various possible ways to deliver research results to your intended audience.

Why not use the power of computer software to help you research and to provide research facilities to others? This chapter explains the mechanisms you can use to create custom applications using Google.

Knowing Your Audience

In order to answer a research question satisfactorily, you need to understand the needs of your audience.

The kind of research client you are dealing with has broad implications about how you should deliver the answers to your research questions. (I tend to use the terms *research client* and *client* very broadly. All I really mean is audience.)

Certainly, research answers are delivered in many contexts. For example, if you are handing in a term paper in a graduate course, then the term paper is the answer to research questions and the professor is the research client (you would be smart to figure out the best way to meet the needs of the assignment and ask the right questions before you begin researching and writing the paper). If your manager asks you to research a business idea, then your manager is the research client (and you need to figure out both the right research questions and the deliverables up front). If you can appropriately do so without irking your boss, get the parameters of your research assignment laid out in writing at the very beginning of the project. Also, find out who your point person is if things go awry midway through the research process. You need to be able to go to a single person for clarification so that you can stay on schedule and deliver the correct product.

Here are some of the more common kinds of research clients, with an indication of the range of formality you are likely to encounter when presenting answers to these clients:

- ✔ **Government agency:** Usually requires a formal presentation involving reports and documentation

- ✔ **Government agency (risk assessment):** Ranges from very informal to elaborate presentations and documentation

- ✔ **Academic (high schools, colleges, and graduate):** Requires formal documentation such as a term paper or peer-reviewed article

- ✔ **Business (competitive and strategic intelligence):** Ranges from very informal to highly structured, involving in-person presentations and extensive documentation

- ✔ **Business (product management):** Informal assessment of course of action, PowerPoint slide presentations

Refining Research Questions

The first — and sometimes the hardest — task of the researcher is to find the right questions. Even if you can find the information you need without using query techniques, if you don't know the question or questions your research is supposed to answer, you won't know whether you have succeeded — and you won't have an agreed-upon reference point to objectively determine success or failure when you meet with the research client.

So how do you find out what questions to ask to successfully resolve a research project? Well, there's no single answer to this question (ha ha). Experienced professional researchers develop their own, individual methods and techniques for drilling down to the heart of an assignment and coming up with the right list of questions. Intuition plays an important role. The best researchers have developed a sixth-sense about the questions that should be asked and answered.

TIP

Asking who, what, when, where, why, and how?

Journalists are traditionally taught to ask six questions, the so-called "six Ws": who, what, when, where, why, and how? If you are at a loss about where to begin a research project, start by asking questions. Unsure which questions to ask? Start with these six; they work well for researchers, too (although they are primarily designed to work for journalists who are writing about stories involving people).

If you draw a blank during a research assignment, you can do a great deal worse than falling back on the six Ws. Use these questions as filters to probe you research subject, examine it more carefully, and arrive at more detailed questions about it.

Ask "who" in the spirit of finding the person who did something. If "who" is a good research question for your project, you should go further and find out about traits, characteristics, history, and so on.

"What" is often as simple as the question, "What happened?" But, more expansively, you can ask, "What does it mean?", "What is its purpose?", "What are its causes?", and so on.

"When" is often a question of straight chronology. But you can also ask when an event will happen again, why it happened when it happened, and so on. You might also want to ask in relation to chronology, "What new events have happened recently?" and "Why is this important now?"

"Where" usually describes a place. But you can elaborate: Is it part of a larger place? What is special about the place? This question can help narrow the scope of a research project. If you don't know how to answer it, it is probably a good idea to go back to your research client for further "where" information.

"Why" is the question researchers (as opposed to journalists) most often want to know, because if you know why something happened, you know the most important thing about the event. "Why" asks for a reasoning process, and for conclusions (in other words, you may ask "why" when you're analyzing your primary research, but you're not likely to arrive at a direct causal relationship as the immediate product of primary research). You can elaborate on the "why" question to ask about proximate causes, underlying causes, motivation, objectives, and alternatives. Or you can use it to pose a hypothesis. (Sometimes the why is given by your client: Provide evidence that our product is not destroying the ozone layer.")

"How" as a question opens the areas of method, procedure, and process. You can use "how" to find out about goals and objectives, how things work, and whether they are repeatable.

A researcher is a kind of detective. You may have noticed that detectives in the movies are often presented with situations that are not what they at first seem. Some degree of misdirection is okay at the beginning of a project; if everyone knew right away who committed the crime, there would be no suspense — and no reason for a detective. The same thing is true for a researcher.

Your first job is to cut through the veil of confusion (and sometimes outright misrepresentation) in the initial presentation of the research problem. In other words, find out what the *real* topic of research is.

The task of finding out what results your client is after is often accomplished through the effective use of a reference interview. I show you how to conduct a reference interview in Chapter 10.

You simply must get your client to tell you what he or she is really, really looking for. (This advice applies in spades if you are your own client: Understand your motivation.) For example, if a client comes to you with a general question about the methodology used in voting exit polls, you should find out what the client really wants to know, and whether the client has a political affiliation or an ax to grind.

Here are some important do's and don'ts based on the experience of top professional researchers:

- ✔ **Do** always assume that the initial set of questions posed by your research client only scratches the surface of the problem. Dig deeper!

- ✔ **Do** always start by asking "why" many times. Be like that 4-year-old child who wants to know why the sun rises. Ask the question over and over again until you fall over or get an answer, whichever happens first.

- ✔ **Do** make sure that each question you ask can be answered. Most good research questions cannot be answered simply, or with 100 percent assurance of accuracy, and that's okay. But don't attempt to answer something that is unknowable based on current human knowledge (for example, the geologic composition of a hypothetical asteroid on the other side of the galaxy).

- ✔ **Don't** forget to set your parameters. If a question cannot be answered with precision, make sure you understand what kinds of answers are acceptable. (I tell you more about how to deal with this issue later in Chapter 10.)

- ✔ **Don't** ask vague questions. If a question is ambiguous, or capable of being interpreted in multiple ways, rephrase the question so that it reasonably can only have one meaning. For example, if Ms. Client says "Tell me about the property impact of the underground water ordinance," rephrase the question: "Will Ms. Client be able to transfer her real estate without problems even though it is within 30 feet of a Class B culvert after the legislation passes?"

✔ **Do** look for hidden ambiguities. Make sure your list of questions contains no words with unclear meanings. For example, the client who asked about "property impact" may really be using those words to see if there is a legal impediment to the conveyance of clear title. Words can be tricky, slippery things, particularly — as is often the case with research topics — when technical and legal fields are involved. As the researcher, you need to pin the ornery beasts down.

✔ **Do** strive for clarity; simple questions that call for concrete answers are best.

✔ **Do** double-check your questions. If your research is not finding answers, go back and check that your initial questions make sense. For example, if your client is trying to answer the question, "How do I sell software in Romania?" and you can't find any answers, perhaps the problem is that there is no way to sell software in that country (perhaps because everyone there uses free, open-source software and isn't interested in paying for anything).

Presenting Research Results

How you present research results depends upon many factors, including the circumstances of the research assignment and what the client has requested (and what you are being paid to do).

Some possibilities are to personally present information, write up a paper, provide a PowerPoint presentation, use e-mail, present information on the Web, or create a Web-based application for presentation. You may also want, need, or be required to combine these research delivery mechanisms.

In some cases, the format of research assignments may be determined by your client, depending on the industry the client is in. For example, if your client is a business that does biomedical research and it wants you to research the effects of Prozac on teenagers, you may need to follow APA (American Psychological Association) style, with an abstract and appropriate citations. Or, if you're doing research for an academic publisher, you may have to use MLA (Modern Language Association) style.

Here are some of the common formats for research question and answer deliverables (see Chapter 12 for more details), roughly ranging from least formal to most formal:

✔ Informal answer to an ad-hoc question, delivered in person, by phone, or via e-mail.

✔ Compact verbal report, either on the phone or in person.

✔ Summary e-mail.

✔ Web delivery of initial results.

✔ Executive summary.

✔ PowerPoint presentation.

✔ Extensive in-person presentation.

✔ Formal written report or paper, with or without formal sourcing information.

✔ Statistical information, such as quantitative information entered into a spreadsheet program using Excel.

✔ A software program, with or without data, perhaps created using the Google APIs, as explained in Part IV. For example, to answer a question about changing popularity of specific words and concepts on the Web over time, you might present to your client a modified version of the program I show you in Chapter 18.

Making assumptions about the format for presentation delivery is unwise. In fact, the results could be disastrous if you don't meet the client's expectations. Always ask your client what his or her preference is. For example, the client might require the information to be posted on a Web site with plenty of cross-referenced links; if you present the answer to the client as a PowerPoint presentation, your answer may be useless, even though it contains the correct information.

Writing Software That Uses Google

Software makes life easier for everyone, and software for researchers is even better. You can create custom software that helps you (and others) obtain research results. You can also use software to analyze and present research results.

The following sections explain the basics of writing software that uses Google.

Scripting

When you enter search terms on the Google home page and click the Search Web button, Google uses the search terms you've entered to create a URL

(Uniform Resource Locator). Your search results are generated by opening this URL in a browser (which Google does automatically in a standard Google Web search).

For example, if you want to search for the term *harold davis,* the following URL is used to open the first page of search results in your browser:

```
www.google.com/search?hl=en&q=Harold+Davis&btnG=Google+Search
```

The URL for the results page is viewable in the Internet Explorer Address Bar (see Figure 3-1).

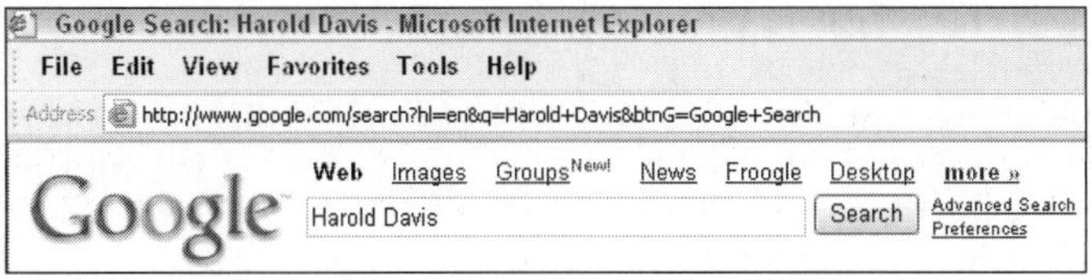

Figure 3-1:
You can see the URL generated by a search in Internet Explorer's Address Bar.

This URL tells Google that the search results are to be in English and that the search is for both terms (*harold* AND *davis*). (See Chapter 4 for more information about Google's default conjunction operator, represented in a search query by a space, +, or AND.)

All this stuff about URLs is interesting, but what's the point? You can use the Google search results URL in the HTML of your own Web pages.

For example, you could create a hypertext link with the text <u>Find Harold Davis</u>, as shown in Figure 3-2. When the user clicks the link, the Google search results page opens in the user's browser.

Figure 3-2:
The hypertext link opens the Google search URL (shown here on the status bar).

Bottom line: Google search queries do not have to be hard-coded into HTML. You can generate the query part of a Google search URL with a script on your Web page.

When you combine scripts that generate portions (or all) of a Google search result URL with HTML forms, you can create very useful applications (including research tools) that are relatively simple.

In Chapter 5, I provide an example that uses a scripted Google URL to create a box that searches only a single site. You must specify the site in your code (in my example, I specified fbi.gov). In Chapter 13, I show you how to use scripting, HTML forms, and a generated URL to create an application that uses Google's Language Services to translate Web pages.

Introducing the Deskbar

Perhaps you've found that working with the Google Toolbar has made your Google research more efficient and fun! (See Chapter 1 for information about how to download, install, and use the Google Toolbar.) Well, there's another bar you might also find useful.

The Google Deskbar works pretty much like the Google Toolbar, except that it's not part of your Web browser. You can download the Google Deskbar, which is officially a *beta* product (unfinished and subject to change at any time with no notice), at http://deskbar.google.com. The Deskbar is different from the Toolbar in three significant ways:

- ✔ **You don't have to open Internet Explorer to conduct a search.** If you're writing your novel in Word and you want to find information about yetis (specifically which hand they favor), you don't have to toggle over to Internet Explorer and search for *ambidextrous yeti*. You can type your search term in the Deskbar's search box and click the Search button (which looks like a pair of binoculars, as shown in Figure 3-3).

- ✔ **Your results are presented in a mini-viewer.** By default, when you perform a Google search using the Google Deskbar, a special mini-viewer opens on your desktop. (That's right: It's a mini-viewer, not mini me!) The mini-viewer looks just like a Google Web results page, as shown in Figure 3-4, but it doesn't take up the entire computer screen (hence the mini aspect of the viewer).

- ✔ **You can create customized plug-ins to automate a variety of activities involving your computer.** See "Programming the Deskbar," later in this chapter.

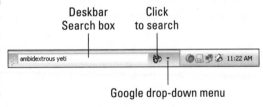

Figure 3-3: The Google Deskbar is positioned on the Windows taskbar.

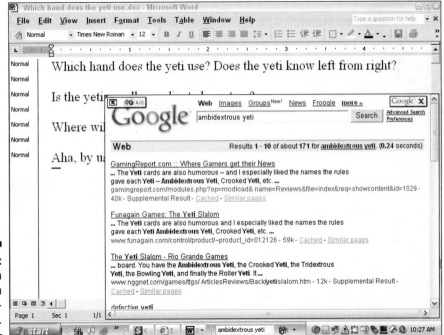

Figure 3-4: Your search appears in the mini-viewer.

You can configure the Deskbar so it opens in Internet Explorer instead of in the mini-viewer.

To change the Deskbar options, select Options from the drop-down menu next to the Deskbar search window. The Google Deskbar Settings window opens. Choose the Mini-Viewer tab to change the default method the Deskbar uses to display results.

Programming the Deskbar

You can extend the useful nature of the Google Deskbar with custom programs, called *Deskbar plug-ins,* using .NET languages such as C# and Visual Basic.

Each Deskbar plug-in is a .NET single-assembly DLL (Dynamic Link Library) that is placed in the Deskbar's `Plugins` folder. Custom searches created with a Deskbar plug-in implement the ICustomSearch interface.

You can download the Google Plug-In Developer Kit from `http://deskbar.google.com/help/api/plugin_download.html`. The Developer Kit provides a sample C# .NET project and some (pretty skimpy) documentation.

If you want to see the documentation without downloading the Development Kit, you can view it at `http://deskbar.google.com/help/api/plugin_documentation.html`.

To give you a taste of what the plug-ins can do for you, here's an example. You can create an application that generates passwords of the length you specify; each generated password displays in the Deskbar window on the Windows taskbar.

And that's just the tip of the iceberg. You can add tons of functionality to the Deskbar — essentially, if you can program an application in a .NET library, you can add it to the Deskbar.

Unlike the Google APIs (which I show you how to use in Part IV), you can't use the Deskbar plug-ins to create custom searches of Google itself. For this reason, I don't go into a description of the applications you can create with the plug-ins. I encourage you to test them out, though.

Using the Google APIs

The Google APIs are Web methods that can be used (in conjunction with the Google Web APIs service) with any programming language and development environment that can work with Web services.

The Google APIs comprise the Google Web APIs service. The three Google APIs are

- ✔ **doGetCachedPage:** Returns a page from the Google cache

- ✔ **doGoogleSearch:** Performs a Google search based on the query passed to it and returns the results in an array

- ✔ **doSpellingSuggestion:** Returns a spelling suggestion (if Google has one)

The most important Google API is doGoogleSearch, which can be used in conjunction with sophisticated Google search strings to create a wide variety of research tools using the information that a Google search makes available.

In order to use these APIs, you need a Google developer key. (See Chapter 14 for information about obtaining a developer key and downloading the Google APIs software development kit (SDK).

You'll find a great deal of information about building applications that use the Google APIs in Part IV and the appendixes.

Part II
Crafting Queries and Using the Google Research Tools

The 5th Wave   By Rich Tennant

"Maybe your keyword search, 'legal secretary, love, fame, fortune', needs to be refined."

In this part...

You don't need an advanced degree to search the Web with Google. But knowing how to make effective use of the Google search engine can make your search results a great deal more useful. The universe of Google also consists of worlds within worlds, and the research tools provided by some of these "mini-Googles" can be surprisingly useful.

Chapter 4 explains how to create effective searches by making good use of some of the simple operators Google provides.

Chapter 5 continues along this course, and shows you how to pinpoint search results with precision using advanced Google operators. You also learn how to create a simple client-side script that lets you add Google's searching capabilities to your site (provided it has been indexed by Google).

Chapter 6 shows you how to use Google Answers for your research, Chapter 7 shows you how to make the most of the Google Directory, and Chapter 8 explains how you can use Google Images to get some surprising results — which don't always have to do with pictures.

Finally, in Chapter 9 you learn how to put these research tools and techniques together to use information publicly available on the Web to create a company and industry competitive intelligence profile.

Chapter 4

Building Simple, Effective Queries

Simplicity is often best, and simple queries often produce the most useful research results when you use the Google search engine. In other words, you don't need to know anything fancy to use Google, as millions of users worldwide have proved. I often find the research answers I need just by typing a few words in Google and clicking the Search button.

Even in this realm of easy searching — think of it as the "fast food" of researching — some simple concepts and techniques can make your searches much more effective. This is the difference between frustrating searches that lead you to page after page of search results without ever finding what you need, and "love at first sight" searching: The first page of returned results contains a number of links pointing to exactly the information you need.

In this chapter, I give you information about straight text searching and show you how to get more out of your search. I show you how to craft the perfect keywords to get the results you need.

Understanding how to use the simple Google operators, quote phrases, and use Google wildcard characters can improve your search results without much effort. This chapter offers handy techniques in all these areas. And if you want to get a little fancier with your searches, you can use the Google Advanced Search page, which I also show you in this chapter.

You also need to know what Google results mean. In this chapter, I explain Google results sets, what cached results are, and how to conduct further searches within a results set of an initial search.

Speeding Up Basic Text Searches

As you likely know, the basic way you use Google is to enter *search terms,* also called *queries* or *keywords,* into the Google search box, shown in Figure 4-1. Then click the Google Search button or press the Enter key on your keyboard.

There's no point in formulating your words as a question, even if you want a specific question answered. For example, suppose the director of a science fiction thriller taking place in Antarctica asked you to find out whether there are ants in Antarctica (somehow the plot turns on the presence of these ants in a space training station on the polar ice fields).

As a researcher using Google, it should be simple to answer the question:

```
Are there ants in Antarctica?
```

However, the only words in this question, also called a *query,* that Google pays any attention to are *ants* and *Antarctica.* So save yourself the trouble and don't bother with the whole question. Just go ahead and type the important words, or *keywords.* Google searches its index for Web pages containing both keywords. (See Chapter 11 for an under-the-hood glimpse of how Google does its job.)

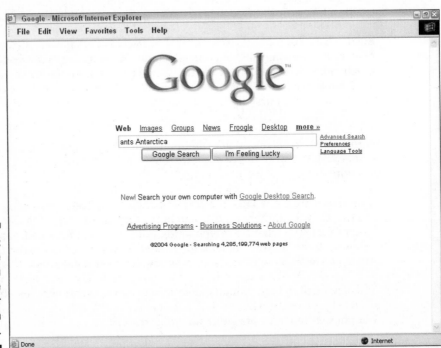

Figure 4-1:
Enter the words you want to use for your search in the box.

If you don't specify otherwise — I explain how to do so in "Introducing Simple Operators" — Google assumes that two or more keywords in a query are connected implicitly by the AND operator; Google searches for pages that contain all the keywords.

Creating more simple, specific search queries

When you use Google in its simplest form, you should follow some basic search rules:

- ✓ **Punctuation doesn't count.** In fact, it is stripped out of the query automatically.

- ✓ **Keywords aren't case sensitive.** Uppercase and lowercase letters are considered equal, so *Antarctica* is the same as *antarctica*.

- ✓ **You're limited to ten words.** Everything after the first ten words is truncated and ignored (see "Working with Wildcards" for a way to get around the ten-word limitation).

- ✓ **Avoid misspellings:** If you misspell a keyword in your search, then you won't get the results you expect. If Google thinks you've misspelled a search term, it gives you the benefit of the doubt by searching for the misspelled word and proposing a spelling correction when it presents results.

- ✓ **Be specific:** The more targeted your keywords, the more likely you are to get usable search results. A search for *sanitation Alameda County CA* is more likely to yield results having to do with sanitation issues within Alameda County than a search for *garbage Northern California*.

- ✓ **A *thing* is not many *things*:** Singular and plural forms are different keywords to Google. If a search using a singular form (ant) doesn't provide the results you are looking for, you should consider using the plural form (ants) instead. As an example, the query *ant Antarctica* doesn't tell you anything about whether there are ants in Antarctica, but *ants Antarctica* returns many pages that provide this information.

- ✓ **Google ignores most common, short words:** Don't bother to pose questions in your search queries; Google throws out all the *stop words* anyway. *Stop words* include most articles (such as *the, and,* and *or*), prepositions (*after, in,* and so on), pronouns *(I), how, it,* and forms of the verb *to be* (*is, was, will be,* and so on). Some single letters are also eliminated. (If a word is omitted from your search terms on these grounds, a message to that effect appears at the top of your search results.)

These words are excluded to keep searches fast and to keep focused on the most important search terms in the query. So if you want to search for the movie *how the west was won,* be sure to enter your query phrase wrapped in quotes *("how the west was won")* so that the stop words won't be ignored (although you'll still get some relevant results without the quotes while *how, the,* and *was* are ignored as stop words).

Use keywords that are distinctive and important. If you need to search using a stop word, you can wrap the phrase that includes the stop word in quotes, as I explain in "Quoting Phrases," or wrap the stop word itself in quotes.

When stop words are excluded from a search, Google notes the fact on the results page, just below the search box.

In "Understanding Results," later in this chapter, I explain how to analyze Google results in detail. For now, you can see in Figure 4-2 the initial results for a search for *ants Antarctica.*

The Google search results include excerpts from the pages Google deems relevant. This is very helpful to you as a researcher because you can scan these excerpts to decide for yourself how relevant a results page is without having to open the page.

Figure 4-2: Google search results include excerpts from the text of the relevant Web pages.

What happens behind the scenes of a Google search?

It's fun, and sometimes useful, to know what happens when you click the Google Search button. Google spits out a Uniform Resource Locator (URL), also called a Web address, that consists (in large part) of your search keywords, and sends the URL as a form GET HTTP request to the Google Web server. For example, here's the URL generated by the *ants Antarctica* query that I made:

```
www.google.com/search?hl=en&q=
    ants+Antarctica&btnG=Google
    +Search
```

If you are using Microsoft Internet Explorer as your Web browser, you can easily view the generated Web address by making sure that the Address Bar option is checked to display on the Toolbar submenu of the View menu. You can then see the Google generated URL for the results page in the Address Bar.

Another reason this function is useful is because you can tell at a glance whether all the information you need in order to answer your simple query is present in the first Google set of results. Right away, you can let the film director know (from the third and fifth results on the Google results page) that "Native ants can be found everywhere in the world, excluding Antarctica . . ." and that there are more than 9,000 species of ants in virtually all regions of the world except Antarctica.

Avoiding the I'm-Feeling-Lucky pitfall

An alternative to the Google Search button is to click the I'm Feeling Lucky button. Clicking this button brings up the Web page that Google feels is the best answer to your query (in other words, the first page in the return results set) without going through the intermediate step of returning a results set of links. (For more information about how Google determines the order of its return results set, and therefore the best page match, see Chapter 11.)

Think of the I'm Feeling Lucky button as the Clint Eastwood button from the film *Dirty Harry*. Ask yourself, "Do you feel lucky today, kid?"

The "Clint Eastwood" button is popular among many everyday Google users. But if you're doing heavy-duty research, you are likely to find (as have many others) that it usually doesn't provide helpful results to your queries. As a matter of fact, the Clint Eastwood result to the *ants Antarctica* query shows me a nice picture of an ant, and a map of New Zealand, but it doesn't tell me anything about ants in Antarctica.

By the way, Google search results are not static, meaning you don't always get the same thing over time for a given search. The relative PageRank of pages does change, and therefore Google's estimation of which single "best" page to return to you may also differ with time. So if you try this, you may get a different "best" page than I did.

Obtaining Google Desktop Search results

If you're like me, one of your biggest organizational challenges as a researcher is *relocating* information you've *already* found once, hidden in the files of your desktop computer.

The Google Desktop Search tool greatly helps with this problem. You can use Google Desktop Search to retrieve information from the files on your hard drive as a stand-alone program, or have it integrate the results from searching your personal files with your Web searches.

By comparison, the search feature built into Microsoft Windows is slow, has a complex and hard-to-use interface (particularly if you need to find information within a file as opposed to the name of a file), and doesn't integrate with your Web search results.

To install Google Desktop Search, you need to download it from `http://desktop.google.com`.

When you first run Google Desktop Search, you need to tell it which kinds of files to include in the index that it creates (and which you use when you search your desktop). Later, you can change your Google Desktop Search settings using the Google Desktop Search Preferences page, shown in Figure 4-3.

When you first install Google Desktop Search, Google must index the files you specify on your computer. This process can take hours, but the good news is that you can keep on working while the indexing process goes on in the background.

Click the Show Desktop Search Results on Google Web Search Result Pages check box in the Integration section of the Preferences page to determine whether files and documents from your own desktop also appear in the results set when you conduct a Web search with Google.

After your desktop content has been indexed, you can search specifically for local content by opening Google Desktop Search (click the icon in the Windows system tray).

And if you set up Google Desktop Search to display local desktop results when you search the Web, local documents appear alongside Web results, as you see in Figure 4-4. As you can also see in Figure 4-4, a link to the 132 results on your local computer appears at the top of the Web search results (along with the top two local links). If you want to see all the items on your local computer, click this results link.

If you are only interested in a Web search for a particular term, you can suppress the local results by clicking the Hide link, next to the summary of local results, shown in Figure 4-4.

Google says that the privacy of your information is secure. Specifically, the index to your information is stored on your own computer, and won't be shared with Google or anyone else without your permission. (For further information, see http://desktop.google.com/privacyfaq.html.) Still, if you are concerned about privacy, you'll have to take Google's word that it hasn't made use of what it finds on your computer. (Google's word is good enough for me!)

Google Desktop Search is a great took for you to use if you need to go through your own data repositories. Now there's never any reason to have to find the same information twice!

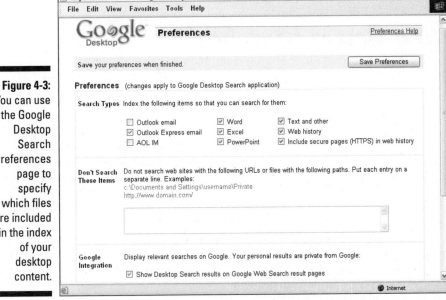

Figure 4-3:
You can use the Google Desktop Search Preferences page to specify which files are included in the index of your desktop content.

Crafting Better Searches

There's a craft to finding the right search terms for answering a research question. As with any craft, after a while you get a feeling for the best way to do things. In the meantime, these suggestions will help:

- **Pose answerable queries:** This one seems obvious, and even a little circular — how do you know if there will be search results without first searching? What I mean is that you should make sure that your search terms are unambiguous. Have you given Google enough information to answer your query? For example, what about a search for *lemon?* Do you mean lemon tree, lemon cake, lemon candy, the color of a lemon, a car that is a lemon, Lemon laws, or other alternatives?

  Google can do many things, but it can't read your mind. If you need help being specific, try answering the question "What kind of . . . ?" before you conduct a search. For example, ask "What kind of lemon?" and see how your answer changes your query.

- **Don't describe; use keywords:** Google search terms should not be a description of what you want to find, so don't search for *round yellow fruit* if you're looking for information about how well lemon trees grow in Wisconsin. Rather, consider the words that a Webmaster might use. For example, if you're looking for a good lemon tree that won't die in the winter, you might want to search for *lemon tree climate gardening*.

✔ **Enter search terms in the order they are most likely to be found:** Yes, Virginia, the order of search terms does make a difference. In the example of the lemon tree, I chose the order of my keywords to be hierarchical. The most important term is the lemon tree. The two last keywords, if searched outside the context of lemon trees would do nothing for me.

✔ **Understanding implicit** AND **word linkage:** Google search terms are implicitly linked as if the Google AND operator (see "Introducing Simple Operators") had been used. This means that when you search for more than one word, you search for pages that contain all the words (*lemon* AND *tree* AND *climate* AND *gardening*).

✔ **Use unlikely word combinations:** Sometimes unlikely word combinations return the best results; as long as all the words used are relevant, they cut way down on spurious results. For example, I found some basic information when I searched for *lemon tree climate gardening,* but because I know that gardeners categorize climates into zones based on temperature, I changed my keywords to *lemon tree gardening zone 5.* The result at the top of the results set told me immediately that growing any citrus tree in a colder climate would be a very bad idea.

✔ **Change your search terms or search within results:** If you're not getting the right results, change things around. Search terms are implicitly linked, so adding to an existing keyword can narrow the scope of a search. Alternatively, with the same effect, click the <u>Search within results</u> link at the bottom of the results page and enter your new keyword.

Introducing Simple Operators

Operators are used in conjunction with Google search terms and have a special meaning to Google. They are not included in the subject of a search, but rather change how Google works when it performs a search. Thus, the operator AND signifies that two words should be searched for together. The operator OR looks for one term or another to show up in the search results.

I talk about AND, OR, +, and – operators in this section.

Although words entered as Google search terms are not case sensitive, Google operators are. You must type **AND** or **OR**. You cannot enter them as **and** or **or**. (Alternatively, you can use the pipe operator, |, as the OR operator.)

Understanding Google operator options

Google uses a rather simplistic set of query operators that do not correspond completely to standard Boolean or SQL systems. (For more information about Boolean operators and Boolean logic, try searching for those terms on Google. SQL, or Structured Query Language, is used for interacting with databases.)

For example, in contrast to traditional Boolean operators, Google doesn't provide a *negation operator* as such. Google does have an exclusion operator (see the section called "The exclusion operator" for more details). In other words, with Google you can match results to a search if any of the search terms appear in the pages (see the section called "The OR operator"), but you can't create an exclusive, or *match* — in which the search matches if the result contains one, and only one, of the search terms. In other words, Google doesn't allow you to do a search for either *bananas* or *gorillas* that does not exclude pages that have both *bananas* and *gorillas* on them.

With Google, simplicity is the name of the game. Keeping the search operator syntax simple means that searches are speedier, but you don't get the full spectrum of operators that are available with other engines.

The average Google user probably doesn't need to worry about operators at all; but as a researcher, you do; Google's limited syntax means that you must use what they've given you with as much skill as possible.

Understanding the AND operator

The AND search operator is the explicit conjunction operator that tells Google that the terms on either side of the AND operator should be included in search results. By default, even if you don't use an operator, Google provides search results for multiple keywords as if you'd used the AND operator (this fact explains why AND isn't used too often). However, using AND instead of the implicit conjunction makes it clear what is going on and makes it easier to transfer your results to a search engine (or database) that does require the explicit use of an AND operator (such as an SQL-driven database).

The OR operator

When you use the OR operator, you tell Google, "Match *any* of the terms connected by the OR operator" (as oppose to AND, which requires *all* the terms to appear in search results).

One of the best uses of the OR operator is when you're not quite sure of the spelling of a term (looking for *autochthonous?*), or when the term has several variations (*email* OR *e-mail*). Or perhaps you want to include both singular and plural forms of a word (*ant* OR *ants*).

Sometimes OR works if an item is known by more than one term. For example, the search

```
wireless device OR computer OR network
```

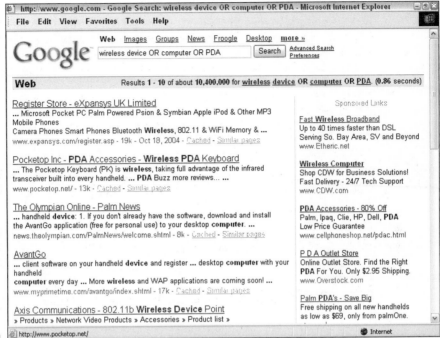

Figure 4-5:
The OR operator returns results that include any of the terms joined using the OR operator.

returns pages that contain the words *wireless* and *device* or *wireless* and *computer* or *wireless* and *network* (wireless and any two or three of the other terms) as you can see in Figure 4-5. In any event, the word *wireless* appears in the results.

The inclusion operator

The *inclusion operator,* signified by a plus sign (+), forces Google to include the indicated word on each page that is returned as a result. The inclusion operator, +, must come immediately before the term to be included, without any spaces.

The inclusion operator is most useful for reinserting the *stop words* that Google leaves out by default. Sometimes you really need to include stop words to get the best results. Never fear; the + is here. For example, if you search for

```
Star Wars I
```

the results omit *I* from the search results. (In fact, Google even displays a message to let you know that *I* is a very common word and was therefore omitted from the search.) If you're really looking for results related to the first episode of the *Star Wars* space opera, it's handy-dandy to be able to enter

```
Star Wars +I
```

and get search results related to *Episode I: The Phantom Menace*.

The exclusion operator

The exclusion operator requires Google to return results that do not include a specified term. This operator is represented by a minus sign (–) before the term to be excluded (no spaces are allowed between the operator and the excluded term).

Exclusion is one of the most useful operators a researcher can use because it allows you to clarify the context of terms. Many words are used across a number of fields. For example, a virus can infect a computer or a person. A search for

```
virus -computer
```

should, in theory, show only biological viruses. If you try this search, you'll see that in fact it includes biologic viruses, philosophic pseudo-religious viruses, and more, as well as some computer virus links. In contrast, a search just for *virus* returns primarily links about computer viruses. So the exclusion operator doesn't always work perfectly, but it does improve results.

Here's another example. Take the search term *fly*. Fly could refer to an insect, fishing, a kind of guy, or an airline. Suppose your research interest is in the fly genome. You can suppress a great many extraneous results using the exclusion operator in a search such as this:

```
fly -guy -airplane -airline -fishing
```

with the results shown in Figure 4-6.

Refining searches with inclusion and exclusion

Of course, you can combine multiple terms along with exclusion operators. This technique is likely to give you better results than just using exclusion operators (the inclusion operator is implied when you add any new term to your query).

Figure 4-6:
The exclusion operator is very useful for making searches more precise.

For example, if you want to find biological but not computer viruses, using a search term that includes *virus* and *biological* and excludes *computer,* like this:

```
virus biological -computer
```

is a good idea. If you are looking for the fly genome, you'll get pretty good results if you include both *fly* and *genome* in your search. (There's really not much point in excluding *guy, airplane, airline,* and *fishing* as I do in the previous section because these terms don't come up in search results when you add the term *genome* to the mix.) But you might want to search for fly genomes that belong to flies other than the fruit fly. If so, you could include *genome* and exclude *fruit,* with excellent results:

```
fly genome -fruit
```

Quoting Phrases

A phrase enclosed in double quotes *"like this"* is probably the most commonly used special syntax in a Google search. In a typical search, if you type **chocolate malt**, the words *chocolate* and *malt* can appear anywhere on the Web pages in the results set Google presents to you — so you can end up at a page that discusses chocolate mousse and malt liquor. When you place double quotes around a phrase, Google finds pages that contain the exact phrase *chocolate malt* with the words together in all their happy ice-cream goodness.

Within a quoted phrase, punctuation and capitalization are still ignored, but stop words are not excluded from the search. A search for *Star Wars +I* would yield similar results to a search for *"Star Wars I"*. The difference is that in the first search, *I* can exist anywhere on the pages your search results yield. In the second search, the three terms must be linked together, but any pages that refer to *Star Wars **Episode** I* would be excluded from the results. So the first search is probably slightly better. The moral is that you can change the quality of your search results with minor variations in how you search. You have to decide for yourself whether it is worth the effort to conduct multiple searches with slight variations like this, depending upon your individual research circumstances.

Anytime you are interested in a specific phrase, such as a quotation from a speech, a song lyric, a line of a poem, or a book title, the best way to find it is by using a quoted search.

The classical search with quotes is a search for the phrase *"to be or not to be"*. This phrase is from Hamlet's soliloquy, and without the quotation marks, the exact phrase wouldn't show up in your search results because every word in the phrase except *not* is a stop word. However, a quoted search, with *hamlet* added so that extraneous results are omitted, like this:

```
hamlet "to be or not to be"
```

returns numerous relevant links, as you can see in Figure 4-7.

Applying the *Jeopardy!* approach to research

Although I advise you not to use actual questions in your Google searches, one exception to this rule is when you use quoted phrases that are partial answers to your question.

For example, you could use a quoted search using a partial answering phrase to find the population of San Francisco:

```
"the population of San
    Francisco is"
```

Indeed, the results page for this research contains numerous links to (differing) tallies of the population of San Francisco. While the comparatively simple search for *"San Francisco population"* yields comparable results, you should consider trying a quoted partial answer phrase in some situations.

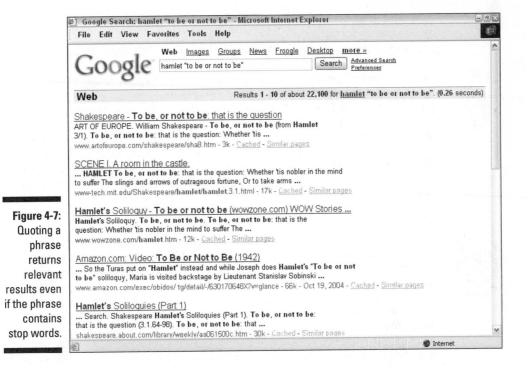

Figure 4-7:
Quoting a
phrase
returns
relevant
results even
if the phrase
contains
stop words.

If you're working on an academic paper, you may be interested to know that quoted phrases are often used by teachers to detect plagiarism. A teacher can use a distinctive phrase or two as the basis for a quoted Google search. Then the instructor can inspect any matches that come up as possible sources from which the student copied text verbatim.

Working with Wildcards

The asterisk, *, is the so-called *wildcard operator*. It is used to match any word. This is extremely useful if you know part of a phrase. For example, searching for

```
"I left my * in San Francisco"
```

provides numerous matches containing the phrase "I left my heart in San Francisco" and a few with other body parts, such as "I left my blood in San Francisco" (don't ask).

You can use multiple stars to represent multiple words. The search

```
"Do you know the way to " **
```

produces numerous links to sites that include the phrase "Do you know the way to San Jose?" as well as others that include phrases like "Do you know the way to Santa Fe?", "Do you know the way to San Andreas?", "Do you know the way to Ban Jose?", "Do you know the way to Abu Ghraib?", and more.

By the way, you can use the wildcard operator either within or outside a quoted phrase. So you get almost the same results if you use the query

```
"Do you know the way to **"
```

Wildcards are not counted towards the ten-word search limit, so you can use a wildcard operator in place of common words to enter somewhat longer search terms.

In Google, unfortunately, the wildcard operator cannot be used to match partial words. So if you want to use a search like *beaut** to match *beautiful, beautician,* and so on, you are out of luck.

Using the Advanced Search Page

Google has many advanced operators, which I show you how to use in Chapter 5. In fact, from the Advanced Search page, you can use most of Google's search operators — the ones I explain in this chapter and the more heavy-duty operators I discuss in Chapter 5. Although you don't get the full functionality of the operators using the Advanced Search page — for example, you have more choices of file type restrictions using operators — you do get most of the operator's functionality. The distinction is that the Advanced Search page offers a different interface for accessing information. So instead of using arcane syntax (+ OR *) you can use a series of text boxes and drop-down menus.

To achieve Google operator functionality without using the Google operators in your search terms themselves, you need to use the Google Advanced Search.

To open the Google Advanced Search page, click the <u>Advanced Search</u> link on the Google home page or to the right of the search box on any Google results page.

In some cases, you may want to use operators as part of your search terms, even if you enter the search terms using the Advanced Search page rather than the usual Google search box, for example, by using the wildcard operator or quoting a phrase in the With All of the Words box.

Take a look at Figure 4-8, which shows the Google Advanced Search page, to see just how many search options are under your control. Ah, the power.

Using the Advanced Search page, you can control search terms by entering text in several different text boxes labeled as follows:

- **with all of the words:** This option is the equivalent of a normal, implicit AND Google search.

- **with the exact phrase:** This option is just like entering a quoted phrase in the Google search box.

- **with at least one of the words:** This is the same thing as using the OR operator between the words in a normal search.

- **without the words:** The words you enter in this box are treated as if they each had the exclusion operator (–) prepended to them.

The Advanced Search page is your first stop if you want to adjust Google settings. For example, you can adjust how searches are conducted, how pages are returned (including the number of results per returned page), and the file formats to be shown as return results. You can also restrict searches to a particular Web domain. (I show you how to do the same thing using the *site* operator in Chapter 5.)

You should know your file format options, especially if you're doing research in records that aren't likely to be associated primarily with the World Wide Web. Google's default is to show you all file formats, but by using the Advanced Search page you can exclude standard Web pages (HTML) and restrict search results to your choice of files in Adobe Acrobat (`.pdf`), Postscript (`.ps`), Microsoft Word (`.doc`), Microsoft Excel (`.xls`), Microsoft PowerPoint (`.ppt`), or Rich Text Format (`.rtf`) formats.

Restricting the file format might lead to improved search results in a number of situations. For example, if you are interested in scholarly or academic research papers, it is a good bet that you'll find these saved as Postscript files, so you can restrict your search to just look for this file type.

Understanding Results

Understanding the results page that Google displays when you make a search is very important to researchers. If you know what you are looking at, you can save a great deal of time — and also glean valuable hints for refining a search to help achieve your research goals.

Figure 4-9 shows a typical results page. This page shows the first ten search results for the query

```
traffic patterns "North Berkeley" BART
```

This query might be used in a research project to analyze how to improve traffic flow and increase pedestrian safety around the North Berkeley BART (Bay Area Rapid Transit) station.

By default, Google only gives you ten results per page. You can change your settings so that you see more results per page. Simply click either the Preferences link or the Advanced Search link on the search results page (see "Using the Advanced Search Page").

Results are returned in the order of their PageRank in Google's index. Pages with the highest PageRank are at the top of the list. I explain the details of how PageRank works in Chapter 11. For now, you can think of PageRank as Google's evaluation of how the Web as a whole evaluates the merit of each Web page.

Each search results page provides statistics in the upper-right corner (above the actual search results) that show you how many results were found in total and how long the search took.

Web search result block — Statistical information

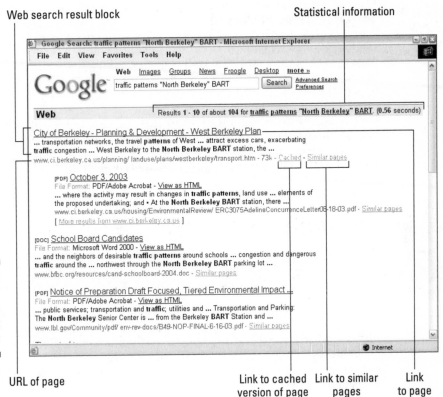

Figure 4-9:
A typical
Google
results
page.

URL of page — Link to cached version of page — Link to similar pages — Link to page

The total count of search results is an estimate, not the precise number. It would take Google too long to figure out the actual number of results each time.

In addition, the statistics part of the results page provides links to each of the terms in a multiword search; these links take you to the definition of the term at Answers.com. The Answers.com definition page provides a link back to the most popular Web sites for the term (using Google of course!), so this can be a speedy shortcut if you decide you need to broaden a search.

Each of the results on the page is represented by a snippet of text from the Web page the result points to. A link to the Web page is also provided, with the title of the page as the text for the link, if it is available (the page's URL is used if it is not).

Each result also provides a <u>Cached</u> link (see the upcoming section, "Cached results") and a <u>Similar Pages</u> link (see "Refining your search," also coming up).

Using the results

Obviously, one way you can use the results presented on a search results page is to click through to the Web page that is linked to each result. But the results page, and each result on the page, contains a great deal of useful information itself.

First, most researchers know to ignore ads and sponsored links for the most part. It can be fun to click through on sponsored links, but technically speaking these are not research results — they are paid-for placements and lack the research validation of a page returned because of its PageRank.

The snippet of text returned as part of a result should help you understand whether the page referenced by the result might contain what you are looking for. Your search terms appear in bold type in the snippet.

If your search terms do not appear in bold in the snippet, it is because the search terms do not appear in the text of the page, but are associated with the page in some other way — for example, as the text of a link pointing to the page.

The snippet itself may, in fact, contain the information you need (for example, the population of San Francisco, or the fact that there are no ants in Antarctica). If you can find what you need in the snippet, there is no need to click through to the actual page, and you can save some time. (Of course, you can better evaluate the credibility of a Web page than of a snippet from that page, although even a snippet provides some clues about its credibility. Credibility of Web sources is a difficult topic, discussed in Chapter 11.)

If the various snippets reveal contradictory information (for example, I mention earlier in this chapter that you'll find differing figures for the population of San Francisco depending on the source), this will alert you to the existence of methodological issues.

One of the best ways to use snippets is to gather ideas for further searches, based on the words and phrases you find in the snippets. For example, the phrase *excess cars* in one of the snippets returned by the *traffic patterns* search shown in Figure 4-9 might be a good search to use to find general information about traffic flow issues. Or you might see something about *bus and car circulation* that spurs an new query.

Snippets can also be used to assess the credibility of a page before you open it. For example, you may want to avoid pages in which the snippets include misspellings or words that are all capitalized.

If a snippet does not appear as part of the result, the page has not been *cached* by Google. This might happen if Google hasn't downloaded the page yet into its Cache servers, but has downloaded pages that contain links to it. See Chapter 11 for more information about how Google's caching works.

You can also scan snippets to (sometimes!) avoid opening pages that are unlikely to produce good research results. These types of pages include

- **Spam pages:** Spam pages are pages placed by sites that contain decep-tive keywords intended to fool Google into thinking they are legitimate. In fact, these pages actually exist for the sole purpose of displaying advertisements. Google is pretty good at eliminating these pages, and you can report them at `www.google.com/contact/spamreport.html`, but some spam pages do get through on occasion. You can usually iden-tify a spam page because it contains the keywords you are interested in but the text is nonsensical and/or repetitious. For example, the following return result is clearly pointing to a spam site:

```
2u Rack Mount Chassis - info on 2u Rack Mount Chassis...
split level. london hotel. limited express. hotel. drop
        ship
wholesale. phone silver or keyboard bracelet. new york
angelina ballerina. vacation. cream polish. ...
host.bagelox.com/2u_rack_mount_chassis.html - 25k -
- Cached - Similar pages
```

- **Commercial pages:** Commercial pages are pretty clearly trying to sell something, which is fine if you are looking to buy it — but usually not very helpful to a researcher, unless the research assignment is to investi-gate the product that is being sold. Just because a site is a ".com" site doesn't make it necessarily unhelpful to a researcher, and there are of course many sites that provide useful information on a for-profit basis. But a site selling, for example, candles or widgets is unlikely to be help-ful to a researcher unless the research topic is candles (or widgets).

It's usually pretty easy to identify commercial sites from their snippets because they often contain product descriptions, prices, and links to pages hosted by well-known retailers. Here's a typical snippet pointing to a commercial page:

```
Amazon.com: Electronics: Linksys BEFW11S4 Wireless-B
Cable/DSL ...... Amazon.com Product Description The
        EtherFast
wireless access point and cable/DSL router features a
        router,
a 4-port 10/100 switch, NAT firewall, and an IEEE ...
www.amazon.com/exec/obidos/ tg/detail/-
        /B00005ARK3?v=glance -68k - Oct 18, 2004 - Cached
        - Similar pages
```

✔ **Logon pages:** These pages usually contain the word "Logon" (or "Login"), references to signing in, or references to lost passwords; they are easy to pick out. Here's a pretty typical snippet that obviously refers to a logon page:

```
Forgot Your Password?Help. Forgot Your Password? Your
        User
Name. Send my Password to: The e-mail address registered
        to my
account A new e-mail address (This ...
www.ezboard.com/help/form_forgotpassword.html - 8k -
        Cached - Similar pages
```

✔ **Error pages:** Error pages usually contain the word "error" in their snippet, and may describe a specific kind of error, such as an access error. Here's a typical error page snippet:

```
Sign-in Access ErrorHotmail. Sign-in Access Error.
        JavaScript
required. The browser that you are using does not support
JavaScript, or you may have disabled JavaScript. Help.
        ...
www.hotmail.com/ - 11k - Cached - Similar pages
```

✔ **Page moved pages:** Page moved pages usually include some of the phrases "Page Moved," "Site Moved," or "Redirect" in their snippets, so they are easy to pick out.

```
PageAmerican Association of Home-Based Businesses is now
accessible from a new site... In 3 seconds, you will be
automatically redirected ...
www.aahbb.org/ - 2k - Cached - Similar pages
```

Cached results

If you click the <u>Cached</u> link in a search result, a copy of the Web page that Google has downloaded and saved in its cache servers appears. (In Chapter 11, I explain how parts of Google work together behind the scenes, and where the cache servers fit in.)

The copy of a Web page that is opened from the Google cache server is a snapshot frozen in time — the time when Google downloaded it. So if the Web page in the "real world" has changed since then, those changes aren't reflected in the cached copy.

Figure 4-10 shows the upper portion of a Google-cached page, which provides information about when it was cached, how to link to the cached page, and the terms in the page that are highlighted, as well as a link to the "live" version of the page.

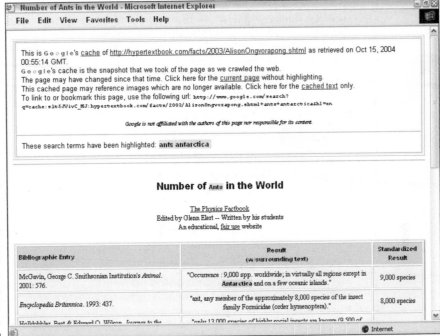

Figure 4-10:
Google
highlights
terms from
your
search
in its
cached
pages.

So why open a cached version of a page rather than the page itself? For the most part, there's no particularly good reason to do so; however, cached pages provide a potential resource that researchers should know about:

✔ The fact that search terms are highlighted in the cached result (of course, they are not in a live page) can be helpful.

✔ You can usually open cached pages more quickly than you can access its live analog because Google's servers are faster than almost anybody else's.

✔ If you can't access the live Web page (perhaps because the Web server is down, or because the page has been removed), you may be able to find the cached page. Still, you need to be aware that the cached page you are viewing is not necessarily up to date. (Of course, if you are looking for removed information, this may be what you want.)

Refining your search

According to some studies, if you don't find search result you need within the first 25 results returned, you need to change or refine your search. In other words, assuming that the number of results per results page has been left at the default of ten, there's no point in looking past the first three results pages.

In my own experience, I sometimes find useful results farther down in the ordering of a results set than 25. However, at some point fairly early on (and by early on I mean within the first half dozen pages of your millions and millions of results pages) you hit the law of diminishing returns. Efficient research practice says it is better to refine your search earlier than later.

There are many ways to refine a search. After your initial search, you may realize that you need to change directions and rethink how to proceed. If nothing pops into your mind as a way to change or refine your search, the following methods can help you get better results:

- **Click the <u>Similar pages</u> link provided by the return result that is closest to what you are looking for:** This action provides a list with results similar to the initial resource, particularly pages from competitive sites.

- **Add a word at the end of the existing search term:** Doing so instantly generates a search within the existing results because the added word implicitly uses the AND operator. (See "Understanding the AND operator," earlier in this chapter.)

- **Start over with a new search based on new keywords you picked up from the snippets:** Do a new search using terms suggested by the return snippets from your original search.

Chapter 5

Achieving Precision with Google Operators

. . . .

In This Chapter

▶ Using the synonym operator

▶ Searching for similar pages with `related:`

▶ Effective searching with `in:` and `allin:`

▶ Using operators to find specialized information

▶ Searching within a site

▶ Building a Site Search box

. . . .

*B*eyond the valley of the "simple" Google operators that I explain in Chapter 4 lies a vast and beautiful landscape of Google operators that can be used to achieve precision in your searches.

This chapter tells you how to get the most out of some of the most sophisticated Google operators. You learn how to use

    ✔ The synonym operator (~) to perform flexible searching

    ✔ The `related:` operator to broaden the horizons of your searches

    ✔ The occurrences operators (beginning with `in:` or `allin:`) to achieve pinpoint results

I also show you how to use specialized operators to find definitions of terms, restrict the file types in search results, find all the links to a given page, and locate the phone numbers for people and businesses.

Sometimes you don't want to search the whole Web. Maybe you just want to search a particular site. I show you how to easily do this with the `site:` operator and I also show you some useful related techniques. Best of all, I show you how to use the `site:` operator, along with a little JavaScript code, to add a Google site search to an HTML page. This is a great little tool — add it to your own Web site if you want users to be able to search the site with Google. You also can use it as an easy research tool if you find yourself often searching a particular site.

You can achieve much — but not all — of the functionality I explain in this chapter by using the Google Advanced Search form. In some cases, there's no other way to obtain the research results shown in this chapter except by using the operators that I explain.

Using the Synonym Operator

When you place the synonym operator, ~, directly in front of a search term (without any spaces), the search matches Web synonyms as well as the given search term. Using this operator can make crafting a search term a great deal easier if you suspect that your search term is close to a word that will deliver the result you are looking for (but not quite the word).

The synonym operator symbol, ~, called a *tilde,* means approximately in mathematics (which is why Google chose the symbol for this purpose).

One way you can think of this operator is as equating words with similar meanings. For example, suppose you have a research project in which you need to find hard, statistical data related to vehicular traffic patterns. The term data has several synonyms; by placing the ~ symbol in front of *data,* you open your search up to many more relevant results. A search query like

```
traffic ~data -site
```

matches not just *traffic data* but also *traffic statistics, traffic information,* and so on.

I added the -site: exclusion term to this example to exclude the word *site* so that I would get results mostly related to vehicular traffic rather than Web *site* traffic. (I explain the exclusion operator, -, in Chapter 4.) If you use the synonym operator, you should try to also use exclusionary terms to avoid making your search too broad. I added the -site: exclusion to this search after discovering that, without it, I was getting a large number of network traffic results (as well as the desired results relating to vehicular traffic).

In this search, -site: is an excluded term, not the site: operator.

As you've probably realized, you could use the OR operator, together with all the alternative terms you wanted to use, instead of the synonym operator. (I explain how to use the OR operator in Chapter 4.) But to use the OR operator as if it is the synonym operator, you'd need to know all the possible alternative terms that you might want to search on. The great advantage of the synonym operator is that you don't need to know these words in advance. You just have to trust that Google does.

Of course, if there are no synonyms for a term, using the synonym operator isn't going to help you. For example, as Gertrude Stein wrote, "a rose is a rose is a rose." A search for ~*rose* on Google leads to the same results as the simpler search for *rose*.

If you expect that Google gets its synonyms from a synonym lookup table, otherwise known as a *thesaurus* in the offline world, you're wrong. In the universe of Google, synonyms are determined by Web usage of the terms. If Google finds that on several pages two terms appear in close proximity to each other, Google thinks of the terms as synonyms — even if they are far apart in meaning.

This method of discovering synonyms sometimes leads to some pretty weird results. According to Google, there are really no synonyms for the search term ~*giraffe* besides *giraffe*. But if you enter the term ~**zebra**, you'll find that *bar code* is a synonym of *zebra* — because of the Zebra bar code technology.

Would you believe that if you enter ~**patient**, you get *doctor* as a synonym? (And not as in "Doctor, heal thyself?") Sometimes the synonym operator in fact yields antonyms (as in this example).

The synonym operator does not necessarily work equally in both directions. For example, if you type ~**cheap** you discover that *buy* is its synonym. (In some cases, Google synonyms only go in one direction: You won't find *cheap* as a synonymous result if you enter ~**buy**.)

The synonym operator is a valuable research tool. Just keep in mind, the synonyms it comes up with are based on Web usage patterns, and are not the synonyms you'd find in a thesaurus.

There are a bunch of wacky Google games out there. For example, I tell you about GoogleFight later in this chapter. Right now, I want propose a new one: Find the wackiest Google supposed synonym. Please send me your wacky Google synonyms at `research_google@bearhome.com`.

The Related Operator

In Chapter 4, I explain how to use the return results set from a search to show you similar pages. All you need to do is click the <u>Similar pages</u> link (see Figure 5-1).

Under the hood, the <u>Similar pages</u> link invokes a fresh search using the `related:` operator and the page you've selected.

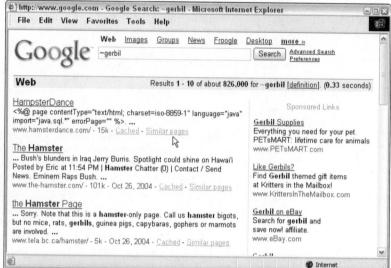

Figure 5-1:
Click the
Similar
pages link
in a return
result
snippet to
see related
pages.

If you like this idea, you can skip a step and request to see similar pages when you enter your initial search query. To see all the similar pages of a given page, use the `related:` operator followed by the original page (without any spaces). For example, the search

```
related:www.google.com
```

returns 31 results that are, for the most part, search engines that compete with Google. If you are curious, the top returns for this search (at least when I searched) are, in order: Yahoo!, AltaVista, Lycos, Excite, AlltheWeb, DogPile, WebCrawler, Northern Light, and MSN.

The *related:www.google.com* search includes a few "similar" page results that are obviously not search engines, and omits some of the search engine and meta-search engines you would find on a broader keyword lookup like *Web search engine*. Why this is true is anyone's guess. But the point is that a broad search returns many results — there are more than 7,000,000 results for *Web search engine* search — versus the handful pulled in using the `related:` operator. This makes the `related:` operator an effective tool for broadening a search in a pinpoint fashion.

As you might expect from a search engine that relies on context and ranking to give relevant results, the `related:` operator works better on well-known pages with a high PageRank, such as `www.google.com` or `www.nytimes.com`, than it does on more obscure pages because it's sometimes not particularly clear what a similar page is.

Working with Occurrences Operators

Unless you specify otherwise, Google matches your search terms to keywords located anywhere in the text of a Web page — and in a lot of other places, too, including the HTML elements used to create the page. This means that you sometimes don't get the most precise results when you use the default tools. For example, if you search for *best programming practices,* you may end up with a page that lists results of all three words in different locations, one in the header, one in a link, and another in the name of the page. In lower-ranked results, you may end up with pages that contain only two of the words, not located together. As I note in Chapter 4, you can put the search term in quotation marks *("best programming practices")* to ensure that resulting pages contain the terms together, which improves your results considerably. However, with the *occurrences operators,* you can get even more specific with your directives to Google. For example a search for:

```
allintitle: best programming practices
```

returns results with all three words in the HTML title of a page, an even more pinpointed result than quoting the terms (because the fact that the words are in the title means that the Webmaster who created the page feels that they best describe the page).

The occurrences operators are used to pinpoint the occurrence of search terms in specific elements of Web pages and Web links. For example, you use one of the four occurrences operators beginning with allin: when you want *all the terms* in a search to be in a page or link element (such as the title of the page). You use one of the occurrences operators beginning with in: to make sure that *a single search term* is found in the specified page or link element.

Operators that apply to a single term, like intitle:, must immediately precede the term without any spaces. On the other hand, some operators (for example, the allin: operators and define:) refer to all the terms in a search. These operators must go at the beginning of a search, can't be combined with other search operators, and they're usually (but don't have to be) followed by a space before the search terms they apply to.

You can specifically target four possible page and link elements with either the allin: or the in: operator. These groupings are shown in Table 5-1.

Table 5-1	Grouping the Occurrences Operators			
Where to Look for Terms:	**Text of Links to Page**	**Text of a Web Page**	**Title of a Web Page**	**URL of a Web Page**
allin: (all search terms)	allinanchor:	allintext:	allintitle:	allinurl:
in: (single search terms)	inanchor:	intext:	intitle:	inurl:

Here's a quick rundown of what these four terms mean:

- ✔ **anchor:** An anchor is the text that accompanies or makes up a description of a link. This is sometimes also called *link text.* The Web page that is opened when a user clicks the link is called the link's *target.*

  From an HTML perspective, an anchor (or link text) is everything between `<a>` and `</a>` tags.

- ✔ **text:** The stuff written in the actual HTML document that is in the body of a page and not part of an HTML tag itself.

- ✔ **title:** The name the Webmaster has given the HTML file, found in the `<head>` section of an HTML page between the `<title>` and `</title>` tags.

- ✔ **URL:** The *Uniform Resource Locator,* or address in human-readable form on the Web, of a Web page.

If you think about it, you only really need the `in:` operators: an `allin:` search of all terms within a specific element could be constructed using the AND operator with each search term. But having the `allin:` operator sure makes life easier for researchers! For example, the search *allintitle: harold davis* is exactly the same as the search *intitle:harold intitle:davis.*

Table 5-2 shows all eight of the occurrences operators, what they mean, and an example of how each is used.

To get a better feeling for the examples in Table 5-2, you can use Google to search with them and take a look at the results.

Table 5-2	Using the Occurrences Operators	
Occurrences Operator	*What It Does*	*Example Query*
`allinanchor:`	The pages returned are linked to by pages with all search terms in anchor text.	*allinanchor: best research tools*
`allintext:`	All search terms must appear in the text of the page.	*allintext: HTML tag*
`allintitle:`	All search terms must appear in the title of the page.	*allintitle: Form 1120*
`allinurl:`	All search terms must appear in the URL of the page.	*allinurl:easter island statues*
`inanchor:`	Term *(deciduous)* must appear in the anchor text of links to the page.	*inanchor:deciduous trees*
`intext:`	Term must appear in the text of the page.	*intext:HTML*
`intitle:`	Term must appear in the title of a page.	*intitle:10-k*
`inurl:`	Term *(CIA)* must appear in the URL (Web address) of a page.	*inurl:CIA population density*

How you can best use the occurrences operators (and the examples shown in Table 5-2) may take a bit of getting used to. The following sections offer a bit more explanation.

Finding your links: `allinanchor:` and `inanchor:` operators

Suppose you want your search to return only pages that are the target of links when the link text matches your search. To do so, you can use the `allinanchor:` and `inanchor:` operators. These operators search only text that consists of clickable links on Web pages.

Another way of putting this is that the text being searched falls inside `<a>` `</a>`, or *anchor,* tags in the underlying HTML. Less formally, an anchor is a term or phrase that identifies a document in a noncomputerese language so that when people click the link they know what they're getting. Few Webmasters would write an anchor like *Mr. McGee's Fishing Site* if they were linking to `www.acmeknitting.com`; an anchor such as *Visit Acme Knitting* would be more probable.

Because anchor text is reasonably likely to contain a straightforward description of the content of the page being linked to, using anchor text for pinpointed research often makes good sense, even though the return result is the site being linked to (for example, `www.acmeknitting.com`).

To take this a little further, if you already know you are interested in Acme Knitting, it's easy to end up on the Acme Knitting site. But suppose you want to find the best site about knitting in general. A search for

```
inanchor:knitting
```

returns pages that are the targets of links that have the keyword *knitting* in link text somewhere on the Web pages, including Acme Knitting. The order of the search results tells you the most-linked sites — a gauge of popularity, and a rough indicator of quality on the Web.

In another example, suppose a Web page contains a whole bunch of text and the phrase <u>Times Square in New York</u> is a clickable link. If you want to find all Web pages that are linked to with anchors that contain the words *New York Times* in clickable links, you use the `allinanchor:` operator, along with the three words *New York Times* in your search; the page linked to by the *Times Square in New York* anchor shows up in the results set.

The `allinanchor:` and `inanchor:` operators are probably the most useful of the occurrences operators, but they can also be the most difficult to wrap your brain around.

The anchor operators match a keyword, multiple keywords, or a search phrase with the text that accompanies a hyperlink. The returned page is the one pointed to by the hyperlink, not the one containing the text. For example, suppose that the HTML for the page `www.braintique.com` (like thousands of other sites) contains a link to the New York Times Web site (`www.nytimes.com`):

```
I get my news from the
<a href="http://www.nytimes.com">New York Times</a>!
```

An `allinanchor:` search for the phrase *New York Times*:

```
allinanchor: New York Times
```

returns a list of sites that are the targets of links on pages that use the terms *New, York,* and *Times* in their anchor text. Not surprisingly, the New York Times Online site itself is one of these targets, and as a result of its popularity, the New York Times site appears at the top of the return results set for this search.

A few things you ought to remember about the `allinanchor:` and `inanchor:` operators:

- ✔ **Resulting pages are targets, not originators of the anchors.** The `allinanchor:` and `inanchor:` operators return results pages that are the *targets* of pages that use your search term in their anchors; to repeat in a different way, the results aren't the pages containing the anchors, but the targets to which the anchors point.

- ✔ **Search terms don't have to all appear in the same link text (anchor).** For example, this search:

  ```
  allinanchor: Groups Froogle
  ```

  finds the main Google page, which includes Groups in one link, and Froogle in a separate link. (Don't be fooled because the results set includes the Google page; the links on the page with the *Groups* and *Froogle* text themselves point to Google, which is why Google is returned.)

- ✔ **Use quotes to get exact links.** If you want to find pages with link text that includes an exact phrase, you should use the `inanchor:` or `allinanchor:` operator (either will do) combined with a quoted phrase. For example:

  ```
  inanchor:"New York Times"
  ```

  returns pages with the literal phrase *"New York Times"* in a single anchor, not potentially divided up in a bunch of different anchors with *"New," "York,"* and *"Times"* in the different anchors.

  Mind you, without the quotes, keywords don't have to be in order, either, so without quotation marks you risk the possibility of finding results such as the target of an anchor to the *New Times* or the *York Times.*

In essence, the `allinanchor:` and `inanchor:` operators let you obtain search results based on the links leading to a site. From a research perspective, you can use this team of operators as your own personal version of the Google PageRank popularity determination (see Chapter 11 for more about the Google PageRank). For example, in Table 5-2, the example query for

```
allinanchor: best research tools
```

returns a list of sites with research tools good enough that someone has bothered to link to them with the text *best research tools* in the link (you can see some of the snippets pointing to these research tools in Figure 5-2).

Figure 5-2:
Other sites
have linked
to these
research
tools, so
they ought
to be good.

The search

```
inanchor:deciduous trees
```

looks for the word *deciduous* in the text of a hyperlink and the word *tree* somewhere in the text of a document, and returns a much more pinpointed list of sites with information about deciduous trees, rather than a straight search for the keywords *deciduous trees* — because the sites in the results set were linked to with text that included the word *deciduous*.

These operators allow you to harness the power of hyperlinking on the Web so that you can hone your research results.

The in: operators *must* precede the term they modify without a space. In contrast, the allin: operators are allowed a space (these operators refer to all terms and must appear first in the search query). It's better form to keep the space for allin: operators.

Getting into the text: allintext: *and* intext:

The allintext: and intext: operators, which return results when all search terms (allintext:) or a single search term (intext:) match within the text of a page, are probably the least useful of the occurrences operators.

You should know that you can use a variety of other elements in Google to make a search match besides the text of a page. Google can look into the HTML (meta tags, `alt` parameters of `img` tags, and more) and within inbound link text (which is where the `allinanchor:` and `inanchor:` operators come in). A default Google search without operators does look at all this stuff, and not just the text on a page.

The word HTML appears in almost every single document on the Web, since almost every document starts with the `<html>` tag. But what if you want to search for the word HTML in the text itself and not in the tags? You can use the `intext:` (or `allintext:`) operator.

When you use these operators, Google doesn't look at any other elements in addition to the text in a document. When you're searching for a term like *HTML,* limiting the search to the document texts (and excluding HTML tags) is very useful. The search

```
intext:HTML
```

returns only pages with the term *HTML* in their text, with vastly different results than you would get if you simply constructed a search query for the term *HTML.*

Finding forms: `allintitle:` *and* `intitle:`

The `allintitle:` and `intitle:` operators search for terms, or a single word, within the title of a page. These operators can be extraordinarily effective in conducting searches with laserlike precision when you are looking for something that is likely to be in a page title. A good time to use either the `allintitle:` or `intitle:` operator is when you're looking for specific bureaucratic forms. If you want to find information about Form 1120 (a — yawn — corporate income tax form), distributed by the U.S. Internal Revenue Service, as well as other information about completing the form, the search

```
allintitle: Form 1120
```

gets you just what you want. If you are interested in the SEC's 10-K form, which is used for filing corporate annual reports with the U.S. Securities and Exchange Commission, the search

```
intitle:10-k
```

gives you links to the SEC's site describing the form, to online databases containing the form, and to much more information related to 10-K filings.

In contrast, a straight search for the term *10-k* returns all sorts of extraneous results, like sites about running 10-K races and sites about 10-K dollars.

If one of your search terms includes a hyphen, you might want to try searching with the hyphen and without the hyphen. For example, you'll get different results if you search for *10-k* (which Google regards as one word) than if you search for *10 k* (which Google treats as two words). You can omit the hyphen from a search within a title for a hyphenated word (such as `intitle:10-k`) with the `allintitle:` operator, for example: `allintitle: 10 k`. Bottom line: There's no correct way to treat hyphens, only different ways. Each search makes as much sense as any other, and each produces unique results, so I recommend experimentation.

Narrowing the search: `allinurl:` *and* `inurl:`

Suppose you want to search only the addresses of the Web pages and not the text of the pages. In that case, you would use the `allinurl:` or `inurl:` operator. For example, suppose you want to get back a results set that contains only pages whose addresses have the words *dummies* and *books* in them. Here are some sample pages you might see in such a results set:

```
www.ccc24k.com/dummies-books.htm
www.linux-directory.com/ perl-books/Perl-for-Dummies.shtml
www.evsdesigns.com/online-deals-kws/ books/for-dummies/1.html
```

In fact, probably the best way to really narrow a search is to use the `inurl:` and `allinurl:` operators, which make sure that the word (or words) in the search term appear in the URL of all the results pages that turn up. Searches with these operators can be very efficient, but you may miss results that interest you because not all Web sites have addresses with URLs that reflect their contents. For example, the Dented Reality site (with the URL `www.dented reality.com.au/`) is the home of XooMLe, a great tool for working with HTTP and the Google APIs (I explain how to use it in Chapter 15), but you'd never know it from the URL (or, in this particular case, from the site title either).

For example, the search

```
allinurl:easter island statues
```

returns 38 results. In contrast, a straight search for *easter island statues* without being modified with an operator, returns over 27,000 results. Most of the 38 results returned from the pinpointed search are on topic, while the broader search results contain a mélange of the relevant, irrelevant, and plain old spam sites. Pinpointing your search makes culling through search results less burdensome because they are more likely to be on topic. Besides, 38 is a reasonable number.

If you want to know what the U.S. Central Intelligence Agency has to say publicly about population density, the search

```
inurl:CIA population density
```

works well because results are restricted to Web sites with the term *CIA* in the URL and containing *population density* in the text (or some other element).

Including and excluding with the occurrences operators

Mixing and matching occurrences operators can be a very effective method of arriving at just the right search results, while at the same time excluding the results you don't want.

For example, to find pages about Google that aren't originated and managed by Google, you could create a search that includes *Google* in the page title, but excludes it from the URL:

```
intitle:google -inurl:google
```

If you want to get around the party line about a company or institution, a search that includes the company name in the page title and excludes it from the URL will probably find the dirt on the company, that is, if there is any dirt to be dished.

For example, the search *intitle:walmart -inurl:walmart* returns *The evil that is Walmart, Does Walmart avoid paying its workers for work done?,* and so on, in the first ten return results. These sites are inherently biased, but then that's the point of this search — to bring up the dirt anyone is saying about a company or other institution. Just because someone has put up a Web site doesn't mean the material on the site is true. (I show you how to evaluate the credibility of Web sources in Chapter 11.)

You can also use occurrences operators with a combination of inclusions and exclusions to pin down an otherwise ambiguous search. This technique is especially useful for words have multiple meanings.

For example, it's possible to surf waves, or to surf the Internet. The search

```
intitle:surf -intext:internet
```

returns results relevant to the ocean, but not to the Internet.

Getting Definitions

What does that word mean? Even accomplished researchers don't always know, particularly if they are in the early stages of learning about a technical and complex subject.

As I explain in Chapter 4, Google search results contain links to online definitions (supplied by Answers.com) for each word in the search phrase.

You can also use the `define:` operator in Google to quickly get a so-called Web definition of a word (or phrase) — with or without doing a search. That is, you get linked to a compendium of definitions of the word or phrase on the Web, along with links to the Web page that originated each definition.

Often, seeing someone else's definition of a word (even if you already know what the word means) generates new research avenues and keywords.

To view the Web definition of a word or phrase, start with the `define:` operator and then add the word or phrase (you can add a space after the operator if you'd like). For example:

```
define: class interface
```

provides a definition of *class interface* culled from the Web, as you can see in Figure 5-3.

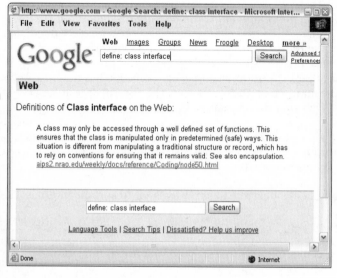

Figure 5-3: When you use the `define:` operator, Google gives you definitions from the Web.

Because these definitions are taken from a variety of Web sources, they are not always good or authoritative. For example, the definition of class interface shown in Figure 5-3 could certainly be improved.

If you leave the colon off the operator, for example typing **define class interface**, Google shows you search results as well as Web definitions. Ultimately, you may learn more about the subject from some of the search results than you do when you use the define: operator.

Restricting File Types

In Chapter 4, I explain that you can use the Advanced Search form to restrict a search to a specific type of file. For example, you can restrict your file types to Adobe Acrobat (.pdf), Postscript (.ps), Microsoft Word (.doc), Microsoft Excel (.xls), Microsoft PowerPoint (.ppt), or Rich Text Format (.rtf) formats.

The filetype: operator provides the same functionality as the File Format drop-down list in the Advanced Search form. It also allows you to restrict searches to some additional file formats.

To restrict a search to a specific format, use the filetype: operator followed by the file extension, and then type your search term.

Restricting a search using file format can narrow results and make the search more accurate under the right circumstances. For example, if you're looking for a scholarly paper, restricting your search to Adobe Postscript might make sense. If you expect to find answers in a business presentation, it might help to restrict your search to Microsoft PowerPoint files.

Owners' manuals and other documentation found online are often meant to be view as Adobe Acrobat (.pdf) files. So restricting your file format to Acrobat might make sense if you are looking for product documentation. For example, suppose you want to find the operating manual for a Panasonic High Definition Plasma television. If you know the television's model number, you can do the most precise search possible by narrowing your search down by file format, like this:

```
filetype:pdf TH-42PX25U/P
```

This search returns all PDF files that contain the string *TX-42PX25U/P*. Included in the results set is a link to the product's operating manual, as you can see in Figure 5-4.

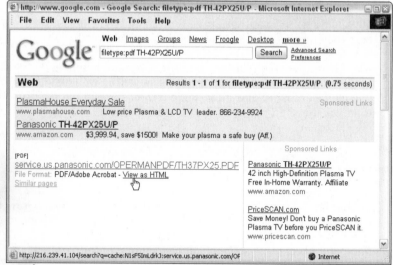

Figure 5-4:
Restricting
file formats
can help
you find
authoritative
information,
such as this
product
manual.

Google has the ability to automatically convert the files it understands to HTML (or to text if they cannot be converted to HTML). This means that you don't need to have any special software to view these files. For example, suppose you don't have Acrobat Reader and want to view the PDF file whose snippet is shown in Figure 5-4. Simply click the View as HTML link.

Backtracking with the Link Operator

The link: operator returns pages that link to the specified page. For example, the search

```
link:www.researchbuzz.com
```

returns sites that contain links to www.researchbuzz.com, as you can see in Figure 5-5.

Webmasters can use the information provided by the link: operator in a number of ways:

- ✔ To help understand their own page's PageRank

- ✔ To find out about the sites that link to their site

- ✔ To find out which sites link to competitors' sites (and perhaps can be persuaded to add another link as well)

Figure 5-5:
The search
using the
link:
operator
returns
more than
1,700 pages
that have
linked to the
Research
buzz site.

Researchers can use the information provided by the link: operator as:

✔ **A rough indication of a site's credibility:** You can generally regard pages with many links as inherently likely to be credible — or at least many Webmasters have thought so. The fact that researchbuzz.com has links, also called *back links,* from some 1,700 other pages makes it a credible source for information about the online research business. But researchbuzz.com is not as credible as the New York Times, with more than 73,000 back links. (By comparison, www.google.com has over 2,500,000 back links.)

✔ **A helpful navigation tool:** The link: search results for a page can also provide navigation help. Suppose a page in a multipage article doesn't provide a link to the first page of the article, or to the table of contents for the material that includes the article. Provided the site has been indexed by Google, the back links for the page should provide this navigation information.

Finding a Phone Number

Researchers often need to find a phone number for a person or business. You may have any number of legitimate reasons for needing this information; you might need to confirm something your research has found, talk to a background expert, or maybe you've been asked to find financial information that involves a person or business.

The Google phone number operators currently only work for the United States (not for Canada or the rest of the world). So if you are looking for a phone number that's outside of the U.S., you are out of luck, at least with these operators; you can find many phone numbers in the U.S. and around the world with another type of Web search.

Google provides the three operators shown in Table 5-3 to locate the phone number of a person or business.

Table 5-3	Finding a Phone Number	
Operator	*What It Does*	*Example*
bphonebook:	Locates business phone numbers	*bphonebook: Google CA*
phonebook:	Locates business and residential phone numbers	*phonebook: D Smith NY*
rphonebook:	Locates home phone numbers	*rphonebook: Larry Page CA*

To search for a phone number, choose the operator you want to use (refer to Table 5-3) depending on whether you are looking for a business number, a residential number, or (in some circumstances) both. The phonebook: operator needs to be the first term in the search. You must include some geographic information when you conduct the search. You don't have to include the state, but if you include just a city name, you may end up with listings from several states. Obviously, the more specific you are, the more likely you are to come up with the phone number you want.

Entering a city and state give you more pinpointed results than just entering a state. Also, you don't need to include a comma between the name of the person and the geographical information (however, adding a comma doesn't affect results, so if you are mindlessly accurate with punctuation, don't worry).

For example, a search for

```
rphonebook: Larry Page CA
```

returns a number of listings for people named Larry Page living in California.

Because a search for a common name like Larry Page generally yields more than one result, you may not know which residential number belongs to Larry Page, the cofounder of Google. Perhaps none of them do. You wouldn't know for sure without trying the number and speaking to someone at the other end of the line. I'm certainly not going to bother Larry, or anyone else, without a good reason, and neither should you!

This leads me to some inherent limitations in the Google phonebook search. These include the following:

- ✔ Google cannot return unlisted numbers.

- ✔ You won't get meaningful results unless you include a state, which can be written out *(California)* or entered via its two-letter abbreviation *(CA)*.

- ✔ If a name is common, a phonebook search returns many phone numbers. Particularly with residential searches, being sure which result goes with the person you're interested in finding can be difficult. For example, searching for

  ```
  phonebook: D Smith NY
  ```

  returns roughly 30 business and 600 residential listings. If you know a town (or city), you can include this along with the state, for example:

  ```
  phonebook: D Smith albany ny
  ```

  Even this search yields 36 results — too many to make a guess. Pretty much the only way you can pick between these numbers is if you already know the street address of the person or business you are looking for.

- ✔ Multiple phone numbers are often returned for a single business. For example, searching for

  ```
  bphonebook: Google Ca
  ```

  returns four different numbers. As the Ghostbusters say, "Who ya gonna call?"

- ✔ There can be inaccuracies in the underlying telephone directory data that Google uses. For example, my own listings in the Google phone directories are inaccurate. These errors and omissions can make it harder to find specific people or businesses.

You can find a list of sites with directories for finding people and phone numbers by searching Google with the keywords *find person*. Using the keywords *find business* results in sites that claim to locate (and provide information about) businesses.

If you really hit a dead end, there are also a number of services on the Web that will help you locate, and find information about, a person or business for

Finding phone numbers with other Web sources

If you don't find the phone number you need using Google's phonebook: operator, try looking for the listing with Google's Web search. A surprising number of phone numbers, along with address information, do show up on the Web.

Doing a Web search of the company name and the city and state is particularly helpful. For example, the search string *Google Mountain View CA* shows a Local Results item at the top of the results set, and the item contains Google's phone number. Pretty cool!

Because not all online phone directories use the same underlying data, you should also try other phone directories besides Google before

you give up your phone number search. A good online directory to try is www.switchboard.com. Because Switchboard is well connected in the U.S. telephone industry, it tends to have comprehensive listings in the United States. There are, of course, many other phone directory sites on the Web; you can find many of them by searching Google for related:www.switchboard.com.

Switchboard (like Google) only includes U.S. telephone numbers. If you are interested in phone numbers outside the U.S., Infobel (www.infobel.com/world) is a good site to try. Infobel provides links to phone directories for most countries in the world.

---

a fee. You can easily find these services by looking at the sponsored links when you do a *find person* or *find business* search on Google. *Caveat emptor!* It's up to you to investigate these services before you try them out.

Google also supports reverse phone lookups. This means that if you have a U.S. phone number, you can just enter it as a search into Google.

With a reverse phone lookup, Google shows you the name and address associated with the number. (Figure 5-6 shows you the results of a reverse lookup for 408-363-0186, one of the numbers I found for Google.)

Reverse lookups are, of course, useful if you have a phone number but lack other information. You can also use the information provided by the reverse lookup to eliminate possible numbers. (Because the Google mothership is docked in Mountain View, and the 408-363-0186 number resolves to San Jose, it is probably not a primary Google phone number.)

If you really want to find a business's phone number, the easiest way to do so would probably be to look through the Contact Us section of the company's Web site.

In addition, you can use reverse lookups to get more information about the person or business associated with the number. (For more information about a variety of numbers you can enter directly into the Google search box, see Chapter 1.)

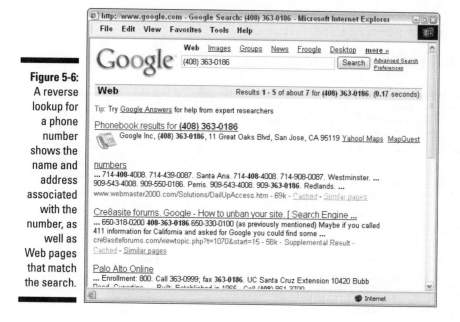

Figure 5-6:
A reverse
lookup for
a phone
number
shows the
name and
address
associated
with the
number, as
well as
Web pages
that match
the search.

Combing a Site

It's often the case that a researcher needs to find information about a particular site, along with information contained on the site. For example, suppose you are researching information that the U.S. FBI has about white-collar crime. For the time being, you are only interested in FBI information, so you need to limit your searches to the FBI site (`fbi.gov`).

The following sections explain how to *comb* a site — go through it with a fine-tooth comb looking for every reference to your search term.

Getting all of Google's information about a site

The first thing you might want to do is find out what Google knows about the site you want to comb. For example, if you're interested in combing the U.S. FBI's Web site, you start by entering **fbi.gov** as a search term in Google. The results shown look a lot like Figure 5-7.

You can search for either *fbi.gov* or *www.fbi.gov* and get the same results.

The return results for the domain search, shown in Figure 5-7, provide you with a link to the domain's home page, as well as links to

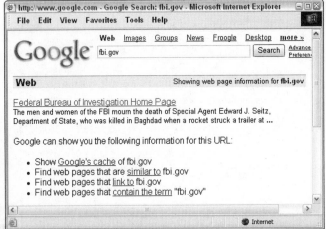

Figure 5-7:
Google can
tell you lots
of things
about a
Web page.

✔ The cached version of the site (see Chapter 4 for an explanation of caching, and when you can benefit from using a cached version of a site).

✔ Similar pages to the site (such as *fbi.gov*). These are the pages you would get with a `related:` search, and mostly belong to government organizations.

✔ Sites that contain a link to the site (such as *fbi.gov*). You get the same results as if you had used the `link:` operator.

✔ Pages that include the text in your search (such as *fbi.gov*).

You can use these return results as a kind of command central so that you don't have to do individual searches to access this information.

Using the `site:` operator

You use the `site:` operator to restrict searches to a site or a *domain*. You can restrict searches using the `site:` operator to domains such as `.com`, `.edu`, and `.org`. As examples, it might make sense to do this if you are looking for information and suspect it will be found within a school or university (`.edu`), or in a not-for-profit organization (`.org`).

For example, you might want to restrict a search for tools that help detect plagiarism to `.edu` sites, because plagiarism is a problem that most often impacts students, schools, and universities:

```
site:.edu plagiarism tools detect
```

Going local

Even when you don't need a phone number or address, a time may come when you need to keep search results pinpointed to a specific geographic area. Google provides several mechanisms for helping you get geographic data.

If you add a zip code after your other search terms, the first few results Google returns are local results within the zip code you specified. These local results are indicated with a little compass icon (I discuss this feature in Chapter 1).

Alternatively, you can use the Google Local service by opening the URL `http://local.` `google.com`. Although it has been around a while, the Google Local service is still technically in beta, meaning it has not been officially launched yet.

With the Google Local page open, you can enter a local search term, and a location (using city and state, or zip code), as you can see in the following figure.

Click the Google Search button. Google returns numerous local listings, along with a map showing locations, and some other relevant local information.

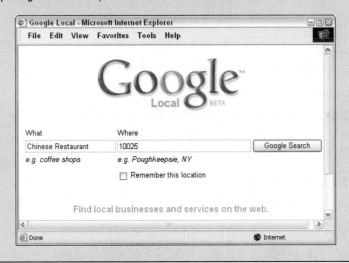

Make sure not to put a space between the `site:` operator and the domain or site to which you're restricting your search.

You can use the `site:` operator to search the FBI's site for information about white-collar crime with a search like

```
site:fbi.gov white collar crime
```

Search results (except for sponsored links) are restricted to pages on the `fbi.gov` site, as you can see in Figure 5-8.

Figure 5-8:
Google can tell you lots of things about a Web page.

Building a Site Search Box

You can easily use the `site:` operator and a little JavaScript code right in an HTML page to create a search box that uses Google to search within any site it has indexed.

Building your own Site Search box this way has a number of potential uses. You can use it to extend the functionality of Google.

Using ready-made functionality

Two sites that use simple client-side code to extend the functionality of Google's searches are FaganFinder, `www.faganfinder.com`, and GoogleFight, `www.googlefight.com`. (Although neither of these sites specifically use the `site:` operator to implement searches within a Google-indexed site, they both show how easy it is to use the technique to extend Google's functionality.)

FaganFinder allows you to do a typical Google search, but supplements Google with other searching resources.

In the case of GoogleFight, I use the phrase "extends the functionality" loosely. GoogleFight is a novelty site. Users enter two different Google search terms, and GoogleFight displays which of the terms gets more research results from a Google search. For example, *Open Source* beats *Bill Gates* by 14,800,000 to 3,300,000 research results returned.

Analyzing Google's search string

If you're a Webmaster, you can use a Site Search box to add site searching capabilities to their own site (provided it has been indexed by Google). That way, researchers can use a Site Search box to run searches against any site, so they don't have to repeatedly enter the site address.

The first thing is to notice the URL that is generated when you click the Google Search button. Essentially, clicking this button sends the search string to the Google server. To create your own search box, you can easily send your own search string to the Google server. To see what this search string ought to look like, look at the string, or URL, that Google actually sends when you initiate a search:

1. **Open the Internet Explorer browser and choose View➪Toolbars to select the Address Bar option so that it has a check mark next to it.**

2. **Initiate a search in Google such as** *site:fbi.gov white collar crime,* **and click the Search button.**

   The search string in the URL is sent to Google in the Address Bar (see Figure 5-9). For example, the keywords *site:fbi.gov white collar crime* yield the following string:

   ```
   http://www.google.com/search?hl=en&q=site%3Afbi.gov+white
                        +collar+crime&btnG=Google+Search
   ```

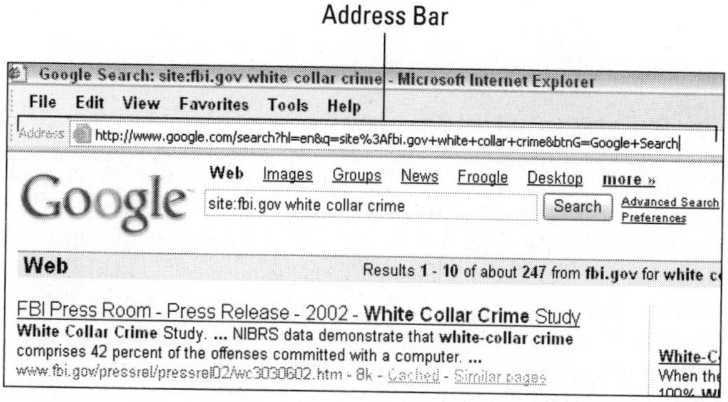

Address Bar

Figure 5-9:
You can see the search string in the URL sent to Google.

If you deconstruct the URL sent to Google to initiate this search piece by piece, you can see how to construct your own searches without using a Google search box.

In the URL, *search?* tells Google to start a search.

Next, *hl=en* specifies the language for return results (you'll probably want to skip this when you write our own).

Everything after the *&q=* is the actual search query. The word *site* is the `site:` operator. The rather obscure *%3A* is the *URL encoded* version of a colon (:), which will be recognized as a : when it is sent to the Google server.

The search terms themselves are separated by plus signs (+).

Finally, *&btnG=Google+Search* tells Google that the inquiry was initiated by clicking the Google Search button. You won't be needing this if you create your own search.

Recreating Google's search string with JavaScript

You can re-create the parts of this search that you need using JavaScript by *hard-coding* — or putting the URL in code rather than letting the user enter it — the site to be searched, letting the user enter the search terms, and using the JavaScript `window.location` property to open the generated search in the user's Web browser.

To learn more about JavaScript objects — such as `window.location` — and JavaScript programming, you can do a Google Web search for **javascript**, and follow the resulting links.

Here's an FBI search page that uses a search string created in JavaScript:

```
<html>
<body>
<table cellspacing=8>
<SCRIPT language="JavaScript">
function goGoogle(term){
var siteURL = "fbi.gov ";
var googURL = "http://www.google.com/search?q=site:" +
    siteURL + term;
window.location = googURL;}
</SCRIPT>
<tr><td><h2>Harold's FBI Search</h2></td></tr><tr>
<form>
    <td align=right><input type=text name="theSearch"
size=40></td></tr>
<tr><td align=right>
```

```
      <input type=button value="Search the FBI"
            onClick='goGoogle(theSearch.value);'>
    </form>
   </td></tr>
 </table>
 </body>
 </html>
```

You can change this to search your own site, or any site you choose, by changing the value of the variable siteURL to whatever site you'd like:

1. **Open the FBI search page in your Web browser and enter a search term.**

   See Figure 5-10. For the sake of variety, and to show that this actually works, I've entered a new search term in my example. Instead of the key-words *white collar crime* I am using the search term *most wanted*.

Figure 5-10: You can open the FBI Search form in your browser.

2. **Click the Search the FBI button.**

   The return results from the Google search appear in your browser window, all restricted to the fbi.gov site, exactly as if you'd entered a site search in Google itself (see Figure 5-11).

The remarkable thing about all this is exactly how easy it is to use client-side scripting techniques to modify Google's searching capabilities for your own research purposes. So go out, get messy, and have fun with adding search boxes that implement Google operators and searches under the hood!

Figure 5-11:
When results of the site search are returned from Google, you can't tell that they started in your own custom search box.

Chapter 6

Using Google Answers to Learn Google Research Techniques

● ●

In This Chapter

▶ Understanding Google Answers

▶ Paying for research using Google Answers

▶ Searching Google Answers

▶ Learning Google techniques from Google Answers

▶ Becoming a Google Answers researcher

● ●

You may not know that Google maintains a marketplace in information. This marketplace is Google Answers, or as Google cofounders Sergey Brin and Larry Page put it, an online "Question Economy." In short, as a result of Google's really cool experiment with Google Answers, you can pay to have your questions answered by researchers that are under contract with Google.

Google Answers utilizes a bidding mechanism. After you pay the 50-cent listing fee, you say how much you're willing to pay for an answer to your question. You can bid anywhere between $2.00 and $200.00. You can also leave a financial tip — just as you would for great service at a restaurant — for the researcher if you really like the answer.

Google chooses its researchers carefully; these researchers really know their stuff. You can also check out the feedback that paying customers leave about researchers.

The more you are willing to pay for an answer, the more likely it is that one of these researchers will decide to answer your question. Questions worth more are also likely to get more immediate attention.

Taking a Look at Google Answers

The information in Google Answers does not appear as part of the search results for a plain-vanilla Google query. You also can't access Google Answers using the Google application programming interface, or API (see Part IV for information on using the APIs to build automated research tools). Google Answers is a world more or less unto itself!

If you're a paid researcher yourself, you may not want to pay someone to query Google for you. After all, armed with the information in this book, along with your own skills in the research field, you should be as good at researching using Google as almost anyone. (Better than anyone, I'd say, but I don't want to boast!) In fact, just in case you have an interest in becoming an approved Google Answers researcher yourself, in this chapter I explain how you might become one (see "Becoming a Google Answers researcher").

So why take a look at Google Answers if you can't use it to answer "normal" Google queries and if you can't build research tools with it?

There are several good reasons for exploring Google Answers:

 ✔ **You can search the answers:** Google Answers is a trove of information that can be searched or browsed. This info isn't searched in a regular query, so you may find it worthwhile to do a separate query in this area of the Google universe.

 ✔ **You can find new research leads:** By looking at the results other research professionals are generating, you can learn about good sources for information that you may not have thought of.

 ✔ **You can study others' research methods:** You can learn about how best to conduct Google research from the answers to questions posed in Google Answers.

 ✔ **You can get technical information quickly:** Google Answers is a great, speedy alternative if you need to know the answer to a highly technical question. Consider this option if the technical answer is a small, but time-consuming, portion of your research project.

Google Answers researchers have been selected as knowledgeable by Google — so they tend to know their stuff. Because they receive feedback on the quality of their work, the Google Answers researchers pride themselves on coming up with good information, and they usually go out of their way to explain the steps they took to find an answer to your question — including full search queries, the logic behind the queries, and links to sites with relevant information.

In the Google Answers universe, an answer that can't be validated is not a very good answer. This makes Google Answers a great school for Google researchers in general!

Navigating to Google Answers

You have your choice of three ways to open the Google Answers application:

- ✔ In your Web browser, open the URL http://answers.google.com.

- ✔ From the Google home page, click the More link to open the Google Services and Tools page. Click the Answers link, represented by an icon that looks like an owl in an academic cap and gown.

- ✔ Conduct a search query as you normally would. If Google can find only a few (or no) results, Google gently suggests that you try Google Answers by providing a Google Answers link on the search results page (see Figure 6-1).

Answers link

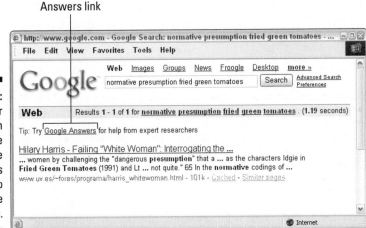

Figure 6-1:
If your search results are nil, Google provides a link to Google Answers.

When you arrive at the Google Answers page, you can browse the questions and answers that are already on the page, but you must obtain a Google Answers account before you can pose your own question. (See "Signing Up for Google Answers.")

Signing Up for Google Answers

However you get there, when you open the Google Answers home page, shown in Figure 6-2, you can get started right away looking for questions and answers.

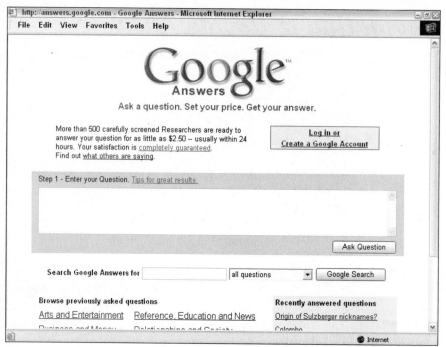

Figure 6-2:
The Google
Answers
home page.

But you can't reap all the benefits of the Google Answers service without an account. There are some substantive advantages to creating a Google Answers account. For example, you can

- ✔ Post research questions (see "Posing your question").

- ✔ Make comments about a research question. Comments are not paid for as research answers are, and any registered Google Answers user can post them. Sometimes the comments ask for clarification on the question. Others respond to the answers that have been offered. Comments are great because they create an interesting dialogue in the Google research community.

- ✔ Track questions you've asked. Google saves all your queries in your account so that you can go back and review all the questions you've posted, along with their answers.

If you already have a Google Groups account (Google Groups is a free online community and discussion group service), or opened an account to obtain a Google APIs key (I explain this process in Chapter 14), you don't need to create a new account to use Google Answers.

To create an account, follow these steps:

1. **On the Google Answers page, click the <u>Login in or Create a Google Account</u> link.**

   The link appears in the upper-right corner of Figure 6-2.

   The Create Account page appears.

2. **Enter your e-mail address and enter a password.**

   Your password must be at least six characters in length. It can contain numbers and letters. You must also retype the password for verification purposes.

   Don't pick an easily recognizable word for your password. Not only is it a bad idea in general, but also, Google won't let you get away with it. If you pick a password that Google deems "too easy," a notification page appears warning you to try a different password.

3. **In the Word Verification section of the page, verify the characters in the box by typing them.**

   This is an extra security feature. The graphics are more easily read by humans than computers, which means that the process of signing up for an account is less susceptible to an automated hacking campaign.

4. **Agree to the Google Terms of Service (TOS) by clicking the appropriately named button.**

   In a matter of seconds, Google sends an e-mail to the address you provide. The e-mail contains a link that looks something like this:

   ```
   http://www.google.com/accounts/VE?c=899835858525377541
   &hl=en
   ```

5. **When you get the e-mail, click the link.**

   The purpose of the link is to verify your e-mail address — it directs you to an E-Mail Address Verified page.

6. **On the E-Mail Address Verified page, click the <u>Click Here to Continue</u> link.**

   The Google Answers Sign-Up page appears (see Figure 6-3). You need to provide a little more information to start to use your account with Google Answers.

7. **Provide a nickname.**

   The nickname is what will appear on-screen when you post questions and comments in Google Answers. This way, the whole world won't know your e-mail address.

   Google automatically appends *-ga* to the end if your nickname within Google Answers. (When I first looked at all those nicknames ending in -ga within Google Answers, I thought it was some honorific like the Japanese *-san,* as in, "take a deep bow, *Harold-ga.*" I soon came to realize that the *ga* is just short for Google Answers!)

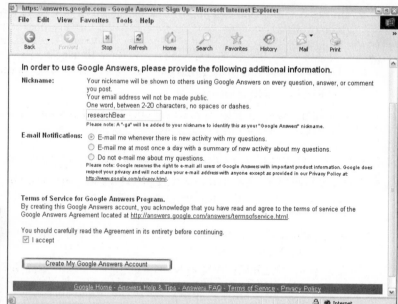

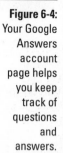

Figure 6-3:
You need a nickname to use Google Answers.

8. **Click the Create My Google Answers Account button.**

   Voilà! Your Google Answers account is created and you're whisked to your Google Answers account page. (As you can see in Figure 6-4, it won't contain much if you haven't asked any questions.)

Figure 6-4:
Your Google Answers account page helps you keep track of questions and answers.

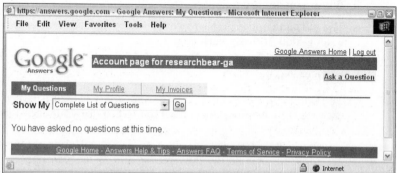

Learning Google Research Techniques

With your Google Answers account in hand, you're ready to begin looking through Google Answers to learn more about researching with Google. As I explain earlier in this chapter, you don't really need a Google Answers account to read answers to questions that have already been posted, but having an account does give you the ability to post comments and to keep track of any research questions you might pose. Plus, if you're using Google as an integrated part of your research, you need an account to use Google Groups, to access the APIs, and to use Google's translation services. There's no harm in obtaining an account, so why not?

You can look through the questions and answers available on Google Answers in one of two ways:

 ✔ Browsing through the Google Answers categories of questions
 ✔ Searching for information that may be in a specific question or answer

Browsing

If you decide to start your Google Answers adventure by browsing, you should know that the categories used in Google Answers are not the same as those used in the wider world of the Google Directory. (I explain how to use the Google Directory in Chapter 7.)

Browsing through categories of information (these categories are called a *taxonomy*) is known as hierarchical searching (because it involves hierarchies of information). In Chapter 10, I show you when it is better to use information arranged hierarchically and when it makes more sense to start by searching using a query.

The top-level categories that you can use for browsing Google Answers are shown on the Google Answers home page (see Figure 6-5). Look for the Browse Previously Asked Questions heading.

If you have a little time on your hands, taking a look at the recently answered questions can be a lot of fun; follow the links shown on the Google Answers home page in Figure 6-5 and see where they lead you. If you have a very specific deadline and need to get on with the research, browsing the categories in this way probably won't yield the best results because the organization simply isn't specific enough. For example, if you click a top-level category like Business and Money, you see that the categorization scheme extends to subcategories like Consulting, eCommerce, and so on. Finding pinpointed information with it isn't exactly a snap. However, research answers tend to make fascinating reading and include oodles of helpful online resources. In some cases, research answers run quite long, and in many cases they are clearly worth the cost.

You can sort questions either by date or by the price offered for the answer (in both cases, you can view them in ascending or descending order). I like to browse by highest-price question first (these questions tend to be the most interesting, and attract the most elaborate responses).

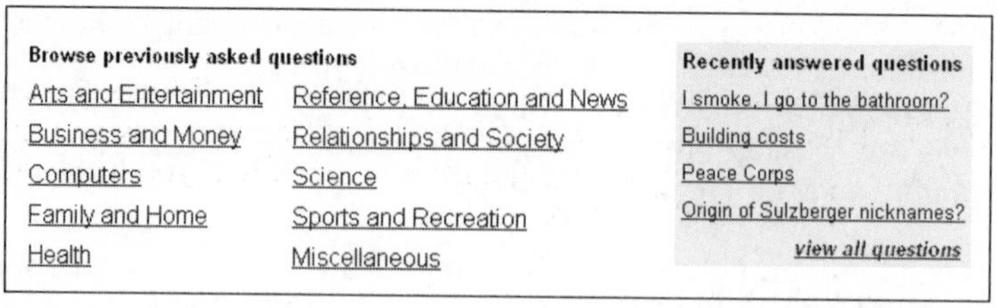

Figure 6-5:
Start by
browsing
the top-level
Google
Answers
categories.

Browse previously asked questions

Arts and Entertainment   Reference, Education and News

Business and Money   Relationships and Society

Computers   Science

Family and Home   Sports and Recreation

Health   Miscellaneous

Recently answered questions

I smoke, I go to the bathroom?

Building costs

Peace Corps

Origin of Sulzberger nicknames?

view all questions

Paying customers of Google Answers get to rate the answers on a one-to-five star scale. If you stick to answers rated four or five stars, you are likely to see more interested and complete answers.

If you like the answer a researcher gave to a question, you can click the link next to the researcher's user ID to view all his or her evaluations (with links to all that reviewer's other answers).

Table 6-1 shows a few questions with answers that I've found extensive and interesting; all these are $200, five-star questions, along with the category for the question and the Google ID of the researcher. You may not be interested in the specific issues addressed in these questions, but you should be aware that these are very complete, generously sourced research responses. If you check these (and other answers) out, I think you will be surprised by their thoroughness, sophistication, and helpfulness.

Table 6-1	Sample Google Answers and Questions	
Research Question	*Category*	*Researcher*
Looking for info about the events leading up to World War I and the Christmas truce of 1914	Reference, Education, and News⇨Teaching and Research	kriswrite-ga
Trying to find out how to get access to the Jstor (www.jstor.org/) and Project Muse (http://muse.jhu.edu/) databases without belonging to an institution that subscribes to them	Reference, Education, and News⇨Teaching and Research	pafalafa-ga
Looking for info about getting a Web page indexed by Google	Business and Money	serenata-ga
Looking for research about the competitive pressures facing the pharmaceutical/biotech industry	Business and Money	easterangel-ga

Searching

You can search for questions and answers from the Google Answers home page. This is a great option because you don't have to pay a dime but you can get much more precise results than you would if you browse the Google Answers categories. Follow these steps:

1. **Enter your search terms.**

2. **Decide whether you want to see only unanswered questions, only questions that have been answered, or all questions.**

   Choose the appropriate option from the drop-down list.

3. **Click Google Search.**

For example, suppose you want to see answers to questions about Google search rank ordering and its relationship (if any) to the AdWords program (in which Google places keyword targeted ads on Web sites) — either to learn how to put up a Web site that appeared higher in search rankings or for research purposes.

You could search to find out about this using the terms *PageRank* and *AdWords,* as shown in Figure 6-6.

Figure 6-6:
Enter
search
terms to
find rel-
evant ques-
tions and
answers.

Such a search leads to plenty of relevant questions with answers containing lots of good information, as you can see in Figure 6-7.

The results set page looks a lot like a results set page from a typical Google search. You can click a link in the return results set to read the specifics of the questions, the paid research answers, and clarifications and comments (if there are any).

At the top of the question, you see a link to the category it belongs to in Google Answers. Clicking this link brings you back to the hierarchical view of Google Answers that I show you in the section called "Browsing," earlier in this chapter.

Figure 6-7:
Google
Answers
returns
questions
that are
relevant to
your search
terms.

Writing a Good Query for Google Answers to Research

If you need to get your work done in a hurry or you know you're in way over your head on a research topic, throwing down some cash with Google Answers may be a great idea. Of course, the higher your bid for answers is, the more likely you are to get a quick answer. But that's not a hard-and-fast rule. You may bid $100 for a question but not get a response because no one understands what you're talking about. Answering questions is not just about money; it's also about clarity in your question.

Good questions should follow these rules:

✔ **Be specific in what constitutes a successful answer from your viewpoint.** For example, say, "I need resources that explain how GPS is integrated into the navigational tools of commercial jetliners. A list of references will do." Don't say, "GPS?"

✔ **Don't cram more than one question into a single question (break up multipart questions into several individual questions).** For example, say, "I want to know more about any international efforts being made to understand the fruit fly genome" in one question, and in another question, say, "I need a single, easy-to-read reference or explanation of how DNA works that I can give to an 8th grade class."

✔ **Don't make questions open-ended.** Save questions like, "What is the meaning of life?" for your next dinner party.

✔ **If relevant, explain what you are *not* looking for.** Maybe you want to find good resources that can help you create a PowerPoint presentation on cell structures. Don't ask for a history of biology in that case.

✔ **If it helps to flesh out your question, provide context.** If you've recently been thrown into a classroom to teach biology and it's been 25 years since you took biology, that's important information to share.

✔ **Provide a sufficient level of detail:** Again, the "What is the meaning of life?" question isn't going to work. But if you want to know how Jean-Paul Sartre would likely explain the meaning of life, you have yourself a good Google Answers question.

✔ **It should go without saying, but be polite:** Saying, "I need to know everything there is to know about routers and networking, but if you're not a very technical person don't bother answering," is not just overly broad, it is also rude. Rudeness doesn't pay on Google Answers.

For more help formulating questions for Google Answers, see the Google Answers Help page, `http://answers.google.com/answers/help.html`.

Verboten questions

You should check out the Google Answers Terms of Service and also check out the FAQs to find out what kinds of questions you are forbidden to ask. Here's a sampling of stuff you can't ask about:

✔ You can't request private information about individuals.

✔ You can't ask for help with illegal activities.

✔ You can't ask questions that sell or advertise products.

✔ You can't ask questions that involve adult content.

✔ You can't use Google Answers to help you with your homework or provide answers to exam questions.

No one at Google Answers will write your term paper if you're a student, and if you're a researcher, the Google Answers people will only take your research so far. It's up to you to do the rest of the work.

Posing your question

The mechanics of asking a question couldn't be much easier:

1. **You can enter a question on the Google Answers home page, as shown in Figure 6-8.**

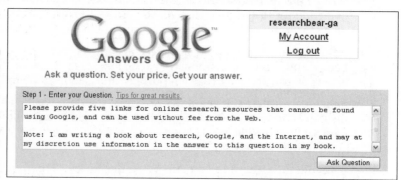

Figure 6-8:
You can enter your question on the Google Answers home page.

2. **When you've completed your question, click the Ask Question button.**

   The Ask a Question page, shown in Figure 6-9, appears.

3. **Provide a subject for your question.**

4. **Indicate how much you'll pay for the answer.**

   A 50-cent listing fee is added to the fee you are willing to pay.

5. **Select the main and subcategories for your question.**

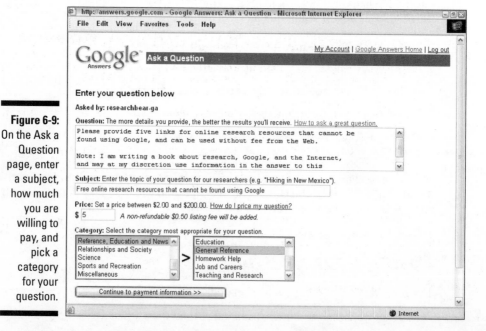

Figure 6-9:
On the Ask a Question page, enter a subject, how much you are willing to pay, and pick a category for your question.

6. **Click the Continue to Payment Information button and enter your credit card information.**

   The 50-cent listing fee is charged immediately, and you only pay the amount you've said you'll pay for the research when the question is answered.

Google offers a money-back guarantee if you do not feel your answer was worth the cost.

You might be wondering how long an unanswered question is listed before it's finally taken off the market. It looks like they stay listed indefinitely. If you don't get anyone to look into your question in a few days or a week, you might need to revise and repost it.

You get another chance to review the listing text and fees. If everything looks okay, click Pay Listing Fee and Post Question to post your question. Your question appears in Google Answers, as shown in Figure 6-10.

If a little lock icon appears in several places in the page displaying your question, it means that a researcher has grabbed the question. It gets locked to make sure that no more than one researcher is working on your question.

Look for this icon to indicate that a
researcher has nabbed the question.

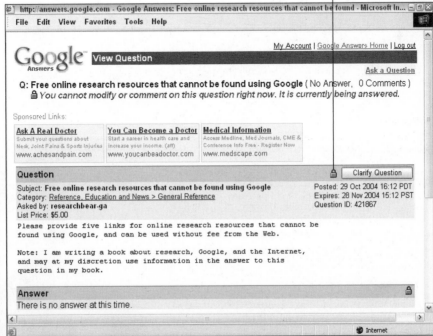

Figure 6-10:
After you
pay the
listing fee,
your
question
appears on
the Google
Answers
page.

Becoming a Google Answers researcher

Not everyone can be a superstar! Google says it has plenty of great researchers, and there's currently no official application process for becoming a Google Answers researcher. As things stand, becoming a researcher is by invitation only (although the Google Answers FAQs suggest that they may begin taking formal applications again at some point).

Right now, probably the only approach if you don't know people who work at Google Answers is to get a reputation for quality comments on Google Answers. This strategy is likely to work better if you concentrate on a specific area, rather than if your comments are on topics all over the map. Google Answers has contracted at least some researchers based on their commenting activity.

Considering the length and sophistication of the better answers on Google Answers, I don't think the researchers are getting rich (although answering these questions is something that can be done on one's down time from anywhere there is an Internet connection). Researchers do the work more for the glory — and are extremely (and rightfully) proud of their work!

If you are a professional researcher, even if you have no interest in working for Google Answers, you should take note: Google Answers represents a new way that the business of research is being run.

Chapter 7

Getting Help from the Google Directory

The Google Directory is a world within Google that presents only Web sites that have been evaluated by editors. Part of the appeal of the Google Directory is that it has intelligently categorized these Web site resources. You can use the resulting catalog to browse for information. You can also use Google's tools to search the Google Directory world (or within a category in that world).

This chapter explains where the Google Directory information comes from and what the philosophy behind it is. I show you how to browse the Google Directory and search within the Google Directory (I also take a brief look at another source of human-generated information within Google, Google Groups).

The gist of this chapter is to show you how to get the most out of the Google Directory when you conduct research.

Introducing the Open Directory Project

The Google Directory is a strange kind of hybrid, neither fish, nor fowl. It is one part automated Web research tool (following Google's usual research approach) and it is part human. Errr . . . I mean humans categorize the knowledge and evaluate the Web sites that the Google Directory supports.

The human part of the Google Directory comes from the ODP (a.k.a. the *Open Directory Project*), which you can visit at http://dmoz.org. The ODP is a giant directory of Web resources evaluated and arranged in a hierarchy by humans (see the sidebar, "Humans do it best!"). The ODP supplies the data the Google Directory uses.

Humans do it best!

The ODP is hosted and administered by Netscape Communications Corporation using *open source* inspired principles. The open source principle is that all the data programming code is freely available and can be modified in any way, shape, or form, with the important proviso that all modifications and improvements (and their source code) be made available under open source licensing.

In fact, taking, modifying, and improving on the existing program is encouraged because rather than having purely financial goals, open source developers focus on building the best model or product with the motivation of having their effort shine before their peers. In addition, it's an advantage to open source because many different developers (not just those from one company) get to review source code. Finally, improvements to a code base under open source get reintegrated back into the code base, no matter who made them.

This contrasts radically with the proprietary model of most software companies — which consider open source development anarchic, with developers making decisions based on what's popular rather than what makes good business sense. The result, in the minds of the proprietary developers, is sloppy software. (Of course, open source proponents can point to some great open source software — Linux and Apache, for example.)

A vast number of volunteer editors (who are subject-matter experts) keep the ODP on track and the project also employs a set of effective internal checks and balances. Any site can follow ODP procedures to get listed and categorized by the ODP for free (see the "Getting

indexed by Google" sidebar). It's also completely free to use the ODP catalog and data (as Google and other Web search engines do) if you have a hankering to build your own Web-based search engine. All you have to do is make sure that you follow the ODP's free-use license and give the ODP credit for its hard work.

The philosophy behind the ODP can best be summed up with the phrase, "Humans do it better." Not only is Web-based information organized and evaluated by actual people, but more importantly, the people at ODP are really proud of that fact. The ODP editors believe that the staggering rate of growth of the Internet means that automated Web searching is increasingly ineffective, and that the "small paid editorial staffs" at commercial directory sites can't possibly keep up with what it calls *link rot* (the dying off of links as information goes out of date, is relocated, or is otherwise modified).

Figuring that if it can't fight the massive growth of the Internet, the least it can do is jump on the bandwagon. The ODP provides a mechanism for the Web to organize itself, using the increasing number of *net-citizens* (its term) worldwide, each of whom is in charge of organizing and presenting some small part of the Web, throwing away rotten content, and keeping good content.

The philosophy that motivates the ODP has been generally inspired by the open source movement, and specifically inspired by the Debian Social Contract. Debian is an open-source operating system that uses the Linux kernel (for more information about the Debian Social Contract, see www.debian.org/social_contract.html).

The ODP and the Google Directory are not the same thing, however. Like many other online search engines, Google uses the ODP's data about how to catalog available Web resources, and follows the ODP's lead in evaluating which sites should be included in its catalog. But that's as far as the Google Directory goes with the ODP's "humans do it best" credo; if you search within a category in the Google Directory, Google uses its sophisticated and automated PageRank algorithm (which the ODP obviously doesn't have) to evaluate the relevance of search results (see Chapter 11 for more information about Google's PageRank algorithm).

The ODP uses a *taxonomy* to categorize and organize knowledge and information. Taxonomies can be searched by browsing larger categories (such as Science⇨Biology⇨Microbiology⇨Virology), and by querying (such as searching for the term *virology*) to find specific information.

You can think of the distinction between a taxonomy and a query as that between a table of contents and an index. A table of contents is an ordered and structured way to find things, but it doesn't contain every important term. In contrast, a good index includes all important keywords, but the terms aren't structured contextually within the index. (I explain taxonomies in Chapter 11.)

No one has yet come up with the perfect taxonomy to organize all human knowledge (or even all the information available on the Web). It's probably not possible to come up with one for a variety of reasons: Things keep on changing; some information cannot readily be pigeonholed into a taxonomic slot; human judgment is fallible; and so on and so forth.

When all is said and done, ODP and its army of volunteer editors have done a pretty miraculous job of categorizing the Web and making sure that the sites in the ODP are of good quality and relevant to their categories. As I show you in this chapter, the ability to use Google's search tools within the ODP data makes the Google Directory a formidable research tool.

Using the Google Directory

In order to make the most effective use of the Google Directory, you need to know how to open, browse, and search the Google Directory.

In this section I show the mechanics of these operations, as well as how to browse Google Groups (like the Google Directory, Google Groups uses human-based categorizations of information and data from the Web).

Getting indexed by Google

Google maintains a Web page (www.google.com/addurl.html) that you can use to add your Web site to the Google index. But it turns out that one of the best ways to get a Web site included in Google (and other major search engines) is to get it cataloged by the ODP.

Before you actually list your Web site with the ODP, you should read the ODP FAQs about suggesting a site. From the ODP home page, click the Suggest URL link. You're led to an FAQ page (http://dmoz.org/add.html) that tells you the steps you need to take to get a site considered for inclusion in the ODP. This page also lists kinds of sites that the ODP will not catalog (for example, sites that are "under construction" or that contain broken links).

To suggest your site, you have to find the category where you think your site fits best. Visit the ODP home page (http://dmoz.org) and maneuver through the ranks. Say you have a

Web site that lists 7,000 unsigned music bands, listed by city, state, region, and country. You might drill down two levels (Arts⇨Music). You really ought to do your best to find the right category for your site, however, so I would suggest drilling even farther down in the taxonomy to increase the chances of your site being included in the ODP (Arts⇨Music⇨Bands and Artists).

When you're satisfied with the category location for your Web site, click the Suggest URL link. On the page that appears, supply your site's URL, a title, a brief description, and your e-mail address. Then click the Submit button.

Of course, there's no way to be sure that the ODP will index your site. (Remember, it is by definition a selective directory.) And, you can't tell whether it has indexed your site without checking back and searching from time to time.

Opening the Google Directory

There are three ways to open the Google Directory:

- ✔ In your Web browser, open the URL http://directory.google.com; this opens the Google Directory home page.

- ✔ From the Google home page, click the More link to open the Google Services and Tools page; click the Directory link or icon (as shown in Figure 7-1). The Google Directory top page opens.

- ✔ Many Google Web searches, such as the one with a results set shown in Figure 7-2, for *units of measurement*, return links to the Google Directory; clicking these links takes you to the inner workings of the Google Directory taxonomy to the position of the topic that was searched for.

Figure 7-1:
Click the
<u>Directory</u>
link or icon
to open the
top page of
the Google
Directory.

This result leads to a Google Directory resource.

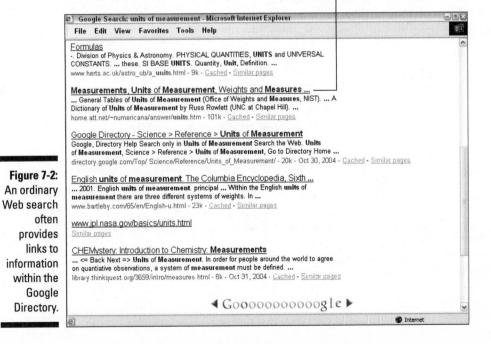

Figure 7-2:
An ordinary
Web search
often
provides
links to
information
within the
Google
Directory.

Browsing the Google Directory

As Google puts it, the Google Directory is "the Web organized by topic into categories." To start browsing the Google Directory, follow these steps:

1. **Open the main Google Directory page.**

   See Figure 7-3.

2. **Choose a category by clicking a link.**

   For example, you can click the <u>Reference</u> link to see a wide variety of categories that fall under the main Reference category, as shown in Figure 7-4.

   The Google Directory structure contains several points of entry to gain access to the same information. That means that even though Reference is listed in the directory structure as a main category, it is also listed as a subcategory of the Science category in Figure 7-4.

3. **Drill down through the subcategories until your heart's content.**

   For example, you may click the <u>Units of Measurement</u> link, as shown in Figure 7-5.

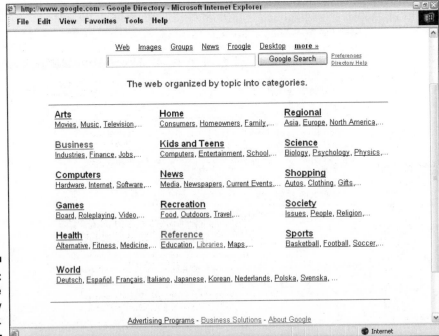

Figure 7-3:
The Google
Directory
page.

The Google Directory is flexible and forgiving. For example, if you start by clicking the <u>Science</u> link instead of the <u>Reference</u> link, you can still get to the <u>Units of Measurement</u> link by choosing the Reference and Units of Measurement subcategories, respectively.

When you get closer to the end of the line (or deeper into the taxonomy, depending on how you want to look at it), you see links to actual Web pages (rather than links to more subcategories). For example, the Scientific Measurement category page shows some links at the bottom of the page shown in Figure 7-5.

4. **Click a link to a page that interests you.**

   These pages are shown by default in Google PageRank order (the PageRank is indicated graphically by green bars along the left side of the Google Directory page).

If you choose, you can order pages within a Google Directory category alphabetically, rather than by PageRank. The ODP's capsule description of a resource is used in the alphabetization. This can help you find a specific resource by what it contains — the ODP descriptions tend to be very concise and good.

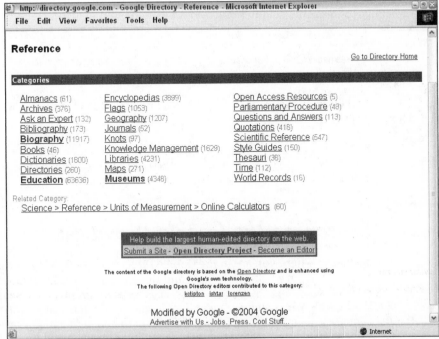

Figure 7-4: The Reference subcategory contains links to more subcategories.

Main category link   Subcategories

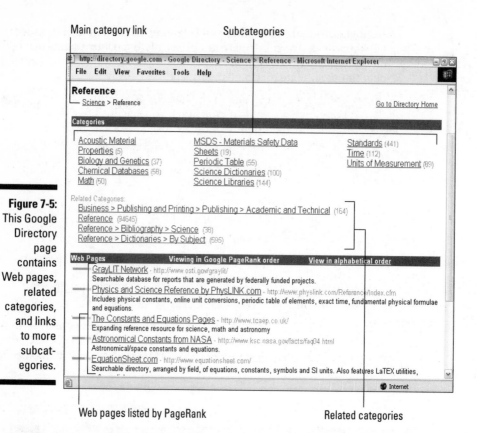

Figure 7-5:
This Google
Directory
page
contains
Web pages,
related
categories,
and links
to more
subcat-
egories.

Web pages listed by PageRank   Related categories

At the top of each Directory page is a link that indicates the position of the page in the Google hierarchy.

By clicking the <u>Go to Directory Home</u> link on the upper right of every Google Directory page, you can navigate directly to the top Google Directory page. You can then start drilling down using another major category.

Searching the Google Directory

No matter where you are in the Google Directory hierarchy, you can search Google Directory using keywords and Google operators. In an important respect, searching the Google Directory works differently than searching the World Wide Web using a typical Google query — when you search Google Directory, your search only finds results in the current category (unless you elect to search the rest of the Web, too). This is very useful for pinpointing search results (see "Making the most of the Google Directory").

For example, a search within the Reference⇨Scientific Measurement category of Google Directory for *Planck's constant* yields only the one result shown in Figure 7-6.

Capitalization doesn't matter (*Planck's constant* and *planck's constant* yield equivalent results), but you should include the apostrophe (because *Planck's* is treated as a different word than *Plancks*).

By way of contrast, a search of the entire Google Directory for *Planck's constant* yields more than 69 results, and a Google Web search shows more than 33,000 results.

To search within a Google Directory, enter your query in the search box towards the top of the page. Make sure that Search Only in Reference is selected rather than Search the Web. Click Google Search (see Figure 7-7).

On the results page for a Google Directory search, your search options change. You can choose to stay within the Google Directory category, or to search the entire Google Directory.

Searching the entire Google Directory is different than using Google to search the entire Web. If you want to search the entire Web, you need to get out of the Directory by clicking the Google Home link at the bottom of the Google Directory results page.

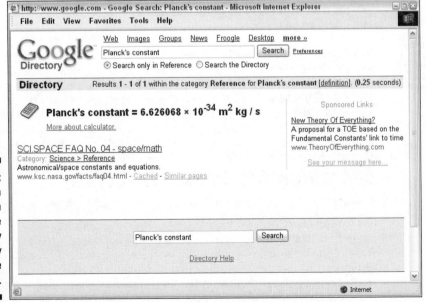

Figure 7-6: A search from within a Google Directory category shows one result.

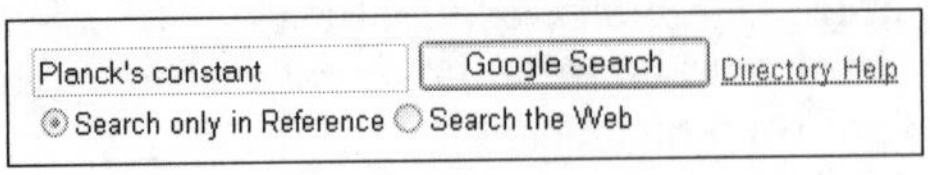

Figure 7-7:
You can
search
within a
category or
use Google
Directory to
search the
Web.

| Planck's constant | Google Search | Directory Help |
| ⦿ Search only in Reference ◯ Search the Web | | |

Making the most of the Google Directory

You may be wondering when it makes sense to use the Google Directory as opposed to the broader Google Web search. One of the best uses for the Google Directory is to familiarize yourself with the landscape of a particular subject matter when you don't know much about a topic. For example, suppose you need to conduct a reference interview (I explain reference interviews in Chapter 10). Suppose you don't have much background understanding of the topic to be covered in the reference interview.

In this situation, Google Directory provides a structure so you can conceptualize how the field of knowledge works. For example, the subcategories under the Business Law category reveal pretty quickly the kinds of professionals who work in business law, as well as the major issues and areas these professionals deal with every day (such as administrative business law, antitrust suits, and so on).

In addition, the Web sites listed in the various Business Law categories have been vetted by editors following ODP guidelines; you don't have to wade through all kinds of irrelevant commercial sites because someone else already has. For example, www.businesslaw.gov is the top-ranked site in the Business Law category. In part maintained by the Small Business Administration, this site is an authoritative provider of legal and regulatory information to America's small businesses. Using Google's Web search, this site is likely to be buried beneath an avalanche of commercial sites with less research value (you can find it, but not on the first page of a typical Google Web search).

Besides the ability to quickly and authoritatively familiarize yourself with an area, Google Directory helps you:

✔ Narrow searches to categories and subcategories.

✔ Get suggestions for keywords and queries. For example, if you're interested in researching traffic patterns, the Google Directory Business⇨Transportation and Logistics⇨Traffic Control category provides tons of ideas for search terms (via related categories, subcategories, and Web sites included in the category).

✔ Find new search directions. If a site is listed under multiple categories, a different category from the one you browsed to find the site may prove a fruitful area for research.

✔ Find comprehensive lists. For example, Arts⇨Literature⇨Authors contains a list that includes thousands of authors alphabetized by their last name.

In addition, you can use the Google Directory to

✔ **Refine your research methodology:** Ask yourself, "Does the way I'm conceptualizing my topic correspond to the organization in the Google Directory?" If not, maybe you can use the organization implied by the Google Directory to improve your process. For example, when I approached writing this book, I observed that topics related to research could be found in the Reference⇨Libraries category and the Reference⇨Education category — not in the Computers category. This categorization helped me understand that I had to focus as much on the research aspects of using Google as on its computer and software issues.

✔ **Understand research deliverables:** Suppose you're researching traffic patterns in a specific area for a client. If you look in the Business⇨Transportation Logistics⇨Traffic Control category, you can find many examples of traffic circulation reports (and get a better example of what they should look like).

✔ **Validate your research results:** As you start to come up with research results, ask yourself two questions:

  • What category in the Google Directory hierarchy does this fit in?

  • Are the results consistent with other information available in that category?

If you have trouble identifying a category, or answer "No" to the question about consistency, you should double-check your research conclusion to make sure that it is right.

Tips for Working with the Google Directory

Here are a few tips that will help you work with the Google Directory:

✔ Don't overlook alphabetized lists in the Google Directory, such as the list of authors, shown in Figure 7-8. This list contains hundreds of authors and thousands of author-related Web links, and is a great way to find out everything you ever wanted to know about, say, Edgar Allen Poe or J.K. Rawlings.

✔ Look under the Regional heading to find categories that are specific to a geographic area. For example, you can find information about the arts in my hometown, Berkeley, California, under Regional⇨North America⇨United States⇨California⇨Localities⇨B⇨Berkeley⇨Arts and Entertainment.

The B stands for Berkeley.

✔ Limit Web page searches to specific categories (or subcategories) to get pinpointed results.

Figure 7-8:
The Google Directory list of authors is arranged alphabetically.

Authors Categorized by Letter
A B C D E F G H I J K L M N O P Q R S T U V W X Y Z

Google Groups: Extending Usenet

The Google Directory puts on a Google face and adds Google tools to the categorization and Web site evaluations supplied by the Open Directory Project. In a similar way, Google Groups adds a Google face and Google tools to a pool of information that Google originally had no part in creating — *Usenet* (or *User*'s *Net*work) newsgroups.

Usenet is a vast group of public discussion forums that is older than the Web itself. It originated in the 1970s as a Unix-based bulletin board system allowing Unix computer users to share information, and eventually came to include hundreds of millions of posts.

Google Groups has archived all the Usenet posts since 1981 and adds myriad Google Groups messages. It currently contains close to one billion messages. Google Groups discussions cover every possible topic. With such a volume of posts, you may not be surprised to discover that there's absolutely no quality control regarding the information posted to the discussions. No doubt you've seen spam in your e-mail in-box. Many Google Groups posts read exactly like this spam. The good news is that you can use some of the Google Groups management features to tackle the spam issue. For example, you can keep a thread private so that only your friends can read and write messages.

Differences of opinion are good, and deciding which tools one prefers to use is based on a variety of personal preferences. I'm not much of a Google Groups fan, but some people are. Acknowledging that they have to wade through a fair amount of irrelevant material, these Google Groups fans feel that the answer to any technical question has probably already been posted to a Google Groups group (so all you have to do is search for it). Others rely on Google Groups for reviews of products so they know what to buy.

Especially if you're not used to wading through this daunting number of posts, and depending very much on the precise discussion thread, finding pinpointed information in Google Groups can be difficult. Accordingly, many researchers tend to overlook it. However, if you want to keep up with the latest gossip about whatever is hot, or need pointers on working a gadget, a Google Groups discussion forum may help. In addition, whatever your research conundrum, someone, somewhere in Google Groups, has probably tackled the same thing. Google Groups may also be a good way to track trends both subjectively and in the aggregate (perhaps using automated sampling techniques). And, if you just have a lot of time on your hands, you can enjoy reading Google Groups discussions about anything you may be interested in.

Accessing Google Groups

You can open Google Groups using the address `http://groups.google.com`, by clicking the <u>Groups</u> link on the Google home page, or by clicking the <u>Groups</u> icon or link in the Google Services and Tools page. With the Google Groups home page open, shown in Figure 7-9, you can create or join a group, browse a hierarchy of discussion groups, or search through the Google Groups archives.

By clicking the <u>Browse all of Usenet</u> link, you can open a more complete listing of the Usenet groups, organized hierarchically by topic, Usenet domain, or geographic location (take your pick) as you can see in Figure 7-10.

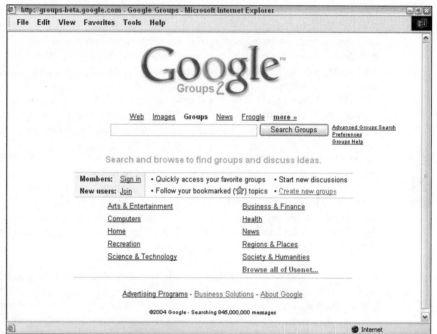

Figure 7-9:
The Google
Groups
home page.

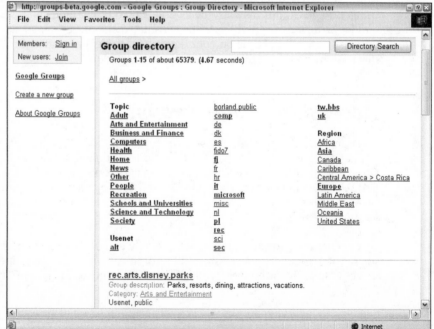

Figure 7-10:
Usenet
groups are
arranged by
topic,
domain, or
geography.

Browsing groups and dealing with post overload

You can continue to browse through the groups (or search), and when you find a group you are interested in, read — or wade through — the postings.

In order to start a Usenet group, post to a Usenet group, or bookmark a Usenet group, you need a Google account (I explain getting a Google account in Chapter 6 and Chapter 14) and a Google Groups nickname.

You do not need to log on to browse or read discussions.

To make dealing with the volume of posts on Usenet easier, Google organizes posts in reverse chronological order and by *thread* — a post with all the follow-up posts that replied to, or commented on, the original post.

Although using Google Groups is likely to be more a recreational activity than a research activity, in some circumstances — if you want to know what people are saying about something — Google Groups can be a valuable research resource.

Chapter 8

Researching Photographs with Google

Google Images is a Google service that lets you use Google's search tools to find pictures — photographs and other graphic images — on the Web.

In this chapter, I show you how to use Google Images to pump up your research results. Along the way, I show you how Google Images works (you may be surprised) and explain why this tool can be so important to providing well-rounded, high-quality research results. I also show you how a neat Google tool called Picasa can help you organize the pictures you already have saved on your computer.

Knowing Google Images Basics

Because nearly one billion images are floating around on the Web, finding the picture you need for your research can be pretty tricky. Google Images helps you manage this difficult feat. In the following sections, I explain what Google Images does and how to use Google Images effectively.

Understanding how Google Images works

Contrary to what you might expect, Google Images has no ability to actually analyze a photograph or other picture on a Web page. Instead, Google Images uses the *context* of an image to determine the image's relevance in your search results. That's right! The picture itself is not considered. The text of the Web page surrounding the image, the content of the `alt` HTML parameter associated with the image, and (most importantly) the caption of the image are the essential clues Google uses to categorize and sort image search results.

Using contextual analysis, Google Images does a surprisingly good job of understanding what an image depicts. Of course, Google Images can't always do a perfect job, and if the contextual elements aren't present — perhaps an image is placed alone on a Web page without any text at all — Google has no way to determine the content of the image.

Google does not consider the filename of an image when analyzing what the image is. So if you have a photo named `billclinton.jpg` on a page by itself, Google won't know that the picture is of Bill Clinton.

Accessing the Google Images tool

You have your choice of a number of ways of opening the Google Images application:

- ✔ Type **images.google.com** into the Address Bar of your browser and click the Go button (or press the Enter key on your keyboard).
- ✔ If you have installed the Google Toolbar (as explained in Chapter 1), click the Google button to open the fly-out menu; from the menu, choose Google Links➪Google Images.
- ✔ On the Google home page, click the <u>Images</u> link.
- ✔ On the Google home page, click the <u>More</u> link; when the Google Services and Tools page opens, click the <u>Images</u> icon or link.

The Google Images home page is shown in Figure 8-1.

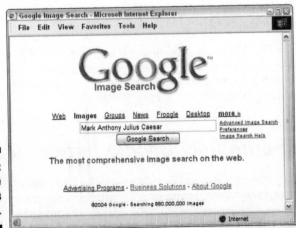

Figure 8-1:
The Google
Images
home page.

Searching for images

On the Google Images home page, you can search for an image by entering a query in the Search box and clicking the Google Search button.

Google Images searches for contextual information about the image, as well as any written content that appears near the image on the Web page; it doesn't have any way of searching the content of images themselves. For this reason, you may need to finesse your search, framing your image searches with language that might be near your desired pictures.

Be aware that words have more than one meaning. Although this is something to consider in all Google searches, pictures can be a lot more vivid (or inappropriate) than you might be expecting. If you want to filter out inappropriate content, be particularly careful when you choose search terms. For example, a search for the term *disney bambi* yields G-rated results, but a search for *bambi* alone might not. Take a look at the section, "Using SafeSearch with Images," later in this chapter for more information on excluding irrelevant or inappropriate content.

Because Google Images works by coming up with pictures that are nearby the text string you entered, search results can return people and objects not remotely in the search terms. For example, the first image returned by a search for *mark anthony julius caesar* is an image neither of Mark Anthony nor of Julius Caesar as you might expect, but rather of Cleopatra, as you can see in Figure 8-2.

Figure 8-2:
A search for *Mark Anthony* and *Julius Caesar* returns a thumbnail image of a poster of Cleopatra.

The operators I explain in Chapters 4 and 5 don't work with Google Images. For more pinpointed searching, you can use the Advanced Image Search window, as well as a couple of advanced image-specific operators (see "Using Advanced Image Search").

Understanding image results

When you conduct a Google Images search, the search results page returns thumbnails of the images that Google Images found.

Each image on the search results page is captioned with its filename (and file format), the URL for the Web page that contains the image, the size of the image in pixels, and the size of the image file.

From this main image search results page, you can change your SafeSearch settings (see "Using SafeSearch with Images") and access the Advanced Image Search window (see "Using Advanced Image Search").

You can also click each image on the search results page. Clicking an image opens an image-specific results page like the one shown in Figure 8-3.

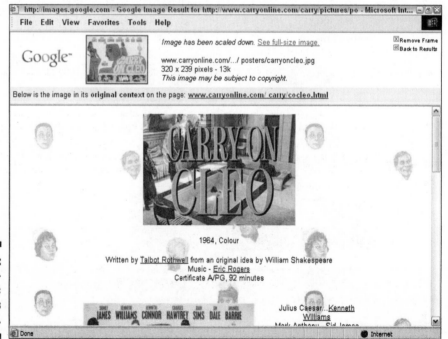

Figure 8-3: An image-specific results page.

Who owns those pictures, anyway?

There's something very important to understand about Google Images. Just because you find a photograph (or other kind of image) using Google Images doesn't mean that you have any right to use the picture. The pictures that Google Images finds are all on Web pages.

The content of these pages, including the pictures, are explicitly copyrighted (if there is a copyright notice on the Web page) or implicitly copyrighted (if there is no notice). Images (and other works of art) are legally copyrighted and owned whether a copyright notice appears on the page or not.

You have the legal right to view the Web page containing the picture. However, that's the only clear legal right you have in relationship to the images that you find during your Google Images search.

Using images belonging to others happens all the time on the Web, and is often tolerated if there are no commercial issues involved. "Fair use" guidelines do allow you to use copyrighted images in limited quantities for noncommercial purposes (to some degree including research).

However, if you want to do anything with an image besides view it on the Web, and your usage is even potentially questionable, you should do the right thing and contact the copyright owner for permission. Depending on the picture you're using, you might just save yourself a lot of grief by always asking for permission before using an image. (Of course, this advice applies to all copyrighted materials, including written documents, audio and video files, and any other content that you find online.)

You can find out more about the U.S. copyright laws and how they apply to images at www.copyright.gov. You can find out about how international copyright laws might apply at the International Federation of Reproduction Rights Organizations, www.ifrro.org.

Each image-specific results page shows a thumbnail of the image, as well as the Web page containing the image. Technically, the image-specific results page is constructed using HTML *frames.* The thumbnail is in a top frame, and the Web page containing the image is in a bottom frame. The frames allow you to simultaneously view both the thumbnail of an image and the context in which it appears.

Downloading images

Downloading images from Google Images — or from the pages that contain the images — is easy enough, but before you do so, please see the sidebar "Who owns those pictures, anyway?"

Depending on your computer's operating system, you can probably drag-and-drop images to your computer. For example, if your computer runs Windows XP, you can drag-and-drop images from the Image Results page to your Windows desktop or to a folder within Windows Explorer.

If you have trouble dragging and dropping the image, right-click on the image and choose Save Picture As from the context menu.

Using SafeSearch with Images

No doubt, you have heard of *content filtering*, software tools that prevent inappropriate content from crossing your desktop depending on your preferences. Although the issue of content filtering is something you may want to consider in all your Google research endeavors, it is specifically and uniquely important to consider when you are conducting a search of images because images can be more viscerally offensive than other kinds of content.

Google uses a content filter called SafeSearch. SafeSearch is designed to remove adult content from Google search results. You can use this filter not only with Google Images searches but also with Google searches in general.

You can set SafeSearch options by clicking the <u>Preferences</u> link on any Google page or by clicking the special link at the top of any Google Images search results page. The link text varies depending on your current SafeSearch settings. You can also set these preferences on a per-search basis when you adjust the setting in the Advanced Image Search window (see "Using Advanced Image Search").

There are three possible SafeSearch settings:

- ✔ **Do not filter my search results:** SafeSearch is disabled.
- ✔ **Use moderate filtering:** The filter excludes adult images but not text (this is the default setting).
- ✔ **Use strict filtering:** The filter excludes adult images and explicit text.

The SafeSearch filters don't always work very well with Google Images. One reason for this is that image searching based on contextual language rather than images themselves is by nature imprecise. Even if you have the SafeSearch filter turned on, results may sometimes include adult imagery — so you may wish to take appropriate precautions if you are searching with children present or while at the office.

Using Advanced Image Search

The Advanced Image Search window, shown in Figure 8-4, provides a way for you to refine your image searches.

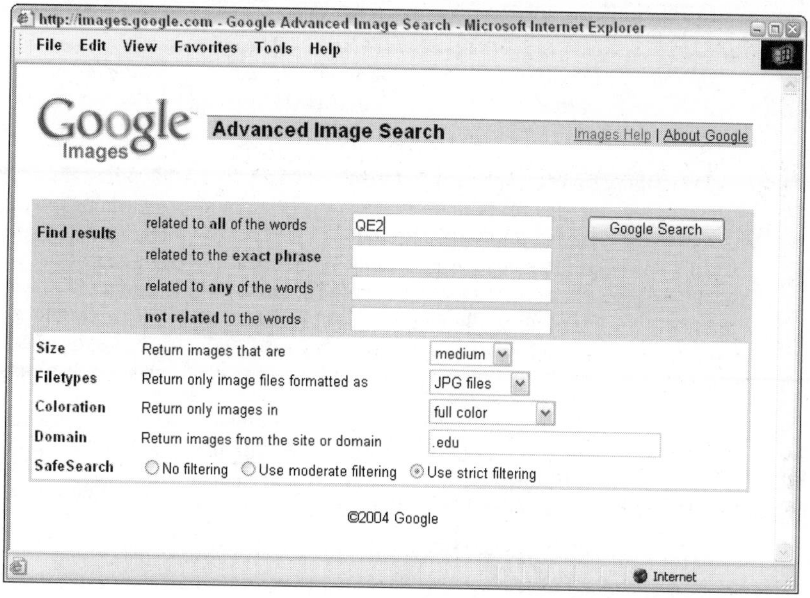

Figure 8-4:
The
Advanced
Image
Search
window.

The upper portion of the Advanced Image Search window (outlined in blue) provides a way to refine image queries. It looks similar to the Advanced Search window you see when you want to make adjustments to a general Google search. The lower portion of the window lets you make some Google Images–specific search refinements; for example, you can determine which file types you want to include in your search. See Table 8-1 for a complete list of refinements. This table also shows related operators that can be used in Google Images searches.

You can adjust any of these categories shown in the table by selecting options from the related drop-down lists. Google Images only returns pictures whose properties match the option value.

Table 8-1		Advanced Image Search Options	
Option	**Possible Values**	**Google Images Equivalent Operator**	**Example**
Size	Any Size, Small, Medium, or Large	n/a	Choose Any Size if you don't care how big or small an image is.
Filetypes	Any filetype, .jpg, .gif, .png	`filetype: particular filetype`	*filetype:any* allows you to search all image filetypes.

(continued)

Table 8-1 *(continued)*

Option	Possible Values	Google Images Equivalent Operator	Example
Coloration	Can be set to any colors, black and white, grayscale, or full color	n/a	If your research requires a certain type of coloration, you can limit your search to some degree.
Domain	Any domain name	`site:domain`	*site:edu* limits your search to images on sites designated as schools or universities.
Safe-Search	Set on a per-search basis to no filtering, moderate filtering, or strict filtering (see "Using Safe-Search with Images")	None, but can be globally set for all Google searches in Google Preferences	Tries to make sure your search keeps you from blushing.

Using Pictures in Your Research

Some professional researchers make it their sole business to provide photographic and illustration research services to publishers, magazines, ad agencies, and other businesses. These so-called photo researchers make up the core membership of the American Society of Picture Professionals (ASPP); have a look at the ASPP Web site, www.aspp.com, if you'd like more information about being a photo researcher.

But if your research job isn't restricted to image services, you surely can see how using images in your research can be helpful. Pictures can be very important to all types of research projects. This section gives you some examples to help spark you on this often untapped research option.

Using Google Images to find written information

If you don't think that using images in your research can be useful when you present results, would you believe that Google Images can help you find written content, too? That's right. If you use it right, Google Images can help you find Web pages with text-based content that you want.

Under specific circumstances, outlined in the following list, you may tap into a goldmine of written information when you use this wonderful tool:

- ✔ If the page doesn't contain a lot of text, the odds of getting enough links to increase PageRank standings aren't good.

- ✔ If the creator of the Web page didn't bother with meta tags or a meta description — HTML tags that are not visible on a Web page, but describe the page to search engines — the page may be pretty far down the return results in any garden-variety Google Web search.

If your search terms are found on the page, and the page contains an image, Google Images might return the page in a far higher position than a Web search.

Finding a specific image

Some time ago I was involved in a major research project that required me to locate and present examples of senior executive fraud at major corporations. I was asked to find copies of the notorious photographs of tobacco company executives standing in a row and swearing before Congress that nicotine was not addictive.

Because most people can evoke these images in their minds, and the photographs are not obscure, finding the images wouldn't seem all that difficult. Unless, of course, you can't remember the dates of the hearings.

Because the big problem was pinpointing the date, I finally had to find the photographs by going down to the library and looking through *The New York Times* on microfilm. Although the side benefit of being a less-than-efficient researcher was that I had an enjoyable stroll down memory lane, I could have saved myself a trip to the library if I'd followed the advice I'm giving you here.

Simply entering the search phrase *tobacco company executives* brought to light several thumbnails of the photograph I was looking for, as you can see in Figure 8-5. (In this kind of search you may want to conduct a regular Web search after you know the date of the hearing to uncover more detailed results, such as a hearing a transcript and the names of the tobacco executives involved.)

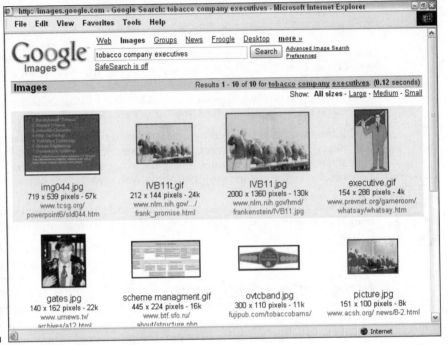

Researching for design

Stage designers for live theater and designers for the movies often need to re-create the look and feel of a particular place in time — or of a specific object, such as the *Titanic*. These, and other, professionals need references for their designs. Reference research for visual collateral is generally carried out by designers — or contracted to research professionals.

For example, a designer might need to re-create the dining room of the doomed ship the *Andrea Doria* (search term *dining room andrea doria*), or create an ambience that echoes 19th-century India (search term *19th century india* — see Figure 8-6). There's no limit to the number and kinds of requests for images that design professionals need for their projects. In aggregate, the Web provides the largest pool of images available anywhere. Google Images provides a very efficient way to search the Web for these images, and meet the needs of design professionals.

It often works best to combine a Google Images search with a Google Web search to find a wide variety of material related to a specific design research assignment.

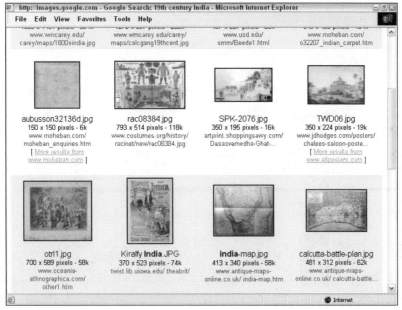

http://images.google.com - Google Search: 19th century India - Microsoft Internet Explorer

File   Edit   View   Favorites   Tools   Help

www.wmcarey.edu/   www.wmcarey.edu/carey/   www.usd.edu/   www.moheban.com/
carey/maps/1800sindia.jpg   maps/calcgang19thcent.jpg   smm/Beede1.html   o32207_indian_carpet.htm

aubusson32136d.jpg   rac08384.jpg   SPK-2076.jpg   TWD06.jpg
150 x 150 pixels - 6k   793 x 514 pixels - 118k   350 x 195 pixels - 16k   350 x 224 pixels - 19k
www.moheban.com/   www.costumes.org/history/   artprint.shoppingsavvy.com/   www.jdhodges.com/posters/
moheban_enquiries.htm   racinet/new/rac08384.jpg   Dasasvamedha-Ghat-...   chalees-saloon-poste...
[More results from   [More results from
www.moheban.com]   www.allposters.com]

otrl1.jpg   Kiralfy India.JPG   india-map.jpg   calcutta-battle-plan.jpg
700 x 589 pixels - 58k   370 x 523 pixels - 74k   413 x 340 pixels - 58k   481 x 312 pixels - 62k
www.oceania-   twist.lib.uiowa.edu/ theabrit/   www.antique-maps-   www.antique-maps-
ethnographica.com/   online.co.uk/ india-map.htm   online.co.uk/ calcutta-battle...
other1.htm

Internet

Figure 8-6: A search of Google Images returns these results.

Organizing your pictures with Picasa

In the summer of 2004, Google acquired a company named Picasa. Picasa's signature software organizes images on your computer into albums.

You can download and install Picasa for free from the Web site www.picasa.com. The first time you run Picasa, the software indexes all the graphics files on your computer (whether they're from your digital camera or saved from the Web). In this way, it acts a lot like the Google Desktop, which I show you in Chapter 5, except that Picasa focuses its operations on image files.

Within Picasa, every folder in your computer that contains images is listed as an album. The albums are displayed, sorted by date, along the left side of the main Picasa window. You can easily "move" pictures into new albums or combine albums by clicking and dragging. (The image files themselves are not moved, just the references to them in the Picasa catalog.) And,

of course, you can change your preferences so that the albums are not sorted by date.

Picasa provides rudimentary image-editing capabilities. For example, within Picasa you can remove *red-eye* from photographs (red-eye is that voodoo-Vampire look caused by looking directly at the flash when a photo is being shot). Picasa is a great, simple, organizing program and is sufficient for basic image editing, but (as you can probably imagine) Picasa is not Adobe Photoshop. If you plan on making major changes or adding effects, this isn't the program for you.

As you'd expect, Picasa provides pretty good tools for searching for images on your computer — particularly useful if you do a lot of image-focused research. It's a safe bet that the future will bring greater integration between Picasa's ability to organize pictures in a user-friendly way, and the great image-searching capabilities of Google Images.

Chapter 9

Providing Competitive Intelligence: Researching an Industry

• •

In This Chapter

▶ Getting information about a public company

▶ Profiling an industry

▶ Providing useful information about industry players

▶ Reading between the lines

• •

Although the term *competitive intelligence* sounds a little subversive, providing competitive intelligence is one of the most common tasks undertaken by research professionals. I'm sure you understand why — in any industry, research is used by companies to justify costs. Competitive intelligence research can reveal information of strategic importance, giving a company an important edge in stiff competition.

This chapter assumes that you're a working research professional about to be hired to deliver competitive intelligence. In this chapter, I present a case study. In real life, you'd probably use a mixture of information resources to fulfill your assignment (see Chapter 10 for information about some of these sources), but for the purpose of this chapter, I assume that you're mostly using the tools provided by Google to perform your preliminary research.

So imagine it's a dark and stormy evening. The shadows are strong in the harsh lights of your office. You're sipping your last cup of coffee when suddenly the telephone rings with a new assignment. . . .

Finding Out About a Company

The voice on the telephone identifies itself as the vice president of strategy for Global Widget Corporation (GWC). She explains that GWC has some new products in development that can be used to control pressures and flows in pipes. GWC would like help researching potential customers for these products in the energy business; the company also wants information about potential pitfalls it may encounter if it enters the energy services market.

You set up an appointment to conduct a reference interview later in the week at GWC's corporate headquarters in downtown San Francisco. A reference interview is an initial face-to-face conversation between researcher and client. This meeting lays out parameters, deadlines, and other important details of the research project. (I explain conducting reference interviews in Chapter 10.)

As you hang up the phone, you scratch your head. Who are these people? What do they really want? And, how do you tell them anything about the energy services industry that they don't already know?

The real information that a competitive intelligence research client would like is usually not disclosed on first contact. The researcher must rely on intuition, experience, and intelligence to ferret out a client's true needs and expectations. Find out what you can about the company immediately so that you know what you're getting into!

Here are some initial general searches you should consider running:

- ✔ A quick Google search of the company (GWC). Type **Global Widget Corporation** or **GWC** (or another, more realistic company name) into the Google Search box.

  When you enter **Global Widget Corporation,** you get a surprising number of search results (12,000+) for a company that doesn't really exist (see Figure 9-1).

- ✔ A quick search about the company's VP of Strategy. Investigate this person at the corporate Web site, and type this person's name into the Google Search box to find out more about his or her professional history.

- ✔ A general search about the energy services industry. This is a good opportunity to conduct a Google Directory search (as I explain in Chapter 7).

Asking (and answering) crucial questions

Of course, the Global Widget Corporation doesn't exist beyond its generic use as the fictitious name of a fictitious business in case studies. That said, if the company did exist, you'd probably want to know a few things. Probably you'd like to know

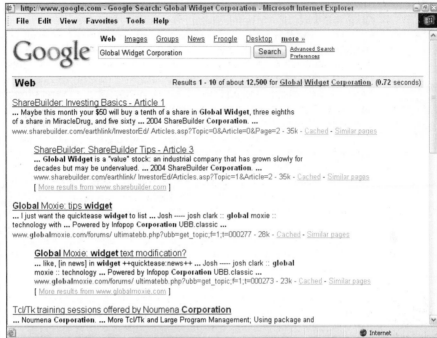

Figure 9-1:
Even though
there is no
Global
Widget
Corporation,
you still get
results
when you
search for
it using
Google.

✔ What businesses is it in?

✔ How big is GWC? How many employees?

✔ How many branches? Is it truly global as the name suggests? Where are its offices and operations?

✔ Is it publicly traded (and, if not, who owns it)?

✔ What is the big financial picture? Is it solvent?

✔ What are its annual sales and net revenues?

✔ Is GWC in trouble, or are there areas of particular concern?

✔ Who are the most important decision makers at GWC, their titles, and backgrounds?

You can make an educated guess at anything you can't find hard data about, such as the relationship between decision makers, by reading between the lines. One place to look for tips about this is in the relative details of compensation packages and option grants — information that is publicly disclosed for the top executives of public companies. Wide disparity between important names signals who is really in power (and may also hint at possible internal conflicts).

For example, when you enter **Cooper Cameron** (a real corporation) into the Google Search box, the first result returned is a link to the company's Web site. The top return results include links to a variety of sites with profile information about the company.

Don't forget to search the recent news about a person or organization you are investigating. Google News, which you can open from the Google home page (or by typing news.google.com into your browser), lets you quickly search for recent news items. You can also use the Google News Alerts service to have news items, as they hit the wires, sent to your e-mail inbox. You can sign up for alerts at www.google.com/alerts.

Look for general business information on the company's home page. On the home page of Cooper Cameron's Web site, for example, the <u>Investor Relations</u> link provides general business information, information about the company's officers, links to public financial filings, and most press releases that involve the company. Companies are not required to have an Investor Relations category on their Web site, put almost all public companies do.

Getting financial information

In all likelihood, all the general information you need about a company is available in an easy-to-digest format on the company's Web site. For example, the Investor Relations pages provided by Cooper Cameron provide all the information I list in "Asking (and answering) crucial questions." All the information, that is, *except*, "Is the company in trouble, or are there any areas of concern?" Finding financial data won't instantly answer this question, but it can give you some hints.

A publicly traded company's filings — such as its annual report — provide a tremendous wealth of information. But to make the most of the information in these filings, you need to know how to read financial statements, and also how to read between the (usually upbeat) lines to understand what is really being said.

If a company is privately owned, finding good quality information might be more difficult. You should do Google searches on the privately-owned company and its owners and top executives. (If you can't obtain information about ownership and officers from Google, this info is on file with the Secretary of State in any state the company does business in, provided the company has any size at all.)

Google searches for information about privately held companies may require refinement and pinpointing (see Chapter 4 and Chapter 5 for more information) to get the best, most accurate results. You should also expect to go well beyond the "third page of results" rule, and dig through page after page of Google resulting links.

To learn more about reading financial statements, you can do a Google search for the terms *financial statement, income statement,* and *balance sheet.* Follow the resulting links to get a bit of background. Or you could use a third-party financial profiling site, such as Yahoo! Finance, `http://finance.yahoo.com`. Figure 9-2 shows the profile page for Cooper Cameron in Yahoo! Finance.

If you enter a publicly traded company name or ticker symbol in the Google Web search box, you'll usually get links to the Yahoo! Finance profile page for the company among the top search results. Yahoo! Finance is a great site for financial information, but it is far from the only game in town. You might also want to try the sites listed in the sidebar "Sites that offer useful financial information."

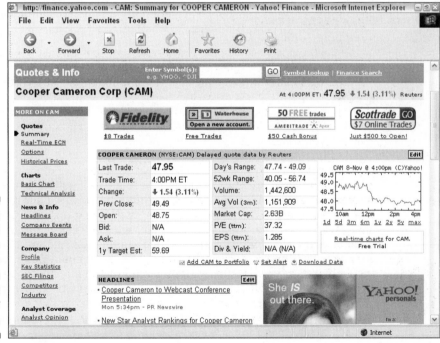

Figure 9-2: Yahoo! Finance provides capsule information about major companies.

Sites that offer useful financial information

Many sites provide useful financial information, some by aggregating content from a variety of sources, others by making on-the-record public information (such as SEC filings) more accessible, and still others by providing opinions (and even rumors).

Here are some of my favorite sites that provide information about businesses, finance, and the stock market (in addition to Yahoo! Finance, which seems to be the preferred general financial information provider when you do a Google search):

- CBS MarketWatch: `http://cbs.market watch.com`

- Fortune: `www.fortune.com`

- Hoover's Online: `www.hoovers.com`

- MSN Money: `http://moneycentral.com/investor/home.asp`

- NASDAQ: `www.nasdaq.com`

- The New York Stock Exchange: `www.nyse.com`

- The EDGAR Database: `www.sec.gov/edgar/searchedgar/webusers.htm` (EDGAR is the official database of the Securities and Exchange Commission and can be used to find all formal filings of publicly traded entities.)

- Silicon Investor: `www.siliconinvestor.com`

- TheStreet.com: `www.thestreet.com`

- The Wall Street Journal Online: `http://online.wsj.com`

Some of these sites are free to use, some offer mixed free and paid content, and others (for example, the Wall Street Journal) offer access by subscription only.

You should know that some of these sites offer bulletin boards. Yahoo! Finance is notorious for the wild postings on its stock bulletin boards, and Silicon Investor's claim to fame is almost entirely based on its bulletin boards.

Bulletin boards provide people who have an ax to grind a place to rant and rave — and to pump the stocks they own, or dump on the stocks they've sold short. It you filter everything you read through a hefty dose of skepticism, bulletin board posts can also offer unique windows on rumors about specific companies, and provide advance warning of information — both good and bad — that hasn't made its way into the news yet.

Your financial research checklist

To find out more about a company, there's no substitute for good contacts in the industry. If you don't have these contacts, you'd be surprised how easy it is to make them. From there, you can learn a great deal of information that isn't generally known. If you have time, you can attend a trade show or convention in that particular industry. See "Understanding an Industry" for more information. I recommend doing the following to find financial information:

✔ **Conduct an** intitle: **not** inurl: **search for dirt on the company.** For example, type the following into the Google Search box (see Chapter 5 for an explanation of how this works):

```
intitle:"cooper cameron" -inurl:coopercameron
```

This search returns pages that have Cooper Cameron in the page title, but not its Web address (the page URL). If anyone is really annoyed at the company — annoyed enough to publish a Web page — this search almost certainly finds it.

✔ **Carefully read news items involving the company.** You can find recent headlines on financial aggregation sites such as Yahoo! Finance or many of the sites listed in the "Sites that offer useful financial information" sidebar; you can also search http://news.google.com for news items. If the company faces any serious financial troubles, you'll probably glimpse a hint of them in the news.

✔ **Check a chart of the performance of the company's equity.** If there are any large movements in either direction during the past few months, see if you can determine the cause. For example, Enron stock started to drop precipitately long before the news of Enron's troubles made the news. If there is negative information about a company, *someone* always knows about it and acts on it by selling stock — and telling friends, who also act on it. (Of course, if you're not a financial analyst, you're not an expert, so it's best not to make too many assumptions without an expert's help.)

✔ **Use financial filings to make sure that finances are not deteriorating.** Check out the suggestions earlier in this chapter for finding resources to help learn about filings, or get competent help if you are on shaky grounds with financial statements.

✔ **Check security analysts' reports, many of which can be found using a Google Web search:** But bear in mind that analysts tend to be optimistically biased.

✔ **Search Usenet (Google Groups) to see if there are any rumors or other information about the company.** I discuss Google Groups in Chapter 7.

Much of the time, you won't find anything "wrong" at all with a company because there is no "bad" news to find. The point isn't necessarily to verify whether a company is squeaky clean; it's to achieve a thorough sense of its operations and its role in the larger industry. (By the way, Cooper Cameron is squeaky clean.)

After you understand an industry (see "Understanding an Industry") and know its players (see "Knowing the Players"), you can consider contacting competitors to see what they have to say.

A sample financial profile

The idea behind doing all this background research is to then summarize your findings so that you have them in a convenient, easy-to-read format. Some benefits of having a financial profile at your fingertips include the following:

✔ When you write down the financial profile, you can get a better focus on what is (and is not) likely to be important to a company.

✔ If the company is a client, then the officers of the company eat, drink, and breathe this kind of information. You may find that writing down this information helps you level the playing field just a bit so that you can impress your clients with your ability to simply summarize what they do.

✔ More likely than not, you will need this material anyhow for your final work product.

✔ You can show your profile to your client, and verify, "Did I get this right?"

Here's a short profile of Cooper Cameron that uses the techniques and sources I explain in this section to answer the questions I posed about Global Widget Corporation (with the profile relating to Cooper Cameron instead):

Profile of Cooper Cameron Corporation

What it is: *Cooper Cameron makes oil and gas pressure control equipment, centrifugal air compressors, gas compressors, and turbochargers, which it sells to major energy, energy exploration and production (so-called "e & p" companies), pipeline, and refinery companies. Predecessor companies to Cooper Cameron date back to the 1830s. With excellent product, quality, and safety reputations, Cooper Cameron currently has a market capitalization of close to $3 billion, with very little debt.*

Ownership: *Cooper Cameron is publicly traded on the NYSE under the symbol CAM. The largest single ownership group is the mutual fund behemoth Fidelity Management, which owns about 14 percent of the company. Cooper Cameron is approximately 90 percent owned by financial institutions.*

Employees: *There are about 7,700 employees worldwide.*

Offices and operations: *Cooper Cameron is a global corporation, with customers in more than 115 countries. It is headquartered in Houston, Texas, and incorporated in Delaware.*

Finances: *With annual sales of about $2 billion growing 5 percent year to year (five year growth rate), income of about $70 million growing 10 percent year to year (five year growth rate), over $600 million in liquid assets, and very little debt, Cooper Cameron is very solvent.*

Decision makers: *This link provides information about officers, members of the board, and the company org chart: www.coopercameron.com/cgi-bin/corporate/organization/ccc_structure.cfm.*

After all this work digging into Cooper Cameron, suppose you want to under-stand a little more about its products (for example, what they are). What better way than to use Google Images to look at some pictures? (I explain using Google Images in Chapter 8).

Some of the thumbnail image return results using the search term *Cooper Cameron* are shown in Figure 9-3. I particularly like the undersea imagery because these pictures show the intensely engineered quality of this com-pany's work.

Figure 9-3: Search Google Images to find out more about a company's products.

Understanding an Industry

Delivering profile information about a company is important, but so is profil-ing an entire industry. Both the fictional Global Widget Corporation and the real Cooper Cameron (which I discuss throughout this chapter) are part of the energy services industry. What does this industry look like as a whole, and how can you apply what you've picked up in this chapter in your evaluation of the industry you're researching? Well, glad you asked. I suggest starting with the Google Directory and using Google to search the Web.

You may want to ask and answer the following questions about an industry:

- ✔ What are the industry products and services?

- ✔ What is the gross revenue of the industry?

- ✔ How profitable is the industry?

- ✔ Who are the customers (for example, consumers, or other businesses)?

- ✔ Is the industry localized? National? Worldwide?

- ✔ What's the general level of education in the industry? (Mining and farming both have rather different average levels of education than software development.)

- ✔ Who are the top five players in the industry? The top 25 players?

- ✔ Is the industry growing or shrinking? Is it in trouble?

- ✔ What political interactions or interventions affect the industry?

- ✔ Is the industry facing any "paradigm shifts," or is it in "business as usual" mode?

Finding out about an industry with Google Directory

The Google Directory provides an excellent starting place to learn about the structure of an industry. (I explain how to open and use the Google Directory in both search and browse mode in Chapter 7.)

To find out more about an industry (such as energy services), follow these general steps:

1. **Click the <u>Business</u> link on the main Google Directory page.**

   See Figure 9-4.

2. **Choose the business category that suits your query.**

   For example, Figure 9-5 shows the Energy and Environment category.

3. **To find more about a business, continue clicking category links.**

   For example, if you're interested in more about the oil and gas businesses, as shown in Figure 9-6, click the <u>Oil and Gas</u> link.

Figure 9-4:
The Business category is the starting place for learning about an industry.

Figure 9-5:
Drill through the business categories.

Figure 9-6:
Pick a sub-
category
like Oil
and Gas.

4. **Select yet another subcategory, and another, until you have a complete financial picture.**

   For example, as you can see in Figure 9-7, a number of subcategories can help you learn about energy and services in the Oil and Gas category.

5. **Peruse the categories that are most likely to give you an industry overview.**

   In the Oil and Gas category, the Industry Resources subcategory is a great place to start because it provides industry overview information. Many of the links in Industry Resources (some of which are shown in Figure 9-8) are to sites that (on a free or paid basis) provide excellent snapshots, thorough analysis, and predictive information about the energy services industry.

6. **Look for company-specific information.**

   For example, in the Oil and Gas category, the following subcategories are likely to be helpful because they offer company-specific information:

   - Operating Companies
   - Services Companies
   - Tools and Equipment

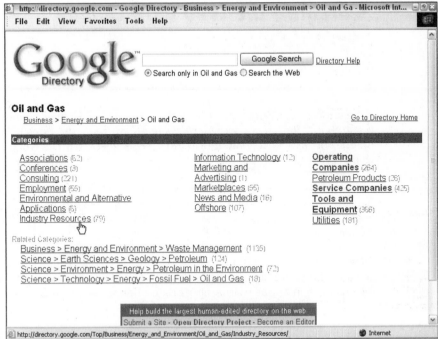

Figure 9-7:
The options
available in
the Oil
and Gas
category.

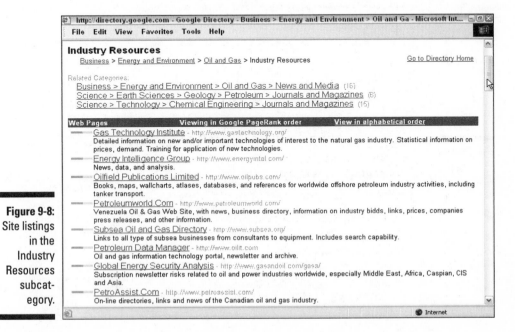

Figure 9-8:
Site listings
in the
Industry
Resources
subcat-
egory.

Searching the Web with Google to profile an industry

One attractive way to gather information about an industry is to use the Google Web search engine. Not surprising, is it?

For example, to learn about the energy services industry as a whole, a search for the terms *energy services industry profile* provides links to a number of sites with great information (see Figure 9-9). The wonderful thing is that the search results aren't the same as those found in the Google Directory.

Some of the best links that come up in the return results shown in Figure 9-9 are to Yahoo! Finance, Business.com, Hoover's, and ZapData (part of Dun and Bradstreet).

Some business information is given away for free, but be prepared to purchase so-called *premium* data such as sales leads. One notable exception is Yahoo! Finance, which at this writing appears to offer all its information for free.

Figure 9-9:
As the search results show, many sites provide industry profile information.

A sample industry profile

Based on the industry information you gather using the Google Directory, and the data you obtain from sites you find searching the Web, you can profile an industry, perhaps as follows:

> ***Energy Services Industry Profile***
>
> *The energy services industry provides products and services to the energy industry in the following segments:*
>
> ***Exploration:*** *Geological, geophysical, and other exploration-related services.*
>
> ***Oil field equipment:*** *Drill bits, pipes, pumps, and so on.*
>
> ***Field services:*** *Well drilling, operations management, clean-up, and more*
>
> *There are about 120 companies of any size (this number includes international and private companies as well as publicly owned companies in the U.S.; for a list see* `http://biz.yahoo.com/ic/oilsrv_cl_all.html.`
>
> *Publicly traded companies in the industry range from the tiny (less than $1 million in annual sales) to the huge, such as Halliburton, which has more than $20 billion in revenue, and Schlumberger, with a $36 billion market capitalization. However, most industry players have market capitalization and revenue in the hundreds of millions.*
>
> *Total size of the industry, based on annual revenue, is estimated to be about $100 billion (see* `www.zapdata.com`*).*

Knowing the Players

Many of the links returned by a search for keywords like *energy services industry profile* provide information about the companies that are players in the industry. For example, Yahoo! Finance at `http://biz.yahoo.com/ic/oilsrv_cl_all.html` provides a comprehensive alphabetized list of companies (see Figure 9-10) linked to Yahoo! profiles of each company.

Unfortunately, finding known companies that have some substance in an industry can be pretty easy, but finding really small businesses in an industry is more difficult; worse yet is the prospect of finding companies that provide single products or services to a variety of industries. These companies can be key players because they have diversified services. In addition, there may be many companies that may be doing research (ahem!) to determine whether breaking into an industry is profitable. Finding these companies in a Google search (without already knowing who they are) isn't easy.

Figure 9-10:
Yahoo!
Finance
provides an
alphabetic
list of
companies
in the
industry.

If you are interested in the larger public companies in an industry, MSN Money provides an excellent free stock screener tool shown in Figure 9-11.

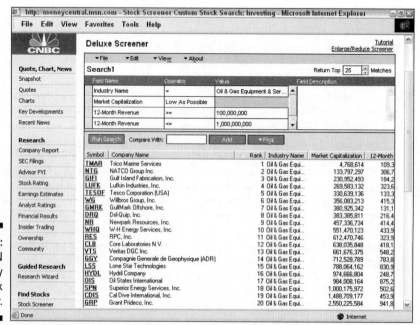

Figure 9-11:
The MSN
Money
stock
screener.

TIP

Reading between the lines

If you read this chapter from beginning to end, you will know more than you probably ever wanted to know about the energy services industry and its players. The idea is that you can apply this information to the industry you're actually researching so that when you meet with the VP of Strategy for (insert name of corporation less example-y than Global Widgets Corporation here) you're ready.

Your initial meeting with your client should be considered a reference interview (see Chapter 10 for more information about conducting a reference interview). During the reference interview, go over your understanding of the industry and its players with your client (to make sure that you got it right). Depending on the situation, I would recommend bringing your company and industry profiles to the initial meeting to verify you've gotten everything right.

You need to find out about the deliverables for this research assignment, and what your client really wants to know. Ultimately, you need to determine why you were engaged. This takes a blend of analysis, effective probing, and intuition — and often, an ability to read between the lines. Use the reference interview to find this out — or at least to begin the process of finding it out!

Using your competitive intelligence about the energy services industry, you're ready to engage in detailed and specific research, and provide the answers and deliverables required by your client. Part III provides the information you need to research like a pro, armed with the research resources of the Web and an in-depth understanding of Google's comparative methodology. Part III also explains the best way to deliver research results.

Find the MSN Money stock screener at http://moneycentral.msn.com/investor/finder/customstocks.asp. What makes this free tool so useful is that you can easily configure it with your own criteria (with a huge variety of criteria) to display only the companies you are interested in, ordered in whatever way you'd like. For example, the screen shown in Figure 9-11 returns energy services companies with annual sales between $100 million and $1 billion and organizes the remaining companies by market capitalization (from lowest to highest).

REMEMBER

I can't think of anything that beats out having contacts in an industry if you want to find out how companies really interact. Key players (individuals in the industry) are simply the best people to tell you which key companies are healthy and which are not. If you don't already have industry connections, consider developing them by attending trade shows or conferences.

Part III
Building Valuable Research Content

In this part . . .

*A*ll the ability in the world to use Google's fabulous research tools won't help you find out what you and your research clients need to know if you don't know how to conduct research in the first place. Chapter 10 helps you research like a pro answering the following questions: What questions should you ask? What research tools are available to you? How can you become a better and more ethical researcher?

Chapter 11 explains how to use the underlying power, methodologies, and mechanisms that power Google to your advantage as a researcher — and avoid the pitfalls that are the fault of the nature of Google itself.

Finally, you need to know how to present your research results. Look no further than Chapter 12.

Chapter 10

Researching Like a Pro

Google, and the World Wide Web itself, are great research tools when you simply use their bare-bones features. But when you realize that you've just scratched the surface with these tools, you'll want to learn more. And the truth is that you can't expect to get the most out of the facilities provided by Google — or even think about automating the Google facilities — without a good understanding of the nature of *research* itself.

This chapter gets to the heart of the matter and helps you take your casual search queries into overdrive. If you're conducting serious research, you can use this chapter to help you determine which questions to ask. And if you're not ready to begin your research project just yet, use this chapter to help you decide which situations are likely to call for research and — if you're working as a professional researcher — which clients are likely to be making research requests.

One truism in the world of software development is that to build a tool that automates a process, you must first understand how the process works manually. Similarly, to understand how to best research using Google, it also helps to have a good understanding of how to use conventional research tools, such as reference interviewing, libraries, and public record repositories. Even if you're already in the know about conventional research, this chapter is a great reference that explains how to employ some of the most useful conventional tools of the trade while using the Google technology. You learn what information is simply not available on the Web (and what tools to use to find this information), and how to approach the so-called *invisible* Web — that is, information resources that are available on the World Wide Web that you cannot access using a search engine such as Google.

Asking Research Questions

You can answer a gazillion casual questions using Google. For example, like millions of people, you've probably found a lot of information about a person by doing a search on Google using his or her name as the search term. Heck, maybe you've even done such a Google search on yourself. Likewise, you can obtain information about products and places (see Chapter 1 for details). And, often, you can clarify a technical concept or process by simply entering the term in the ubiquitous Google search box. In this spirit, as an example, if you need to learn about how "server-side includes" are used in building Web sites, entering the phrase into Google (essentially, the "what is" and the question mark are implied) will probably provide links that give you all the information you need.

Google is a great tool for answering simple questions, but to *search* with Google is not to *research* with Google.

Intense research deals with questions that can't be quantified with a single, simple question. In fact, real research doesn't involve a question at all, but instead involves a topic that is broad and essentially unanswerable as formulated. Generally, this kind of research does not mean original scientific investigation (which is sometimes called *original research*), but rather deep investigation — for example, providing strategic intelligence about a complex industry.

Good researchers drill down, refine, and redefine the research assignment so that it becomes a series of answerable questions that can be answered — possibly by querying Google.

The following sections explain the importance of questions to serious research and how to present the answers. Presenting answers largely depends upon who is asking the questions (in the case of a professional researcher, it is the client). So I also explain some of the issues involved in understanding the needs of the research client.

Why ask questions?

Asking questions is one of the oldest human ways of gaining knowledge, dating back to Plato and the Socratic method, the Talmud (see the similarly titled sidebar, nearby), and the distant past when humans first made efforts to understand themselves, life, and the world. It is one of the best techniques for learning. Asking the right questions is essential to any serious research effort.

The Socratic method, Plato, and the Talmud

Socrates was a fifth-century B.C.E. Athenian philosopher who was sentenced to death by drinking hemlock in 399 for advocating seeking the truth and (supposedly) corrupting the youth of Athens. Socrates left no written record, and his teachings were recorded after the fact, most famously in *The Apology* by Plato, a student of Socrates.

In *The Apology,* which concerns the trial and death of Socrates, Plato wrote that Socrates employed a method of learning that consisted of repeated questioning — often until the person being questioned reached a contradiction, thus proving a fallacy in the original position taken. The questioner never takes a side, and, as Socrates put it, "the wise man is the man who knows he knows nothing." Ultimately, the terms *Socratic reasoning* and *Socratic method* have come to identify a dialectical method of finding the truth by modifying one's position through repeated questioning of those with different ideas.

Plato's early career as a philosophic writer primarily focused on the dialectic techniques he learned as a student of Socrates. Although Plato's later work continued to discuss the ideas originated by Socrates, Plato also explored a diverse range of subjects from the ideal form of government (in *The Republic*) to questions of *ontology* — how we know what we know — and the nature of reality.

The Talmud is a vast written record of rabbinical discussions of Jewish laws, ethics, customs, legends, and more. It is also an extension, parallel commentary, and gloss on the Torah, the first five books of the Hebrew Bible (Genesis, Exodus, Leviticus, Numbers, and Deuteronomy). Taken as a whole, the Talmud is the basis for all subsequent codes of Jewish law. Many people, both Jewish and non-Jewish, consider the Talmud a source of inspiration and moral instruction.

I could say great deal more about Socrates, Plato, and the Talmud. The next time you have some spare time, I suggest you conduct a search on Google for each term in order to learn about these great sources for understanding human reasoning and methodologies.

However, questioning is not the only structure for receiving information (I explain *hierarchic,* or categorized, approaches and taxonomies in Chapter 11). Indeed, in some contexts, questioning is frowned upon and information is only considered valid if it is organized hierarchically.

As a researcher, the ability to ask questions (and get reasonable answers) provides control. If you can't ask the questions, then you don't control the resulting information — it controls you. When you're feeling overwhelmed by a research topic, remember that you can always rely on a standard set of questions (see Chapter 3 for more about finding the best questions to ask) to help you get a handle on the topic, or at the very least, an avenue of inquiry to help narrow the topic down.

Searching hierarchically

In many cases, searching hierarchically is actually easier than asking questions. The difference is like the difference between an index and a table of contents in a book. With a good index, you can look up any phrase or word you like (just as you can search for any word or phrase using Google). You don't have as much freedom using the table of contents, but you do have an organized structure that may help you find what you're looking for because it provides a context.

So, when do you use hierarchical research (by browsing through the categories in a directory) and when do you use the question method (by searching for a word or phrase)? Well, the reality is that nothing is ever that cut-and-dried. The most skilled researchers use a seamless combination of the two methods. In fact, sometimes the hierarchical method is the only way to go if you need to develop some research questions about a topic. Ask yourself the questions in Table 10-1 to determine what you should do next.

Table 10-1	Finding the Right Starting Place	
If Your Research Topic Is . . .	*Then You Should . . .*	*Example*
. . . Unfamiliar to you	. . . Try hierarchic research first (see Chapter 11)	You're a poet who suddenly finds herself studying quantum physics
. . . Fairly well defined, but not likely to produce useful answers as expressed	. . . Ask some questions to make the research focus useful (keep reading Chapter 10); see if you can get a fresh perspective using hierarchical research (skip to Chapter 11)	You're asked to make suggestions to solve the health care mess, in particular how to make sure uninsured people get coverage
. . . A subject you're quite familiar with	. . . Ask questions to drill-down on the research topic to make it more precise	You're a widget industry expert and you're asked how to build a better widget

One of the most important characteristics of the successful research project is an agreement in advance about the questions that need to be answered. See Chapter 3 for help in this department.

Reaching a meeting of the minds with your research clients about the questions that are to be answered is essential to the success of the research process. You should take the lead in coming up with a set of research questions that both you and your research client believe

> ✔ Can be answered
>
> ✔ Will resolve the research assignment

You need agreement with your research client about what questions to ask. This type of contract (whether verbal or written, formal or informal) is comparable to a Scope of Work agreement you might use in any consulting project in any field.

Using Reference Interviews

You don't have time to waste, and your client won't appreciate it if you give results that don't meet his or her needs — no matter how accurate the results are and how well they are presented. So after you've figured out the questions you're going to ask about the topic, you need to give your client a rundown of where you're going to head with the research.

Laying out the details at the beginning of the process (before you actually do the research) saves you and your client a huge amount of hassle and time. I suggest submitting a brief report to your client that specifies exactly what the research plan is. The format of this report depends upon your research client's needs. I tell you more about different clients and their likely needs in the sidebar, "Who needs the answer?" The answers can be as succinct as a verbal "Yes" or "No," or as lengthy as a complex report with extensive backup material.

Conducting a reference interview is one of the key techniques used to determine the questions the client needs answered and the format for the delivery of the research results.

If you're a student, you should consider your teacher the "client." You'll need to come up with the same kind of project scope information that you would for a nonacademic research project. If the assignment does not make all the deliverables clear to you, you should consider conducting the equivalent of a reference interview with the teacher — during office hours, of course.

Interview mechanics and investigative work

If possible, reference interviews should be conducted in person. An in-person interview is better than one conducted over the telephone, which (in turn) is better than a reference interview done via e-mail. Many nuances of communication get lost when you can't see who you're talking to. An in-depth personal interview can be much more effective than one over the phone or across the ether-like Internet. If your initial communication with the research client has been by e-mail or phone, see if you can arrange a face-to-face reference interview. (The other side of this coin is that e-mail is a great tool for gathering factual information with great efficiency. Also, if someone sends you an e-mail message, you have "proof" of what was "said.")

Remember to dress neatly and professionally when conducting reference interviews.

Tape-record reference interviews so that you can listen to them later to make sure you didn't miss something. This is an especially good idea if you're conducting long-term, in-depth research. An interview tape can back you up about what was said, and about the terms of a research engagement, if they are ever in dispute.

Always ask permission before taping a conversation either in person or on the telephone, and record the permission on the tape. Otherwise, you can be inadvertently breaking the law.

If you're tape-recording the interview, you should come prepared to take notes. Notes serve to remind you of some information presented during an interview that you would otherwise forget. (Notes can also serve as backup, although they are not as convincing as a tape recording.)

I can't think of much of a reason to conduct a reference interview if you're entirely ignorant of the subject being discussed. You're not likely to learn much and you won't come across as serious. So if you don't have much background in the area being researched, you need to either learn the basics about the subject before conducting a reference interview, or gracefully find someone better equipped for the assignment.

You can learn basic information about a complex subject using a variety of techniques, including reading a good book that provides a general introduction to the topic, interviewing an expert in the field, and doing initial research using Google. Try the Google Directory, which I discuss in Chapter 7.

Going through the phases of the reference interview

The purpose of the reference interview is to find out about what exactly you'll be researching.

Go into a reference interview with an open mind about what you will learn. You should also assume that it is likely that what you hear from your research client to start with will not be what you end up researching, because research clients often do not understand their own projects. You'll need to help the client understand the true questions they need to have answered.

The reference interview consists of three parts:

1. Reviewing background information

2. Determining the scope of an assignment

3. Repeating back to the client your understanding

Reviewing background information

An example of background information, if you're asked to research competitive business intelligence, would be to learn about a company's products and its industry. Here are some hints for conducting the background portion of the interview:

- ✔ **Ask open-ended questions:** A good technique is to get the client to talk about the projects. For example, you can start by saying "Tell me about ____."

   Researchers often have a favorite open-ended background question. Mine is: "If you were directing a movie about this, how would the capsule review read?"

- ✔ **Get clarification:** If there is anything you don't understand, make sure to get it explained and clarified. If necessary, write down your questions and ask them after the client has finished describing the project.

- ✔ **Put on your thinking cap:** After you have a general sense of the subject matter to be covered, drill down to the heart of the matter by asking "Why?" as often as you can (but not so often as to feel you're being a nuisance). The idea is to look at the topic from as many perspectives as possible so that you can identify potential problems early in the process.

One question you might want to ask early in the background portion of the interview is who your audience is. You need to know if the research is for public consumption, for a marketing team, for the Board of Directors of a major corporation, or for a class full of third graders. Every audience has its own needs, and the research questions you ask (as well as how you answer and present them) vary accordingly.

When you think you have enough background information, summarize what you have found out and move on.

Determining the scope of the assignment

An important goal of this phase of the interview is to sufficiently narrow down and clarify the research topic. As a result of this phase of the discussion, you will produce a list of questions that your research will answer. (If you have trouble coming up with questions, see Chapter 3 for some tips.)

Be careful to make sure that the questions you come up with are questions that your research can realistically answer. This is also the time to make sure that the questions are formulated with clarity and precision.

If your assessment is that the research project involves special difficulties — for example, maybe it requires some kind of public records research — this is a good time to convey those potential pitfalls to your client. In this case, if you decide to continue with the project, you should probably explore what happens if your research hits a dead end.

Here are some topics you should be sure are addressed at this point:

- ✔ **Scheduling:** How long do you have to complete the project? You should talk about schedules, the length of time you'll be working on the project, and any other issues of timing.

- ✔ **Confidentiality:** You should also find out if the information you have been given is confidential, and, if so, respect its confidentiality. You may be asked to sign a written *NDA* (nondisclosure agreement).

- ✔ **Money:** Don't forget to talk about payment, payment schedules, method of payment, and overtime payment. Be prepared to give a fair preliminary estimate of how long the project will take you to complete.

- ✔ **Format:** You should also use the second phase of the interview to determine how the research results will be delivered. Some clients want written results, but they may also want a multimedia presentation prepared. The method of inquiry might shift a little if you're looking for information that can be easily rendered into a visual format.

    Here are some of the common formats for research question and answer deliverables (see Chapter 12 for more details), roughly ranging from least formal to most formal:

    - • Informal answer to an ad-hoc question, delivered in person, by phone, or via e-mail

    - • Compact verbal report, either on the phone or in person

    - • Summary e-mail

    - • Web delivery of initial results

    - • An executive summary

    - • A PowerPoint presentation

    - • An extensive in-person presentation

    - • A formal written report or paper, with or without formal sourcing information

- Statistical information, delivered as part data for software designed to handle quantitative data (a spreadsheet program such as Excel is the simplest example)

- A software program, with or without data, perhaps created using the Google APIs, as explained in Part IV

Making assumptions about format without asking is unwise. In fact, the results could be disastrous if you don't meet the client's expectations. The best way to find out about how a research client likes to get answers is to ask the client. For example, the client might require the information to be posted on a Web site with plenty of cross-referenced links; if you present the answer to the client as a PowerPoint presentation, your answer may prove to be useless to them, even though it contains the correct information.

If you're a professional researcher, it is important to have a written contract as well as an agreement during a reference interview. The Association of Independent Information Professionals (AIIP), www.aiip.org, provides a sample contract and more information about best business practices for researchers.

Research interviews versus reference interviews

Serious researchers tend to spend most of their time online, or in libraries, not conducting interviews. Even movie action hero Indiana Jones, who says "Seventy-five percent of all archaeology is done in the library, researching, reading," has realized this (although he seems to spend most of his time hanging around beautiful women, falling out of airplanes, and so on).

However, sometimes even the most introverted researcher needs to conduct interviews in-person or on the telephone. These interviews differ from reference interviews because they are solely used to uncover information, and they are not conducted with a research client.

Quickly getting valuable background information about an industry, technology, or trend is the most common reason to conduct a research interview. When you interview an expert for this purpose, you should follow the guidelines I explain for reviewing background information in a reference interview.

Another reason to conduct an interview is to find out about something firsthand, from a primary source. Interviewing people who actually witnessed something can yield surprising results, but these results need to be analyzed with care — because human memory is often unreliable.

Conduct an interview with a primary source in a very open-ended fashion. Remember, from a primary source you usually want to find out *what* happened, not an opinion about *why* it happened.

In addition, research interviews are often used in connection with consumer and voter behavior. These kinds of interviews involve a number of special methodological considerations and statistical analyses.

Repeating back to the client your understanding

Make sure to wrap up the reference interview with a recap, in your own words, of what has been discussed and decided. That way both you and your client can make sure you're on the same page.

You should plan to think carefully about your business practices. Although the steps you take depend on many factors, including your relationship with your research client and the project budget, before you start your research you should have a signed contract, a written summary of the reference interview (including schedules, potential conflicts, and contact information), and a list of tools or materials that the researcher is to be provided (if any) to complete the project.

Why Google Is Not the Web

Google is not the Internet and it's not the Web. Actually, even the Web is not the *complete* Web — there is a great deal of useful information that you can't access it on the public Web. Some of this information can be accessed through for-fee databases (see "Using a research database") or (if you've subscribed) via a Web interface (see "Other online research services"). Still other information can only be obtained offline in libraries and government public records repositories.

If you're planning to use Google primarily for your research, you should know how Google works, what its limitations are, and why you might need to use additional resources to complete your research.

Google and other search engines

Web search engines are complex pieces of software. Almost every search engine, including Google, consists of three primary parts:

- ✔ **A Web crawler, sometimes called a spider:** The spider finds and retrieves — meaning, gets and saves a copy of — Web pages.

- ✔ **An indexer:** The indexer indexes all the words on a page, and stores the words in a huge database that cross-references the keywords with the pages in which they appear. As I explain in Chapter 4, short words such as *and* and *how,* also called *stop words,* are indexed, but do not appear in search results unless you override Google's defaults by adding quotes.

✔ **A query processor:** The query processor makes sense of queries entered by users of the search engine, compares the words in your search to the keywords in the index, and returns the resulting matches in some kind of order. (To find out more about queries and how they are processed, see Part I of this book.)

Google's primary innovation when it first became available was a relatively sophisticated way of determining relevancy in the results returned by its query processor. This technique, called the *PageRank* algorithm, depends on the number of Web pages that link to a particular Web page. I explain the PageRank algorithm in more detail in Chapter 11. Essentially, pages that have a higher rank appear closer to the top of the Google search result listings.

By and large, there's not much difference in the way you can implement a spider or an indexer. However, not all search engines have indexed the same parts of the Web. In addition, each search engine's query processor is built differently, using somewhat different principles. That's why different search engines give different results to the same query, and why there are queries that can be answered by a particular search engine, but not by others. Some other search engines license their technology from Google. For example, Yahoo! licensed its search technology from Google for a while until it developed its own search technology. Currently, A9, `www.a9.com`, licenses much of its technology from Google. So if you get almost identical results from several search engines, they are probably using the same underlying technology.

Admittedly, Google is one of the best search engines, run by a world-class team of technologists. But if you can't get relevant results using Google, you should try some other search engines before giving up on finding the information on the Web (see Chapter 2 for a comparison of different search engines).

The "invisible" Web

There are large parts of the World Wide Web that no search engine — including Google — can "see." Providing a good definition of the invisible Web (which is also sometimes called the *deep Web* and *dark matter*) isn't so easy to do. The best way to think of it is simply as material that is on the Web that has been excluded from search engines, specifically from Google, either on purpose or due to technological limitations.

Material on the Web that is invisible to Google will almost certainly be invisible to other search engines as well.

You can easily see why some Web sites — such as those with adult content — might be excluded from Web search engines and thus rendered "invisible." But it may be a little harder for you to understand why sites that contain information of value to researchers are also invisible.

There are a number of possible reasons that Web pages might be excluded from Google (and other search engines). These include

- **Dynamic results aren't easy to read:** If a page is *dynamically generated* and assembled from a database, Google might not return it as a result to your query. Although spiders can access dynamically generated pages, particularly if a page is pulled intact out of a database — and even the returns page from a Google search can be considered a dynamically generated page — spiders can have trouble with any dynamic generation that involves setting multiple fields to return the results.

- **Pages that require logons may not be accessible:** If you're required to log on to access a page and/or a subscription or fee is required to access the page (see "Other online research services"), the results may not come up (because, obviously, Google's spider cannot log on).

- **The page is not connected:** If the Web page is "disconnected," with no other pages linking to it (so a spider cannot find it by following links), it won't show up in a list of search results.

- **The page doesn't have words:** If a Web page contains mostly visual matter, indexing may be limited to ancillary text such as that in `alt` parameters of the `img` tags.

- **Material can be excluded by the Webmaster:** Depending on the site and the information it contains, a Webmaster may mark specific pages as off-limits to crawlers. A file on a Web server named `robot.txt` tells the spider which pages are verboten. For more information about how this works, see the information about Robots Exclusion at `www.robotstxt.org/wc/exclusion.html`.

- **The information is in a format that can't be easily read:** If a file is in a format that is hard for the spider to read, such as an executable file, or a compressed file (such as a `.zip` file), Google may not be able to find it. Google (unlike most other search engines) *does* have an impressive ability to index Acrobat (`.pdf`) and Postscript files, and Microsoft Word (`.doc`) documents.

Other Kinds of Research

If you can't find what you need to know on the Web using Google, it may be time to try other avenues. The following sections give you some suggestions.

Using a research database

Research databases, such as Lexis/Nexus, used to exist off the Web, and would make a specialized client program available to researchers. In other words, you could access the database by physically going to a location that provided access to a research database (usually a library or other professional research institution), or use special software to access it.

The software provided for access to high-quality research databases can provide analysis and retrieval tools that are superior to what you find on the Web, particularly for specialized scientific and technical databases.

These days, more and more research databases provide alternative access via subscription Web sites. So you may have a choice about how to retrieve the information you need.

However you access a research database, you'll most likely have to subscribe or pay a fee unless you have access through an institution that has paid the fees, such as a corporation or university.

A good example of a research database in which having specialized client software (not a Web browser) add value is the Questel Orbit intellectual property service, `www.questel.orbit.com`. Questel Orbit makes patent information in its databases available through its PatReader software, which is a visualization tool for quickly and accurately scanning the full text of patents.

The best way to find research databases is to use a hierarchical approach. For example, have a look at the Reference category in the Google Directory. (I explain using Google Directory in Chapter 7.)

Other online research services

For a researcher, the most important part of the invisible Web is made up of fee-based premium services that provide high-quality information. The information provided by these services may be stored in some kind of database, but to the researcher it hardly matters so long as the service makes a Web interface to the data available.

Some of the best-known online fee-based research services are

- ✔ **DataStar:** `www.datastarweb.com`, a professional research service with an emphasis on companies and industry

- ✔ **Dialog:** `www.dialogweb.com`, an extensive research service that makes more than 600 research databases available either through dedicated software or the Dialog Web site

TIP

Introducing Google Scholar

Google Scholar, a service from Google that is currently in beta release, makes tons of academic, scholarly, and scientific research easily available at no cost (it is supported by targeted advertising).

To open Google Scholar, open the address http://scholar.google.com/ in your browser.

Google Scholar lets you search through a wide variety of scholarly literature, including peer-reviewed papers, theses, books, preprints, abstracts, and technical reports from all broad areas of research. This application returns citations (even if the original being cited is not available on the Web), and uses scholarly citations to help determine relevancy and ranking of its results.

- ✔ **Factiva:** www.factiva.com, an extensive research database with a focus on business, finance, and current events

- ✔ **LexisNexis:** www.lexisnexis.com, perhaps the best known research service, featuring a wide variety of databases covering business, news, and legal affairs

- ✔ **Questia:** www.questia.com, an extensive library of books and periodicals, primarily in the social sciences

- ✔ **Westlaw:** www.westlaw.com, an online legal research service that provides access to statutes, case law, public records, and other legal content

Libraries

Libraries may seem quaint today, particularly when referred to in a book that focuses primarily on using the latest technology from Google to conduct research; but the fact of the matter is that sometimes nothing can beat a good library.

For starters, you'll find archived material you can't find elsewhere, such as old books and periodicals. For example, the research library at the offices of the California Society of Pioneers in San Francisco archives handwritten memoirs of participants in the 1848 gold rush. The only way you can study this material is by physically going to this library.

Often, using the microfilmed copies of major newspapers is the easiest way to learn about something that happened in the past (you won't find much in the way of historical newspapers on the Web).

If you can get access to a good library with open stacks (such as a university library), sometimes browsing in the general area you're interested in leads to more productive results than you can get any other way.

Librarians can be the quintessential professional researchers, and part of their job is to help you. So by all means, if you're serious about research, become friendly with your local librarians. A good librarian is a wonderful resource. Most librarians know a great deal about research sources and truly love research, and love to help people solve tough research questions.

While public libraries where you live may have excellent resources, particularly if you live in a metropolis with fabled libraries, like those in New York City, it is often the case that research universities have the best libraries. Often, university libraries can be used by people living in their community. So if you happen to be based near a major university — or are a student or faculty member at one — consider yourself lucky, and take advantage of the resources the facility offers.

Public records research

Public records include thousands of different repositories of documents that provide information about many subjects, including

- ✔ Lawsuits and legal matters
- ✔ Business information and filings
- ✔ Births and deaths
- ✔ Taxation
- ✔ Property ownership and transfers

Public records research is a specialty unto itself. For starters, while some public record information is available online, much is not. In other words, you may have to physically go to the moldy basement of that imposing old courthouse downtown to find what you need.

Public records research often involves traveling to the locations where the records are kept (this is particularly a problem if the repository is in some other part of the world), and dealing effectively with the record keepers (taking them to lunch may be involved).

In addition, there are no aggregated single sources to tell you where to go to find specific public records information (or where to take the record keepers to lunch!). The online public records that are available are neither comprehensive nor complete.

Public records information is full of errors, and misspellings (meaning that you have to look for alternate spellings of proper nouns such as personal and corporate names when you do your research).

Effective public records researchers are very detail-oriented and will try several approaches to a research challenge if their first tactic doesn't work.

Public records research is subject to legal restrictions, and there are also legal restrictions regarding the use that can be made of the research. So you must make sure that you're familiar with the laws regarding public records research in your jurisdiction before you start a research project that involves public records.

Some of the better online public records research sites include

- ✔ **Choicepoint:** `www.choicepoint.com` (fee-based)
- ✔ **CourtLink:** `www.courtlink.com` (fee-based, provided by LexisNexis)
- ✔ **KnowX:** `www.knowx.com` (fee-based)
- ✔ **Search Systems:** `www.searchsystems.net`, provides free access to over 23,000 public records databases maintained by local U.S. jurisdictions

From Novice to Professional Researcher

If you want to become a professional researcher, you should realize that this is an occupation and a vocation that requires some special personality traits. If you're a researcher by necessity (and not choice), you should read this information. It may save your sanity. The first, most important rule to conducting research without going crazy is to think of the research process as exactly that — a process. If you like to learn (and who doesn't?), you can make it through. If you possess the following personality traits (and who doesn't?), you also have the capacity to complete your project with great acumen.

Want to be a professional? Here is what you need:

- ✔ An insatiable curiosity about everything
- ✔ An eye for patterns in information
- ✔ The willingness to be very detail oriented
- ✔ The ability to use the technology available to researchers, as I explain in this book
- ✔ An ability to work well with people
- ✔ An inclination to cut through the superficial aspect of information and find hidden subtexts

TIP

Towards becoming a professional researcher

Like becoming a professional in any complex field, it would take a book just on the topic to explain everything involved in becoming a professional researcher. As it happens, there is already a good one available: Mary Ellen Bates's *Building and Running a Successful Research Business* (Information Today, Inc.).

You can also find a great deal of good information about becoming a professional researcher by joining the relevant professional societies. In addition to the AIIP, which I mention in "Conducting reference interviews," you should investigate the

Society of Competitive Intelligence Professionals (SCIP), www.scip.org.

If you're interested in becoming a research professional, you should make an effort to understand the different kinds of research assignments that can come up (this book will help!).

See Chapter 3 for information about some kinds of research clients. Do you have the motivation, the curiosity, and an uncanny ability to find information? Then professional research may be for you.

✔ The ability to ask the right questions

✔ The ability to analyze and summarize mountains of information so that it can be presented in palatable forms (See Chapter 12 for more information about delivering research results.)

Ethics and Research

Many ethical issues come up in the course of conducting a serious research project. If you're intending to become a professional researcher, roughly following the guidelines of the AIIP, you should plan to conduct your research in an honest, competent, and confidential fashion. Specifically, you're obliged to

✔ Give clients accurate information on time and within budget

✔ Help clients understand the context in which this information is being presented

✔ Accurately cite research information

✔ Not accept illegal assignments (and educate yourself about the relevant laws)

✔ Respect client confidentiality, as agreed upon with the client

✔ Respect and recognize intellectual property rights

✔ Educate clients about intellectual property rights

✔ Comply with libraries' and online services' rules of access

Chapter 11

Using Google's Comparative Methodology to Your Advantage

In This Chapter

▶ The scope of the information available on the Web

▶ Evaluating information obtained on the Web

▶ The implications of the PageRank algorithm

*T*hink about the way you conducted research 15 years ago and you will have no question that the World Wide Web has changed the way people get their information — probably more than any single innovation in the past. It has also created, for the first time ever, a global repository of information that is accessible to everyone with a computer and an Internet connection.

These changes have hit the field of information research with the force of a cataclysmic tidal wave. Researchers now need to understand how to maximize their knowledge of the Web so that they can use it for research. Evaluating the credibility of information obtained on the Web is another important consideration; you simply can't function as an online researcher without being able to filter out the junk.

If you're interested in automating research, you need to get under the hood — really see how Google works. This chapter explains how to evaluate the credibility of information you find searching the Web with Google. I explain the importance of taxonomies and hierarchical structures of information, and how you can exploit taxonomies when you create automated research tools.

Armed with knowledge about how Google integrates with the Web — particularly with its unique PageRank algorithm — you can speed up your research and ensure accuracy, all while playing to Google's strengths and avoiding its weaknesses.

The Changing World of Research

When an aristocratic Rhinelander named Johan Gutenberg invented the printing press and published the Bible around the year 1450, he changed the worlds of knowledge, books, and research forever. No longer was book ownership (and literacy) restricted to the rich. Books could be produced in identical multiple copies, so that every library individual could own all important works.

More than 500 years after Gutenberg, changing technology has again revolutionized research. The World Wide Web has taken storing and retrieving information into a whole new direction. You don't even have to go to a library to find out what you need to know — all you need is a computer and an Internet connection. The aggregated content available on the Web is far larger than any other body of information.

The great library of Alexandria

The great Library of Alexandria was the largest library of the ancient world. Organized by Demetrius Phalereus, a student of Aristotle, in around 300 B.C.E., the core of the library consisted of Aristotle's collection. The library grew quickly because the Pharaoh of Egypt confiscated and copied all the books and scrolls in the possession of travelers to the new city of Alexandria. By the time of its destruction (according to the historian Plutarch, by fire at the hands of Julius Caesar when he invaded Egypt around 47 B.C.E.), the great library is thought to have held as many as 700,000 scrolls organized following Aristotle's basic divisions of knowledge. The fame of the Great Library of Alexandria has come down through the ages as a shorthand way to reference the biggest of big repositories of information.

At the time of this writing, Google claims to have indexed (and made available) more than 8 billion Web pages. Undoubtedly, the number will be higher by the time you read this.

For several reasons, the number of pages in Google's index can only be a fraction of the information available on the Web at any given time. So presumably the indexable Web is a great deal larger than Google's 8 billion pages.

Many pages can be accessed with multiple URLs. For example, www.barticle.com, www.braintique.com, and www.braintique.com/index.shtml all reference the same Web page. Is it counted once, twice, or three times? Depends. It *should* be indexed once, but sometimes pages like this are indexed multiple times because of the way the links are written. Other times the index isn't sophisticated enough to notice that the links all point to the same site.

Advances in storage technology, effective Web crawling, indexing, and the Google page ranking algorithm have helped tame the sheer size of the Web's information repository — but another problem remains: the quality of the information returned by Google. See "Evaluating the Credibility of Information," later in this chapter.

Aggregated content is a collection of information that hasn't been packaged, organized, and smoothed out. In the era of Gutenberg, however, almost all information was collected, interpreted, cleaned up, and bound together in a nice package — a published book. Categorizing aggregated information using automated software is one of the primary reasons to build research tools (see "Utilizing Automated Research Tools").

Evaluating the Credibility of Information

Unfortunately, I don't know of any magic bullets for evaluating the credibility of information that comes from a Google search. Each page needs to be inspected on its own for credibility. In the old days — before the Internet was everywhere — the bane of a researcher's existence was finding information. Nowadays, you need the hard-boiled skepticism of a Sam Spade to sift through the information so readily available at your fingertips.

Keeping some basics in mind

Here are some factors you face as you conduct research with Google:

- ✔ Anyone can publish Web pages (without a peer or editorial review).

- ✔ The Web doesn't require anyone to follow a standard form for presenting information or for citing sources.

- ✔ Many Web pages are published by those with an agenda; the fact that info is not objectively conveyed may not be immediately obvious.

- ✔ Web sites with questionable information aren't posted merely by crackpots; some sites are committing fraud (financial fraud sites run so-called *phishing* scams). Webmasters of such sites manipulate *meta tags,* the HTML equivalent of index terms, to misrepresent the content of Web pages to Google's spider, and they also include irrelevant words that are not visible to the human eye (but are intended to catch the attention of the search "bots" like the Google spider). Google does a reasonable good job of checking for manipulated meta tags that don't match the contents of a page and also for unrelated text insertions — but of course it doesn't catch all problematic pages.

Proactively assessing Web sources

The following factors are often used by serious researchers to evaluate the credibility of the pages returned from the Web by a Google search. In all cases, the most important thing you can do is verify what you find before you accept it as fact. Start by asking these questions:

✔ **Was the page published by a reputable source?** For example, if the Web source is the March of Dimes or the National Institute of Health, you are probably safe to accept the information.

If the site isn't put out by a well-known source, don't necessarily dump it; the gripes of a disgruntled ex-employee may turn out to be true — just treat them with initial skepticism.

You may even need to pick up the telephone to verify the identity of a Web resource.

✔ **Is the page internally consistent?** Look for obvious errors; do the math if statistics are offered. Obvious errors in grammar, spelling, and punctuation indicate that a page has been thrown together in a hurry. That fact should leave you suspicious about whether the facts were thrown together in an equally sporadic and careless fashion.

✔ **Does the page show an obvious ax to grind?** A page may be created by a reputable source, but that doesn't mean that you can trust the source. Everyone's got opinions, and some opinions always find their way into printed information. Figure out how slanted the information is before you trust it.

✔ **Are "facts" on the page given attribution, either via a hyperlink or in some other fashion (for example, a reference to a book)?** Source citations don't just help you determine reliability; let's face it — they may save you time down the road if you need more material.

✔ **Does the page contain strident ads or X-rated material?** These indicate the site may not be worth your while.

Anyone can find support using Web searches for almost any proposition — remember, Google has indexed upwards of 8 billion pages. There's something for almost every viewpoint within this vast repository. But over time you will develop your own system to weed out unreliable sources and avoid Web sources that don't prove to be credible.

Learning How Google Works

How does Google navigate the vast ocean of information in the World Wide Web and produce useful answers?

The *really* brief answer? They have the world's best computers and tools.

The condensed answer is that Google's superprogram crawls the Web, and on its computers it stores a cache of the pages it finds, all the while building an *indexed lexicon* (or dictionary) of common words. For each word, another

Google supertool creates a list of pages that contain that word. A search for a particular word uses the index to return the list of pages, sorted by PageRank (for an explanation of this proprietary concept, see the section, "The PageRank Algorithm").

The details of how Google works are, of course, proprietary. However, all search engines have major elements in common, and playing around with Google gives some clues about how it works. Also, Google itself has published some information about how it works.

Essentially, Google requires the following in order to be a success:

- ✔ **Speed:** Without fast crawling technology, it's impossible to imagine being able to gather Web documents and keep them up to date.
- ✔ **Accuracy:** A fast research service is all well and good, but without accuracy, what's the point?
- ✔ **Space:** Without efficient storage capabilities that can handle the indexes and underlying documents, queries won't be answered quickly. I'm talking about hundreds (thousands?) of gigabytes of data storage space here. And not just that, efficient, speedy organization and utilization of that space.

The following sections discuss how the various parts of the Google system contribute to making Google the fastest, most accurate Web search system available, with a storehouse of information that simply begs to be trawled by your homemade automated research tools.

Crawling the Web

An autonomous piece of software, of the kind generally known as a *bot* (short for "robot") or *WebBot,* and specifically called the Google Web *crawler* (or *spider*), searches the Web and retrieves Web pages. Google's Web crawler operates continuously to keep its index up to date.

Pulling out the keywords

Meanwhile, the Google indexing software rips through the page and pulls keywords out of it. While the most important function of this software is to throw away words that shouldn't be indexed, such as articles and prepositions (*a, the, for,* and so on), it also performs other functions.

Seeing through hype

As I explain in "Evaluating the Credibility of Information," knowing whether a Web page is on the up-and-up isn't always a simple task. Google does its part in helping you with this evaluation by running pages through content analysis software before you ever see the page to help determine what a page is really about.

Google's fairly intelligent software tries to make sure that Google's indexing analysis is not skewed by measures such as the use of phony meta tags. This hypertext-matching analysis looks at the full content of a page. It looks at formatting, locations of words, fonts, and the subdivisions on each page to figure out the location of each word. Google even looks at the material of related Web pages to make sure that results are relevant. The engine is smart enough to know that words in larger bold fonts (such as headlines) tend to be more important in determining the content of a document, so these words are given more weight than the fine print.

Searching the doc and index servers

A retrieved page is itself cached, or stored, in the Google document servers (called in Googlese the *doc* servers, or doc server farm), along with a PageRank. (The PageRank is used as a measurement to sort documents by importance.) With the text of a document stored in the doc servers, the post-analysis keyword content of a Web page is used to populate the Google index servers. Keywords stored in the index servers point to each document that contains the term in the doc server farm.

When a user makes a search request, the Google Web server sends it on to software that analyzes the request to strip out words that are not indexed (mostly stripping articles and prepositions). It then sends the keywords in the request, with a proximity rating, on to the index server farm. The index servers, along with the doc servers

✔ Determine the documents pointed to by the keywords.

✔ Sort these documents using each one's PageRank.

✔ Provide links to these documents on the Web.

✔ Provide a link to view the cached version of the document in the doc server farm.

✔ Pull an excerpt from the page, using the cached version of the page, to give a quick idea of what it is about.

✔ Return an initial results set of document excerpts and links, with links to retrieve further results sets of matches, rendered as HTML.

By default, Google returns results in sets of ten matches (as an HTML page). You can change the number of results you want to see on the Google Preferences page.

Google prides itself on the fact that most queries are answered in less than half a second. Considering the number of steps involved in answering a query, you can see that this is quite a technological feat. It's no wonder that Google has been said to have more effective computer "fire power" than any other company today.

Figure 11-1 shows how Google works from a broad outline perspective.

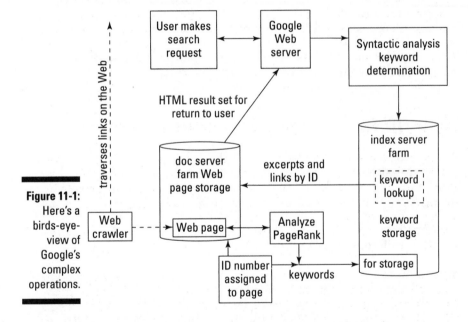

Figure 11-1: Here's a birds-eye-view of Google's complex operations.

The PageRank Algorithm

The *PageRank* algorithm, used to sort pages returned by a request, puts Google's search engine above its competition.

Depending on who you ask, PageRank is either named after its inventor, Lawrence Page, Google's cofounder, or because it is a mechanism for ranking pages.

The underlying idea behind PageRank is an old one that has been used by librarians in the pre-Web past to provide an objective method of scoring the relative importance of scholarly documents. The more citations *other* documents make to a particular document, the more "important" the document is, the higher its rank in the system, and the more likely it is to be retrieved first.

Let me break it down for you:

Each Web page is assigned a number depending upon the number of other pages that link to the page.

The crucial element that makes PageRank work is the nature of the Web itself, which depends almost solely on the use of hyperlinking between pages and sites. In the system that makes Google's PageRank algorithm work, links are a Web popularity contest: Webmaster A thinks Webmaster B's site has good information (or is cool, or looks good, or is funny); Webmaster A may decide to add a link to Webmaster B's site; in turn, Webmaster B might return the favor.

Links from Web site A to Web site B are referred to as *outbound* (from A) and *inbound* (to B). Figure 11-2 gives you a visual representation of outbound and inbound links.

Figure 11-2:
Outbound
and inbound
links.

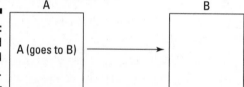

From Web page A's viewpoint, link is outbound.
From Web page B's viewpoint, link is inbound.

The more inbound links a page has (references from other sites), the more likely it is to have a higher PageRank. However, not all inbound links are of equal weight when it comes to how they contribute to PageRank — nor should they be. A Web page gets a higher PageRank if another significant source (by significant source I mean a source that also receives a lot of inbound links, and thus has a higher PageRank) links to it than if a trivial site without traffic provides the inbound link.

A link from a high PageRank page counts for more than a link from a low-ranking page.

The actual PageRank algorithm involves more than simply crunching the number of inbound links to a page, along with the PageRank of each page that provides an inbound link. Although Google's exact method of calculating PageRank is shrouded in proprietary mystery, PageRank does try to exclude links from so-called *link farms,* pages that contain only links, and mutual links (which are individual two-way links put up for the sole purpose of boosting PageRanks).

Getting inside the heads of random surfers

The PageRank formula can be thought of as a model of user behavior of "random surfers." Such a random surfer visits a random Web page, keeps clicking links randomly, never clicking the back button, and eventually gets bored enough to visit a new random page by typing in the Web address into the browser. The probability that the random surfer visits a particular page is its PageRank. The probability at each page that the random surfer will get bored and request a new random page is called the *damping factor*, represented by *d* in the formula.

Put this way, the PageRank for a specific Web page can be calculated by going through all the inbound links to a page, calculating the PageRanks of all these pages, backing up to calculate the inbound links in turn to the new set of pages, and so on, all the way back until there are no more inbound links. A little more technically, a Web page's PageRank can be calculated by iterating recursively through all of its inbound linked pages. This is the fundamental method behind

Google's search engine, although in the real world (as you likely know if you've read this far in this sidebar) there are usually nonrecursive techniques that calculate results more quickly than the corresponding recursive algorithm.

The original formula for PageRank with further explanation is contained in the Brin and Page page (www-db.stanford.edu/~backrub/google.html). Here it is (PR stands for PageRank; A stands for a random page, identified as Page A; T1 ... Tn signifies all the pages that link to Page A; C(A) represents the number of Page A's outbound links):

$$PR(A) = (1-d) + d(PR(T1)/C(T1) \\ + \ldots + d(PR(Tn)/C(Tn)$$

PageRanks form a probability distribution over Web pages, so the sum of all Web pages' PageRanks is 1. The formula for PageRank has, of course, evolved since this formulation, and its exact nature is part of Google's proprietary technology.

You can easily see the comparative PageRank for any Web page if you install the Google Toolbar (see Chapter 1 for more information about the Google Toolbar). With a Web page open, the PageRank is shown in the Toolbar on a scale of 0 to 10. Note that PageRanks are really between 0 and 1, so although the 0 to 10 scale is useful for comparison purposes, it does not represent an actual PageRank number.

Understanding the Implications of PageRank

From a Webmaster's viewpoint, it's easy to understand some of the implications of PageRank. If you want your site to have a high PageRank, then you need to get as many high-ranked sites as possible to link to you. Paradoxically, outbound links reduce the PageRank of the linking site because they reduce overall traffic on the linking site (users are more likely to leave the original site if they have several links they can click).

However, useful outbound links draw traffic to the linking site and encourage other sites to return the favor because they respect the quality of the links the original site provides. Obviously, a whole book could be written about the interesting trade-offs for Webmasters when it comes to providing outbound links.

But you're probably most interested in knowing about the PageRank system from a researcher's viewpoint. Well, there are some interesting implications to the PageRank system for you, too.

Here are some of the benefits of the system:

- ✔ **"Trustworthy" results:** It's virtually impossible for commercial interests to manipulate PageRank. For a page to get a high PageRank, it must convince an important page, or a great many unimportant pages, to link to it. With some limitations, this means that research results returned from Google are more trustworthy — at least in the sense that they have not been explicitly bought and paid for — than results from a search engine that doesn't use PageRank.

- ✔ **Unspecific searches still yield accurate results:** Researchers benefit most when the search is imprecise or underspecified. If you search for *Stanford University,* the search returns numerous results, including publication lists and things (and people) named *Stanford.* However, the PageRank algorithm ensures that the Stanford University home page is listed first in the results set.

Here are some of the system's drawbacks:

- ✔ **The rich get richer:** The most notorious effect of the PageRank algorithm is that popular sites inevitably become more popular. Popular Web sites obtain higher ranks, causing them to get even more popular when researchers visit them. The more popular the site gets, the more people will notice it and decide to add links to it, and the higher its PageRank will go.

  This may in the long run prove to be problematic because the popularity cycle is a hard one to break — and to break into. For now, it's still possible to put up a Web site that draws traffic because of unique and/or quality content. Over time, this kind of site will draw a decent PageRank. However, research is not a popularity poll (as the PageRank algorithm to some extent is). An idea can be popular but false, just as unpopular ideas can be true. (If they'd had PageRank back in the 1400s, the Web site TheEarthIs Flat.com might have had a PageRank of 10 and the Round World.com site a PageRank of 0!)

Although the PageRank algorithm screens out the most blatant financial motivations, it doesn't validate sources, content, or ideas in any meaningful sense. (That's your job.) You need to take the order of document return — which is the work product of the PageRank algorithm — as evidence of Web popularity, but not the underlying soundness of the content of the pages returned (see "Evaluating the credibility of information" for help with this problem).

✔ **PageRank works the same way high-school kids choose a homecoming queen:** Like a high-school popularity contest, PageRank is likely to favor superficial winners. This means that PageRank makes answering superficial ad-hoc queries using Google a snap, but sites with deep but narrow content on the topic may be buried in the results set.

Sites that provide specific content of interest to a relatively small number of people may not be included in important directories, like the Open Directory Project (www.dmoz.org) and Yahoo!, and may not have inbound links from myriad lower PageRank sites. (In other words, small sites with a ton of inbound links are a result of ambitious and enterprising Webmasters; specialized sites are often so busy collecting data that they're not out and about trying to get other pages to link to them.)

When looking for breadth of information, dig deeply into lower-order return results sets. You can also use automated research tools to consider the inherent biases built into PageRank — along with the obvious strength of the methodology (see "Utilizing Automated Research Tools").

Utilizing Automated Research Tools

Human beings, particularly human beings who are good at research, can glance at a document (such as a Web page) and see whether it contains any information that is relevant to the subject of a query. However, this is a surprisingly difficult job for a computer, which has no way to know which subjects are related to other subjects (and which are not).

Comparison mechanisms check to see whether keywords in a document are similar or the same. These mechanisms can sometimes produce good results, but can also be fooled by word similarities and unintentional puns. Even searches on the Web for a simple pair of keywords like *roll over* can bring a huge diversity of return results, ranging from discussions of pets, car crashes, and retirement investing to the creation of graphics for the Web.

To some degree, software can use taxonomies to help sort documents by category (which is why I explain how taxonomies work in this chapter).

Automated research involves creating research tools that sift through voluminous information repositories, returning results without human intervention. Much of the time, for these tools to benefit you, they need to be custom created for you. Depending on what the tool does, you need to know how Google works, understand the tools it makes available, have at least a basic understanding of PageRank, and understand the difference between finding something in a hierarchy as opposed to finding it by conducting a Google search. (Of course, you also need to know how to program.)

✔ Automatically determine whether results returned are relevant to a particular search and a particular subject. This is useful if you are attempting to automate analysis of a large quantity of documents.

✔ Monitor the Web for new information about a specific topic.

✔ Perform market and trend analysis.

✔ Track the popularity of keywords.

Chapter 12

Packaging and Delivering Research

*I*f a tree falls in a forest and there is no one to see it fall, has it really fallen? I guess the answer to this Zen conundrum is probably that the tree really has fallen, but maybe no one will ever know about it.

To the researcher, the analogy is doing effective research and then failing to communicate your findings to your client. You've used your intelligence, curiosity, and research skills; you've worked very hard. What's the point of all this effort if you cannot present your findings in a way that your client can use them?

This chapter explains how to determine the needs of a research client when it comes to the format of the presentation of research results. Interestingly, research clients often don't know their own minds — they don't openly express their requirements because they're simply not sure themselves.

Statistical information presents a particular set of problems when you're delivering it as all or part of your research work product — particularly if your client is not particularly aware of methodological issues involved with statistics. In this chapter, I also show you how to avoid common pitfalls when presenting statistical research results, and how to effectively communicate the gist of statistical issues, which may require the use of software.

Meeting the Needs of Your Client

In Chapter 10, I explain a number of formats that are used to present research results. These ways of "packaging" research results include

- ✔ Orally, in a face-to-face, one-on-one meeting

- ✔ With a presentation to an audience

- ✔ By creating a written report with an executive summary

- ✔ Less formally, via e-mail

- ✔ Using software, a Web site, or a custom Web application to deliver your results

You can't know which kind of packaging to use until you understand who the client is, and what his or her needs and priorities are. In Chapter 3, I list some of the more likely kinds of clients. I explain in Chapter 10 how to conduct a reference interview. This interview is the best time to find out your research client's expectations about how your results will be delivered.

Sometimes, the way you should deliver research results is obvious. For example, if you're in a class and the teacher assigns a research paper, then of course you need to prepare a research paper for delivery. But you can deliver more effective results even in this case if you're clear about the details, for example:

- ✔ What is the research paper about, and what kinds of information should be included?

- ✔ Should there be a bibliography, should it be annotated, and is there a requirement for a specific number of sources?

- ✔ How long should it be?

- ✔ Should it be delivered as hardcopy, on disk, or both?

In general, as the proverb goes, "The devil is in the details." For starters, if you present written material, it should be well-written. Grammatical mistakes and misspellings are not acceptable. If your talents run more in the direction of researching than writing, you may need to get help with editing (or even writing) your research presentations. (However, if you're writing a research paper for school, you certainly can't have somebody else do the writing for you; you'll want to enlist the help of a friend with good editing skills.)

Professional researchers know that real-life situations are often not as fully spelled out as they are in academia. You must understand general expectations and also clarify whether the client has unrevealed expectations or needs. You must rely on your experience, intuition, and communication skills to fully understand what you will be expected to deliver even before you start work on the research.

Most research delivery scenarios involve trade-offs. The most common trade-off is speed of delivery versus depth of information (and longer preparation time). For example, you can quickly deliver a concise, one-sentence summary of research results. But a complete report, full of all the subtleties and nuances you desire, may be very time consuming to prepare. Which one you should deliver depends upon the research client — and the situation. In some cases, you'll need to provide both a summary and a detailed report. The detective who says simply, "I know who did it," without backup has not delivered the level of specificity or proof necessary to convict at a trial or even get an indictment. But in the real world you may have to start at the level of "knowing who did it" — and then be prepared to back up your hunch.

Of course, jumping to a snap conclusion before you do your research can lead to erroneous conclusions. Quite apart from formal issues of *how* research results are presented (the subject of this chapter), you need to understand *what* research question, or questions, are being asked. A good way to make sure that you do is to construct a short version of what you think the research assignment is, and run it by the client to verify that you got it right.

For example, you might ask a research client a question like this: "The assignment is to assess how preservation methods have affected the endangered sea turtle population, right?"

You can learn more about reducing information to the bare essentials in "Getting your elevator pitch down pat." Also, in Chapter 10, I explain how to use reference interviews to become clear about the gist of research assignments.

Google Answers, explained in Chapter 6, provides a nifty way to learn more about refining questions. Browse Google Answers and you can see that the professional researchers who answer the questions posed have clarified any questions that seem unclear to them (and often have restated the question in their own succinct words before attempting to answer it). By reading the requests for clarifications, the clarifications themselves, and the research results in Google Answers, you can learn a lot about how to get to the gist of a research assignment.

Delivering Research Results

How you deliver results depends upon many factors, including the circumstances of the research assignment and what the client has requested (and what you are being paid to do).

Some of the possibilities are to personally present information, write up a paper, provide a PowerPoint presentation, or use Internet output (such as e-mail, the Web, or another Web-based application). You may also want, need, or be required to combine these research delivery mechanisms.

In some cases, the format of research assignments may be determined by your client, depending on the industry the client is in, or presentation formats that are specific to the industry of your client. For example, if your client is a business that does biomedical research and it wants you to research the effects of Prozac on teenagers, you may need to follow APA (American Psychological Association) style, with an abstract and citations accordingly. Or, if you're doing research for an academic publisher, you may have to use MLA (Modern Language Association) style.

For example, I recently completed an assignment for an important technology company in which the goal was to assess that company's competitive strength in a particular field, evaluate competitors and allies, and suggest positioning strategies. Here's what I went through when I presented my results:

1. After my initial conversations with the client, I spent about two weeks conducting research and writing up my results.

2. I delivered my research results by writing a white paper with an executive summary.

3. After submitting the written paper, I had a series of phone conversations with company executives so that I could clarify points and answer questions.

4. As a result of these conversations, I focused on my visual presentation (with an accompanying PowerPoint slideshow, of course) so that it would appeal to a fairly large group of managers and other decision makers.

5. The presentation was followed by an extensive question and answer session.

Presenting research information intelligibly is much more difficult than it sounds, whether you are delivering it orally or in written form. For one thing, the results of your research are likely to be fairly complex and full of nuance. You have to be decisive enough to reach a pithy conclusion, if that is what your research client needs. At the same time, in other circumstances, you'll need to convey, in clear language, objectively researched results that point in several directions, without bias.

Getting your elevator pitch down pat

The idea behind the so-called *elevator pitch* is that any idea worth expressing can be reduced to a sentence or two — the time an elevator takes to get from one floor to another.

Elevator pitches are most commonly associated with sales. You can imagine a professionally attired, articulate salesperson giving his big client a pitch as they travel from the lobby to the second-floor conference room, can't you? Honing your elevator pitch is essential if your client expects a short, verbal answer to the research project.

Even if your client doesn't expect an elevator pitch, you should prepare one to help yourself structure your full research report. In other words, creating an elevator pitch is often more for the benefit of the research than the client.

If you can't craft the equivalent of an elevator pitch (even if your client doesn't expect it), you probably don't understand the subject matter well enough. View your ability to come up with an elevator pitch as a measure of your mastery of the research material.

The elevator pitch should take you less than a minute to spit out. If it's more than three sentences long, you're talking too much; the idea is to cut to the chase, not to explain all the details.

Here's an example of an elevator pitch version of research results about the measures taken to protect a particular species of endangered turtle:

> *After population levels in 2000 had dropped so low that long-term survival was in question, strict enforcement of beach nesting protection has engineered a surprising comeback for this endangered species.*

Note that this elevator pitch — like single-sentence summaries in general — omits many specific details (which turtles? what beach? how far have they come back?). The point here is to be remain as general as possible and still get to the heart of the matter. You can always drill down later to clarify details. Rather than focusing on details, this elevator pitch helps to make sure that you and the research client are on the same page about the general kind of information that is needed.

Here are some helpful tips for preparing elevator pitches:

- Don't start to prepare an elevator pitch until you feel really comfortable with the subject matter of the research and with the research results.

- Aim for an elevator pitch that is one or two or (at most) three sentences long. It may be difficult to do this when the subject matter is complicated, but even the attempt should help you clarify your thoughts. (When you're good at elevator pitches, you can even make them a single sentence long, as in my example earlier in this section.)

- Your elevator pitch doesn't have to provide definitive answers, but it does need to be clear in pointing out avenues of further research and/or a best guess as to what the answer (upon further research) will be.

> ✔ If you get stuck or don't know where to begin, review your notes from the reference interview (see Chapter 10 for more about conducting reference interviews), and ask yourself, "What am I really trying to say?"
>
> ✔ Test your pitch on a trusted friend or colleague. A reaction such as, "Aha! I get it," means your pitch is ready to go. A head-scratching, "Huh?" should send you back to the drawing board.

The acronym KISS — short for Keep It Simple, Stupid — may be mean-spirited on the surface, but it provides the best guideline for an elevator pitch. Just keep things as simple as possible.

Preparing an executive summary

An *executive summary,* sometimes also called an *abstract,* or simply a summary, is a concise statement of your research findings. When it comes to executive summaries, shorter is better. If you can keep it to less than a single page, that's great. In any event, an executive summary should not be long-winded.

Writing well is an art that many people take years (if not their entire lives) mastering. Writing a good executive summary, or, for that matter, any report, correspondence, article, or essay, requires a strong command of the language, a personal style, and precision. If writing doesn't come naturally to you — and even if it does — I suggest picking up a copy of *The Elements of Style,* by William Strunk, Jr. and E.B. White. First published in 1918, this classic is now in its 4th edition; it's a bible for most good writers and a staple used by every English teacher in America.

Expert advice about executive summaries

Writing an executive summary is easiest when you've already written a research report. You can scan the report to understand its structure and content. Try to become clear about the main facets of the research results and prepare an outline that includes key information and concepts grouped in a logical progression. From there, you can build an outline.

With the outline in mind, consider which headings or subheadings you should use to make the organization of the executive summary clear at a casual glance. Try to keep these headings sparse and simple.

Using your outline of key information and concepts, and with the heading and subheading structures in place, fill in the details using a professional style.

Don't forget to read your executive summary aloud to make sure that it makes sense and is consistent. You can hear so many more mistakes when you read things aloud.

Usually, an executive summary accompanies a long research project or *white paper*. (A white paper is a report or briefing, often containing dense supporting information, usually focused on a technology or marketing issue.) Sometimes, there is no paper but only an executive summary accompanied by other supporting material.

You'll find that the best way to prepare an executive summary is to write the full paper first, or at least prepare and organize your research materials. An executive summary needs to be concise partially because it may be the only thing that your research client reads. This is never truer than if your client is a major company and an executive is reviewing your research. That's where the name executive summary comes from — often the busy executive doesn't have time to look at all the details.

Your summary needs to be thorough as well as concise, providing as much detail as you can in a short space. It should:

✔ Include the essential points of your research results.

✔ Follow the framework for your more detailed report, so that readers have a conceptual framework for evaluating research results.

Organizationally speaking, you can divide your full-length research report into sections with headings. These headings can then be used as the basis for the points in your executive summary.

✔ Highlight any recommendations (for further research, or for action) if applicable.

As you write your executive summary, you should remind yourself:

✔ What is the research about?

✔ Why is the research, and the results, important?

✔ What do the research results include?

What you should include in an executive summary depends upon the situation. Obviously, space is limited, and you must decide what is most important to include.

The following are elements often included in an executive summary of research results:

✔ The purpose and scope of research (and research paper if applicable)

✔ Research methodology and any important methodological issues

✔ The results of the research

✔ Recommendations for further research or other actions

✔ Highlighted information about sources

Personally Presenting Results

Personally presenting research results orally with a visual element has the great benefit that you will get an immediate sense of the reaction.

To a great extent, the choice of whether or not there should be an in-person presentation is up to the research client. If you're considering whether to recommend one, you should evaluate whether a presentation can add to the effectiveness of your written research results.

 If you're good with people and you have an opportunity to recommend a presentation, you can use the face-to-face presentation as an opportunity to make contacts. If people remember your face, they're more likely to remember your name, which means that they will think of you if and when they have additional research projects. Of course, a presentation also gives you the chance to do the following:

✔ Answer ad-hoc questions that you didn't already answer

✔ Command the attention of your audience

✔ Correct misimpressions

✔ Suggest areas for further work

The downsides to personal presentation of results are that:

✔ The quality of the information you're delivering can get lost because of presentation issues (for example, you mumble or ramble so that the audience cannot understand what you are saying, you present unprofessional graphics, or you show a "gadgety" slideshow with tons of fades and dissolves).

✔ If you're shy or have a fear of public speaking, you may feel as though you are on the spot.

✔ You can't always provide the depth and detail that are available in a written report.

✔ You can't always accurately provide the sources for your information in sufficient detail so that they can independently be verified.

You can minimize the downsides to personally presenting results if you have also prepared a written report, and refer to it during your in-person presentation. However, you should only rely on this trick if the research client commissioned both a report and the presentation. Don't do more work than you're hired to do.

Unless you are absolutely sure it is appropriate, avoid a one-line, in-person summary presentation of research results. Just because you *can* do an elevator pitch (see "Getting your elevator pitch down pat") doesn't mean that you *should* make it your preferred form of presenting research results. These pitches may be appropriate for the detective in the whodunit, and they are spectacular for helping you focus when you sit down to write out your results, but they don't take you very far in the real world, and they don't demonstrate the hard work you've done.

Effectively using visual information

Visual aids are essential to presenting certain kinds of information, particularly comparative quantitative data. When information is presented visually, it is easier to keep your audience's attention, and studies show that most people retain information much longer when it is presented both visually and orally. Your research clients are likely to be willing to sit through (and respond well to) a presentation that uses snappy graphics; in fact, in the world of PowerPoint presentations, they probably expect graphics and visual aids. Although I assume that you're using PowerPoint to make your presentation, the following sections give common-sense advice that you can also apply to other visual means you might use to display results.

People tend to take things — especially statistical things — at face value. Manipulating apparent research results with pictures and graphics is far easier than in other formats because people are used to believing that anything projected in the wall as a picture is real. However, digital photos can easily be faked. Graphs and charts can be used in a misleading fashion. The moral is to be very careful about the digital imagery you use in presentations, and vet your visual presentation of quantitative data for ways it can be misleading.

Prepare a presentation that includes talking points and visual aids. The easiest way to do this is to create a slideshow in PowerPoint and present it using a laptop computer.

The Slide Notes feature in PowerPoint provides a great way to prepare the talking points for your presentation.

The mechanics of projection preparation

This book can't do justice to all the ins and outs of using PowerPoint or other projection and presentation programs. However, I can give you some basic tips to keep in mind as you save the presentation and prepare to give it. Following these guidelines may help minimize the chances of getting caught in a show stopper:

✔ **Make sure the equipment you need is available:** Check in advance to make sure the client has a projector on-site, set up, and ready to go. You need to know enough about your computer to know whether you can attach your computer to it. If not, you will have to bring your own projector (or beg, borrow, rent, or steal one if you don't own one).

✔ **Get there early and do a dry run:** If you get the chance, test drive your slideshow with the projector you will be using, in the location for the presentation. It's generally a good idea to get to the meeting early, anyway, even if someone else is setting up the equipment. When you make sure everything is set up just right, quickly run through the show.

✔ **Know your connectivity issues:** Check in advance to see if you will have connectivity to the Internet during the presentation. If you do, you'll be able to show some of the basis for your research results by searching with Google in front of the audience.

✔ **Bring several hard copies of your presentation:** Having more than one copy makes losing *all* of them less likely.

✔ **Make a backup:** Use the PowerPoint Pack and Go Wizard (choose File⇨ Pack and Go); the Pack and Go Wizard runs you through the process of saving an independent version of your presentation, which you can save to disk, USB flash, or burn onto a CD-ROM. The great thing about this option is that Pack and Go also packs the viewer, just in case the destination computer hasn't got PowerPoint loaded, or has an earlier version of PowerPoint.

✔ **Make a backup of your backup:** Even if you bring your own laptop computer to the presentation, go ahead and burn the slideshow onto a CD-ROM or save it to disk or portable media (such as a USB flash card) and take that with you, too. Yeah, it may seem redundant, but you never know. In fact, if you don't want to bring your computer at all, you can just bring the CD-ROM.

Preparing a slideshow

Just as you should understand your client's needs and expectations when you do an executive summary, it's ever more important to know the client's needs when you create your PowerPoint slideshow. Because you are physically in the room with your client, you must remember the most important rule — "Don't bore the audience!"

Depending on the topic (and your audience) it can really help to develop a hook, or punch line — in other words, a thematic phrase — that you can use throughout your presentation. Such a hook may help keep your audience paying attention, especially if your topic is technical or complicated.

Creating slideshows involves writing, visuals, and design. These are several elements. Here are some suggestions that will help:

- ✔ **Your slideshow is not your research paper or your speech:** Create a slideshow that consists of *talking points* or *keyword prompts* to help propel your presentation forward. They should not contain the totality of your research, research report, or speech.

  Thou shalt not jam your entire speech into the presentation.

- ✔ **Don't just read the slides:** Verbatim reading of a slideshow is boring, boring, boring and bad, bad, bad.

  Thou shalt rehearse making eye contact, speaking slowly, and being calm.

- ✔ **Present the big picture:** Know what you want to say before you start trying to say it. A PowerPoint presentation is essentially a *white paper,* or thorough briefing about a business, research, or technology topic, in outline form. Each slide should be a topic (if the subject matter is particularly complex, a topic might be divided into subtopics, each of which are represented by a single slide).

  Thou shalt take the time to organize your thoughts before you even open PowerPoint.

- ✔ **Use a simple PowerPoint template:** The simpler the better.

  Thou shalt not reinvent the wheel.

- ✔ **Customize your template:** Creating a personalized template shows professionalism as a researcher. You can easily create a personalized template by modifying a few elements in one of the templates that ships with PowerPoint and by adding your name or logo (if you have one). Depending upon your relationship with your research client, it might alternatively be appropriate to add your client's logo.

  Thou shalt do really simple stuff to customize your presentation.

- ✔ **Aim for readability:** Be careful to choose a background and text colors that make your slides readable at a distance. Font size needs to be big enough so that even those in the back of an audience can read the slides.

  Thou shalt not use a font size less than 14 points — ever.

- ✔ **Be the font of simplicity:** Choose a simple font. (Arial or Times Roman are fine.) Don't mix and match font families (in no event should you use more than two font families. One is better).

  Thou shalt have a very good reason for switching from font to font.

- ✔ **Put your presentation on a diet:** Better presentations are svelte; the shorter the better.

  Thou shalt not ramble on.

✔ **Questions are good:** Craft your presentation to leave room for questions and to encourage a dialogue with your audience.

Thou shalt pause, look up from time to time, and say, "Questions?"

✔ **Intersperse visual aids:** Break up your words with visuals such as charts showing statistical comparisons and pictures.

Thou shalt love pictures.

✔ **Forget about fancy effects:** Don't even think about using fades and dissolves between slides. You also really, really don't need to add individual elements to each slide (such as text loops added one by one). This stuff wastes time and could drive your audience crazy (not in a good way). For success, stick to the facts and present solid research results.

Thou shalt leave special effects to the motion picture industry.

Bring your own water to the presentation. Talking a lot can lead to a hoarse voice, and Murphy's Law says that the right time to get a tickle in your throat is two minutes before the spotlight's on you.

Using E-Mail to Deliver Research Results

In this day and age, researchers often never meet those commissioning research. Contact is made via phone and e-mail — or e-mail alone — and results are sent as e-mail or e-mail attachments.

There's nothing wrong with this, and in fact it is a necessity of doing business in an online world. But you should be aware that e-mail does not convey human emotion. *Emoticons* like the smiley face :-) are supposed to help a little to eliminate the distance created via the written word, but of course they don't really do the trick. Rarely (if ever) would you want to use emoticons in a professional e-mail, anyway.

Now that the Internet has been around for a long time, I am sure you've heard of *netiquette*. No matter how long you've been using e-mail to communicate, you can always use a brush up on keeping e-mails professional but warm.

Here are some tips:

✔ Include salutations and enthusiastic closings. In other words, try to make your e-mails read more like old-fashioned snail mail.

✔ Every e-mail message has its limits. You can only make the message so long and the content so complex. As a practical matter, the maximum length of an e-mail that delivers research results should be one or two paragraphs — somewhere between the elevator pitch and the executive summary.

✔ You can always attach a full report to an e-mail message, and this is sometimes a good idea, particularly if your client is expecting it. But bear in mind that unless it is expected, attachments to e-mails are not always read.

Using the Web to Present Research Results

If you have the ability to create HTML pages and have your own Web server, delivering research results using Web pages — or using a custom Web application — has a number of advantages. Clients appreciate this delivery method because of its easy accessibility. Using a Web page, you can incorporate data and tools derived from Web searches, and use links to provide sourcing data for your information. Although I can't cover this topic completely in this book, in Part IV I show you some techniques for using Web applications for delivering research results in this manner.

If you are using the Web, or a Web application, to deliver research results containing sensitive information, you should make sure that it is adequately protected with passwords or other security mechanisms. Never assume that not publishing link information provides sufficient, if simple, protection. For example, suppose I prepare a research report for a customer and put it on my Web site. I tell my customer to open a specific URL, such as `www.braintique.com/research/private_report.html`. I don't take any special measures to protect the report, and assume that no one else can find it because the address has not been published. This is simply not a good enough way to protect information.

Sourcing Research Information

Sourcing with accuracy and integrity is essential to any research project. There's no issue with this in academia: Authors of academic research papers must always provide references.

The results of your research require both good source information and intelligent deduction processes to reach a conclusion. You can certainly explain your deduction process, and this process can be examined and cross-checked to see if there are any flaws in your logic or methods. Information sourcing is part of this standard.

In Chapter 11, I give you some tips for evaluating Web sites as research sources. When performing research, you need to use these tips, and your common sense, to weigh the quality of information.

Your research clients need to take the same steps. They will want to know whether your research comes from *primary sources* (such as raw data or personal interviews) or *secondary sources* (articles, reviews, interpreted data, and so on). In the case of a secondary source, the value of the information is discounted depending on the integrity and track record of the source. Your research clients cannot perform this evaluation if they do not know your sources.

If a formal research paper is one of your deliverables, the paper should contain a list of sources in a standard format that contains, at the very least

- The author or originator of the source.

- The source's title, if any.

- The date the source was written and/or retrieved.

- The complete Web address. Don't direct readers to the home page of the site if you can get them to the exact page within the larger site.

- The research tools used. If the research in whole or part was obtained using automated tools, then briefly disclose the nature of the tools and the algorithms used.

- If you've used Web delivery as a vehicle, include hyperlinks in your HTML code to Web sites that you used as research sources. Also include a way to invoke any software that you used (or created) as part of an automated research workflow. (This can be fulfilled by providing the actual software on some kind of media or, more frequently, supplying a URL that can be used to run it.)

By all means, tell research clients where you got the information you've used to support your conclusions. Sometimes, hunches go a long way in the research business, and hunches may be good enough for your clients — depending on you, your research client, and the situation — but if your conclusion is based on a hunch, you should say so.

Sometimes there is really no right or wrong answer, and as a researcher you are being asked to provide an expert opinion after reviewing all the evidence. In this kind of situation, your job is to take a stand one way or the other. This is a role that is not comfortable for everyone (or in every situation), so be careful in considering your personality and the specifics of an assignment before you accept a job that requires forming opinions based on conflicting or incomplete information.

When Research Results Are Statistical . . .

Some research projects yield results that are essentially statistical, meaning that the results involve understanding a fair amount of numerical data. For example, in Chapter 18 I show you how to track the changing popularity of Google keywords over time. The popularity of a keyword is represented as a numerical value, with the value varying based on popularity trends. Using and evaluating statistics may enable you to present these changing values over time, and get more informational value out of the numeric data.

Many other kinds of research involve statistics in the results, and in the presentation of results. Determining both consumer behavior and voter polling are essentially statistical in nature. Research that uses automatic techniques to analyze large amounts of data — for example, in trial litigation discovery — relies on statistical measures of accuracy (how close a document is to the subject-matter in litigation may depend on numerical measures of the closeness of vocabulary using sophisticated, linguistic, quantitative measurements refined as time progresses with human input).

Acquiring statistical information can create a few special problems, both in preparation (methodology, number crunching, and analysis) and in presentation. Manipulating statistical information to meet your needs is notoriously easy — Benjamin Disraeli's famous quip, "There are three kinds of lies — lies, damn lies, and statistics," is one of the first things many people think of when they think of statistics. Statistical information can be particularly distorted when economic interests are involved, but even if no one is intentionally trying to distort information, becoming a "statistics whisperer" — someone who listens to what the numbers are really saying — isn't a skill that comes naturally to many people.

You should be careful when you evaluate, calculate, and present statistical research results.

You may also need to consider ways to reformulate quantitative information in light of the needs of a client — but without crossing the border into unethical distortion. For example, if you put together a presentation showing that the client's competition is outperforming the client, you client might not be too happy (depending on whether the client wants the facts, or wants to use the presentation as a sales tool). But if you shift your emphasis to show that the client's sales are catching up to the competition's sales and are projected to pass them in another year, then the client might find the presentation useful (and you haven't distorted anything).

For help with evaluating statistical results for validity, check out the Google Web search results for *evaluating statistics*. To learn more about statistical methodologies, data extraction, and analysis, search Google for *quantitative data mining* (and browse the results). For some great ideas about how to present statistical research results, search for *presenting statistical data*.

A great resource for learning how to effectively present statistical information using charts, graphs, and pictures is Edwards R. Tufte's classic *The Visual Display of Quantitative Information* (Graphics Press, 1992).

Part IV
Building Research Tools Using the Google APIs

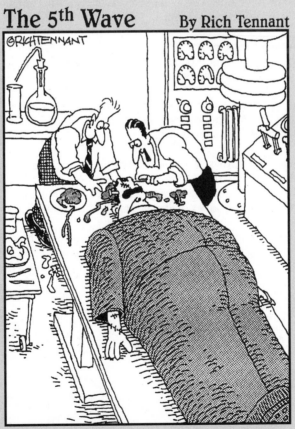

The 5th Wave   By Rich Tennant

"Wait! Wait! Wait! You've got a lung and two eyeballs in there! I thought you said you researched this project on Google?"

In this part . . .

This part explains the nuts and bolts of using the Google APIs Web service. Chapter 13 explains the APIs and shows you how to use the doGoogleSearch method to query Google. Chapter 14 explains how to get your own Google developer key — a necessity if you want to use the APIs in your programming.

Chapter 15 shows you how to work with WSDL (Web Service Description Language) files to get the most out of Google APIs Web service.

Chapter 16 explains the mechanics of creating both Web and Windows applications using C# and Visual Studio .NET to call the Google APIs.

Chapter 17 shows you how to create your own advanced search window that can be integrated into your other applications. You learn the nuts and bolts of creating search strings in code, and how to manage multiple result sets.

Chapter 18 explains how to track keyword result hits over time. Using the techniques in this chapter, you can create your own customized program for tracking the keywords that are significant to you!

Chapter 13

From Scripting to the Google Web APIs

"**I**t was the best of times; it was the worst of times." This chapter is a tale of two cities, or, more plainly, two ways of programming to create research applications:

- ✔ *Client-side scripting* uses simple scripts to construct Google URLs on your Web pages.
- ✔ *Server-side programs* call programmatic methods — the Google APIs — that are the heart of the Google system.

This chapter explains how to create an application that uses client-side scripting in the context of an example (adding an automatic language translation facility to your Web site).

The second half of this chapter is devoted to explaining the programmatic concepts behind the Google APIs (Application Program Interfaces). With this understanding under your belt, you'll be ready to move on to creating research applications using the Google APIs.

Creating Research Applications with Scripts

If you have experience creating Web pages or are a Webmaster, you probably have added scripts to your HTML Web pages, most likely using the JavaScript language.

Adding JavaScript to a Web page is the easiest way to add Google functionality in an application. The application is called *client-side* because the action — programmatic execution — takes place in the Web page on the browser. (In contrast, the Google APIs part of an application is *server-side* because it's executed on Google's servers.)

The advantages and disadvantages of scripting

Client-side programs (such as the one I explain in the following section, "Creating an automatic translation page") work by constructing a Google URL and then opening it in a browser window. The advantages to scripting are

- **It's fun, quick, and easy to create scripts:** Even if you're not very knowledgeable about programming, you may be experienced with scripting — especially if you've dabbled with creating Web pages.

- **You don't need any special tools:** You can create scripts in a simple text editor, such as Notepad.

- **You, and users of your research applications, don't need a Google developer key to create or use a script:** See Chapter 14 for more information about Google developer keys.

- **You can get a great deal of bang for your buck:** Creating scripts is easy, but the results can be professional and spectacular (for example, a number of the applications I highlight in Chapter 19 are created using scripts and not the APIs).

Here are some of the downsides to using scripts to create research applications:

- **It is not a flexible technique:** With the lack of flexibility comes a second downside — what you can do may be too limited for many research purposes.

- **Your code is exposed:** Your source code can be viewed from any Web browser that opens the page containing it.

- **You don't control the display:** Results are displayed the way Google wants to display them.

> ✔ **You don't control the application:** Users end up on a Google page, and are no longer within control of your tool or application.
>
> ✔ **You can't do anything with search results:** You have no way to use, or store, the results of your Google operation for further manipulation in your code.

All these objections are potentially serious. The last one is probably the most difficult to get around for anyone who wants to build research tools. In an application that uses the Google APIs (as I explain later in this chapter), you can do what you want to do with the results of a Google query, even if all you want to do is shove it in a database so you can keep track of changing values. That's simply not possible if you use a client-side script to implement your search.

Flowing with your scripts

In a client-side research program, a script generates a URL in a Web page, which is then opened in a Web browser. The general flow of this logic is shown in Figure 13-1. There's a great contrast with the logical progression of a Google server-side program (shown in Figure 13-2), which uses the Google server to obtain results, and then returns the results (and control) to your program. I go into this topic in more detail in the section, "Creating server-side research tools."

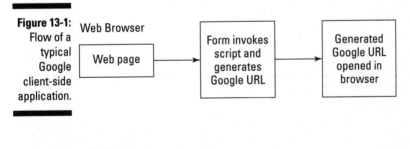

Figure 13-1: Flow of a typical Google client-side application.

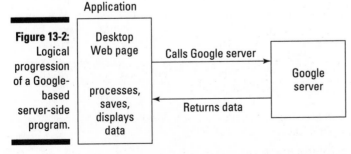

Figure 13-2: Logical progression of a Google-based server-side program.

So why even bother using this option if all these limitations can get in the way? Well, the fact is that in some cases the limitations I describe here don't affect particular applications. So why go to the trouble of building a server-side program that does more than you need? You're probably doing the right thing to build a research tool using client-side code, if only because client-side apps are so simple.

Creating an automatic translation page

Google provides automatic translation services that can (rather roughly) translate Web pages written in French, German, Italian, Portuguese, and Spanish to English (and vice versa). Google can also translate, for example, French to German or German to French. For more information about Google's automatic translations, see `www.google.com/language_tools?hl=en`. You can use Google's automatic translation feature to add automatic page translation to your own Web pages.

Google has started to offer, on a preliminary basis, translation services to and from non-Roman alphabet languages including Chinese, Korean, and Japanese.

Understanding what's going on in a client-side Web program is usually pretty easy because (with certain exceptions) all program code is contained in an HTML-based Web page open in a browser. If you were to build a client-side application that uses Google search technology, the client-side program would construct a URL (uniform resource locator) that involves a Google search and then open the constructed URL in the Web browser.

The programming involves constructing the Google-based URL, and the most painful intellectual work you need to do is figure out how Google search operators work — and how they are put together to construct a URL (I explain Google search operators in Chapters 4 and 5).

In Chapter 5, I show you how to make an easy site-limited search. That is, I show you how to create a client-side program that uses the `site:` operator to create a form that you can use to search a single site. The example I show you in this section does a little bit more than a site-limited search. Well, actually, a lot more! It uses the Google automatic translation facility to translate a given Web page. You provide the Web address and if Google's translation facility can handle the language, you're on your way to Translationville. Figure 13-3 shows using the client-side page that lets users enter a URL for translation and choose a translation language.

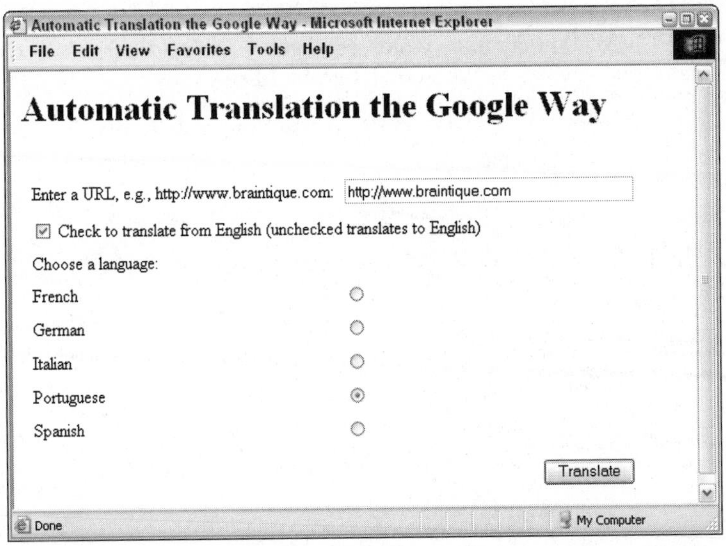

Automatic Translation the Google Way

Enter a URL, e.g., http://www.braintique.com: `http://www.braintique.com`

☑ Check to translate from English (unchecked translates to English)

Choose a language:

French ○

German ○

Italian ○

Portuguese ◉

Spanish ○

[Translate]

Figure 13-3:
In this program, the user enters an address and chooses a language for translation.

Google's automatic translation engine is pretty rough around the edges (as you'd expect from any automatic translation software). Don't get me wrong — the translation is good enough to get the gist of what's on a Web page, but don't expect elegance. Also, Google doesn't have the capability to translate any text that is part of graphics — for example, an image map.

Table 13-1 shows Google's two-letter codes for each of these languages. You need to know these language codes in order to write the code that does the translation.

Table 13-1	Google Language Codes
Language	*Code*
English	en
French	fr
German	de
Italian	it
Portuguese	pt
Spanish	es

If you've ever seen a <u>Translate this page</u> link in a return result snippet (see Figure 13-4), you may have wondered how you could harness the Google translation services for your own needs. Here's how.

Click this link.

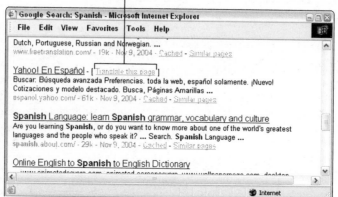

Figure 13-4:
A <u>Translate this page</u> link for a page that wasn't created in English.

If you use a Google service, such as automatic translation, as part of a commercial application, it's possible that you may be in violation of Google's TOS (Terms of Service) agreement; you should check with Google before proceeding.

Clicking the <u>Translate this page</u> link results in an automatic translation using a Google URL roughly like this to translate from Spanish to English (I've stripped some of the nonessential stuff from the URL):

```
http://translate.google.com/translate?hl=en&sl=es&u=http://es
        panol.yahoo.com/
```

The URL at the end of this is the page being automatically translated (`http://espanol.yahoo.com`), the `hl` parameter represents the language being translated into (`en` for English), and the value of the `sl` parameter is the original language (`es` for Spanish).

Try finding and clicking a <u>Translate this page</u> link yourself and viewing the URL that generated the translation. You can view any URL in Internet Explorer by choosing View⇨Address Bar⇨Toolbars.

If you look at the URL used by Google to generate an automatic translation, you'll see that you can easily write a little JavaScript code that uses an HTML form to generate a translation URL for any Web address supplied by a user (refer to Figure 13-3). The generated translation URL would also have to specify the languages for translation.

After the translation URL has been generated, you can tell the browser to open the URL using the JavaScript `window.location` object.

If you want to learn about client-side programming with JavaScript, and how to work with the objects built into JavaScript, have a look at my book *Learn How to Program Using Any Web Browser* (Apress).

Getting your application coded and ready to go

Listing 13-1 shows the HTML form and JavaScript code necessary to automatically translate Web content (to make the code listing easier to read, I've omitted some of the HTML that one might use for formatting purposes, such as Table tags).

Listing 13-1:   Generating an Automatic Translation

```
<html>
<head>
<title>
Automatic Translation the Google Way
</title>
<body>
<h1>Automatic Translation the Google Way</h1><br>
<SCRIPT language="JavaScript">
function goGoogle(theUrl){
var langTo; var langFrom; var theLang;
if (theForm.which[0].checked)
   theLang = "fr";
if (theForm.which[1].checked)
   theLang = "de";
if (theForm.which[2].checked)
   theLang = "it";
if (theForm.which[3].checked)
   theLang = "pt";
if (theForm.which[4].checked)
   theLang = "es";
if (theForm.isFrom.checked == true) {
   langFrom = "en";
   langTo = theLang;
   }
else {
   langFrom = theLang;
   langTo = "en";
   }
```

(continued)

Listing 13-1: *(continued)*

```
var transURL = "http://translate.google.com/translate?hl=" +
    langTo + "&sl=" + langFrom + "&u=" + theUrl
    window.location = transURL;}
</SCRIPT>
<form name=theForm>
Enter a URL, e.g., http://www.braintique.com:
<input type=text name="theUrl" size=40
    value="http://www.braintique.com">
<input type=checkbox name=isFrom value="from" checked>
Check to translate from English (unchecked translates to
    English)
Choose a language:
French <input type=radio name=which value="fr" checked>
German <input type=radio name=which value="de">
Italian <input type=radio name=which value="it">
Portuguese <input type=radio name=which value="pt">
<input type=button value="Translate"
    onClick="goGoogle(theUrl.value);">
</form>
</body>
</html>
```

In addition to the JavaScript code used to find out the user's selection, only one line of code is used to construct the translation URL:

```
var transURL = "http://translate.google.com/translate?hl=" +
    langTo + "&sl=" + langFrom + "&u=" + theUrl
```

After that, all you need to do is make a single statement to open the translation in the user's Web browser:

```
window.location = transURL;
```

As you can see in Figure 13-5, which shows an automatically translated page, you get a great deal of bang for your buck.

As I've already mentioned, not everything in a page can be translated by Google. In Figure 13-5, the image map on the left is not translated, nor is the text in the box on the right side of the page because it is text from a Google ad on Google's server, and not on the page itself.

Why not think up your own application using a Google URL? To get some ideas, use the operators explained in Chapters 4 and 5 and observe the URLs created with them.

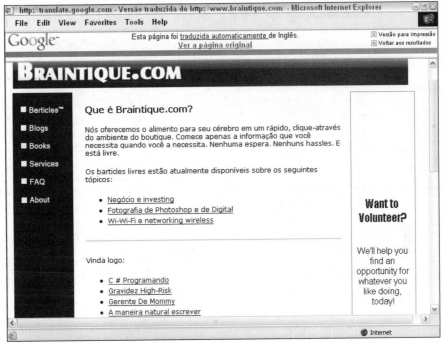

Figure 13-5:
This page
has been
translated
into
Portuguese.

Moving from the Client to the Server

"Never underestimate the power of the dark side, er, the server side!" If Darth Vader had been involved in Web programming, that's what he might have said.

In all networks, there are *clients* and *servers*. For example, your computer (unless it hosts a Web site) is a client computer that accesses the Internet by using a client program (such as Internet Explorer or Mozilla's Firefox) to connect to servers on the Internet.

In a nutshell, client-side programming code is processed on your desktop computer, whereas server-side code is processed on a *remote server*.

In contrast, the Google Web APIs harness the power of the server side by letting your program, running on your own computer, use the Google search engine, running on Google's servers, directly in your code. To understand why this is significant, you need to learn a little more about the difference between client-side and server-side Web programming.

It's important not to dismiss what you *can* do on the client side. One example of the easy functionality that can be created using client-side scripting is shown in the section "Creating an automatic translation page."

Creating server-side research tools

A research tool you build that uses a Google server should, in theory, be written for many kinds of platforms, including Web browsers, Windows XP desktops, and Macs, among others. The Google server has no reason to care what computer your code is running on, what operating system your code requires, and where in the Internet it is doing its thing. This very "don't care" (or *platform independent*) attitude of the Web service software (the Google APIs running on Google servers) is what Web services are all about (see "Connecting everything with Web services" and Chapter 15 for more information).

In addition, your research tool may need to do things that cannot be accomplished easily in a Web browser (you can use the Google APIs in a Windows desktop program).

When your program, regardless of its platform, uses the Google APIs, the following steps take place:

1. Your program queries the Google search engine (which is running on the Google servers).

2. The Google servers return the results of your query to your program.

3. Your program does what it pleases with the results.

So, welcome to the server side! And, may the force be with you!

Connecting everything with Web services

Web services are programs that are used to glue together disparate parts of applications across a far-flung Web. They often join together programs running on several servers, with each of the programs supplying *a part* of the larger software application. Web services constitute a safe and recognizable way to connect the parts of these programs so that they can be used by a wider population. In addition to the Google APIs Web service, both Amazon and eBay offer Web service access to their servers in certain circumstances.

Say you're running a powerful server that provides important and valuable information — such as the servers at Google — and you decide to open some of your server's capabilities to outside programmers, you'd want a *gating* mechanism — a program that lets outside programmers to access only the parts of your server that you want them to access. Additionally, your gating mechanism would be controlled for safety so that outsiders wouldn't be able — intentionally or otherwise — to bring your server down. This kind of gating mechanism is exactly what a Web service is.

A program uses a Web service by remotely calling the functions, also called *methods* or *Web methods,* provided by the Web service over the Internet.

(When a program uses a Web method that is part of a Web service, the program is sometimes said to *consume* the method and service.) For example, an online store might make information about its inventory available via a Web service and Web methods. A hypothetical Web method, `getItem`, might return the price and quantity in stock when passed a product code. A program could use this Web method to display inventory information to end-users.

Of course, to use the Web methods associated with a Web service, you need to know that the service and methods exist. More specifically, in order to code a call to a Web method and Web service, you need to know an address for the Web service, what the methods associated with the service are called, what kinds of values they take, and what kinds of values they return. In other words, to use the inventory Web method example, you need to know that the method is called `getItem`, that it takes a UPC product code, and returns two numbers, one representing the item price, and the other representing the inventory quantity.

As a programmer, how are you going to know this information so you can use the Web service? The good news is that there is a standard way to discover the crucial information about Web methods and Web services.

Each Web service provides a *contract* — consisting of a *WSDL* (Web Services Description Language) file — that provides information about the service and its methods. WSDL files, which I explain in Chapter 15, use *XML* (eXtensible Markup Language) to describe a Web service and its methods. If you have, or can find, a WSDL file, you know how to invoke the methods exposed by a Web service, and you also know what types of values each Web method will return. Using the WSDL file, many modern programming environments automatically generate most of the code you need to use the Web service and its methods.

UDDI (Universal Description, Discovery Integration) is a specification used to create directories for finding Web services. For more information about UDDI, see Chapters 15 and 16.

Google, Amazon, and eBay all use Web services to provide access to portions of their servers and software to developers. Of course, all these businesses, including your pals at Google, only allow access via their Web services under specific conditions (see "Complying with the Terms of Service" for a discussion of Google's conditions).

Introducing the Google APIs Web Service

A few years ago, amid great fanfare, Google introduced the Google Web Service APIs (alternatively called *Google Web APIs service, Google Web APIs, Google APIs,* or even *APIs*). The Google APIs promised to deliver the power of the mighty Google Web search engine to programmers. You're in the midst of a new era of custom applications written around Google.

The term API is short for Application Programming Interface (or Application Program Interface, depending upon who you ask). An API is a *gated method,* or *interface,* for accessing a program, such as an operating system. All this means is that the Powers That Be (in this case, Google) allow programmers access to this program interface, but they don't let programmers access *anything else.*

Since the Google APIs were introduced a few years back, their great promise has only partially been fulfilled. For one thing, the Google APIs remain in beta format, which means that, officially, they are still works in progress. Not too many great applications have been written using the Google APIs (see Chapter 20 for information about some of the best of the best of the Google API applications that do exist).

Why the APIs haven't taken off is a matter of debate. Perhaps software development issues proved too great a challenge — although I doubt that very much — if you have even a little programming experience I don't think you'll find it too hard to create your own Google Web APIs applications. I think the biggest issue is something altogether different. People don't really understand that Google is essentially a research tool and that custom applications built using the APIs only make sense when the programs build research tools that extend Google's functionality.

For example, researchers need a way to hold on to data and to see how data changes over time. They also need the ability to do automated comparisons and correlations.

If you're reading this book, you are likely interested in using the APIs in conjunction with research projects. This makes you an ideal candidate to unleash the true power of the APIs now that the hype and hoopla have come and gone. So what are you waiting for?

The following sections explain what the Google Web Service APIs are and show you how to work with them so that you can create programs to do cooler, better, and more accurate searches. I show you the following:

- ✔ The difference between client-side and server-side Web programming (and why using Google on the server-side is powerful).

- ✔ How you can use *Web services* (programs that are hosted on Web servers and that provide methods that can be accessed by other computers across the Internet) to connect almost everything in the world of software development (you'll find more information about the nature of the Web service beast in Chapter 15).

- ✔ The specific APIs that can be used to query the Google Web service.

- ✔ The limitations of the Google APIs.

- ✔ Why the Google APIs are valuable to researchers who know some programming.

This book mostly uses C# to demonstrate creating applications that use the Google APIs, but you can use any programming language capable of "speaking" to a Web service (see Chapter 15 for more about Web services and the programming languages that can be used with the Google APIs). In Appendix B, I show you how to use Visual Basic .NET to create Google APIs applications, and in Appendix C, I show you how to use the Google APIs from a Java program.

Another way of looking at the Google Web Service APIs is to realize that it is a Web service provided by Google that is formally defined by the filename `GoogleSearch.wsdl`. WSDL stands for Web Services Description Language. See Chapter 15 for more information about this file and about WSDL. The `GoogleSearch.wsdl` file is part of the Google APIs SDK (or software development kit), which you can download from the Google Web site, as I explain in Chapters 15 and 16. You can find out more about the SDK in Appendix A, as well. You can also reference the `GoogleSearch.wsdl` file directly on the Web, so you can use the Google APIs in your code without having to download the SDK (although you will, of course, still need a Google developer key).

If you can do something by searching Google, you can do it in software with a Google APIs application. Want to create an advanced search mechanism? Find changing information over time? You can do these things and much more with the Google APIs (you may get some ideas from the nifty programs that use the Google APIs that I show you in Chapter 20).

Working with the Google APIs

Collectively, the Google Web Service APIs act as a single Web service that contains three *methods,* also called *Web methods,* used for accessing the Google service. You can think of these three methods of the Google Web service as the Google APIs, which is why Google named its Web service as it did.

In "Querying with the APIs" I explain what you can do with each of the three APIs.

The APIs are still in beta — should you care?

The Google Web Service APIs are still in *beta,* like perpetual teenagers about whom great things were expected, but who don't appear to have grown up at all, despite the passing years. Being in beta means that the code isn't officially in its final format, and is still being tested (often you hear about *beta software* that is released to *beta testers* so that it can be tested and tweaked accordingly). Officially, everything about the Google APIs can still change at any moment — the number of APIs, what they do, and even the arguments they take. Google could even decide to end the Web Service APIs completely with no notice (and does mention the possibility in the Google Web Service APIs FAQs).

These possibilities are serious risk factors to consider if you're building applications based on the APIs. Why? Because if things change, your programs might no longer function. Should you worry? Well, yes and no. It probably depends on the effort you put into your application based around the APIs. If it is a huge amount of work with commercial implications, you may want to contact Google to get assurances that they will continue to support the functionality you need (you should get Google's permission anyhow before using the APIs in a for-profit context). Otherwise, I wouldn't worry too much about the issue (but then again, I'm not much of a worrier).

To use the Google Web Services APIs, you need a Google developer key. Getting one is easy (you don't even have to be a developer), and Chapter 14 explains the details.

Complying with the Terms of Service

You can find the Google Web Service APIs Terms of Service (TOS) at `www.google.com/apis/api_terms.html`. The TOS is also included in the Google SDK download (see Appendix A). You must agree to comply with the TOS before you can download the Google APIs SDK.

Besides the infrastructure limitation on the use of the Google APIs (see "Investigating infrastructure limitations"), here are the most significant restrictions:

✔ You may only have one developer key.

✔ You can't use the Google APIs in a commercial application without Google's written permission.

You should know that Google, at least officially, takes a pretty strict view of what constitutes a *commercial application*. The Google APIs are for personal use only (at home or at an office). You're not supposed to use them to sell something or to drive traffic to a site.

✔ This goes without saying, but you're not supposed to use the Google APIs as part of anything illegal.

✔ You can't use the Google APIs along with any product or service that competes with Google's products and services.

✔ You can't alter Google's intellectual property marks as they may appear in the Google Web APIs.

Google explicitly disclaims any liability about whether or not the Google APIs work right, damage your computer, infringe on anyone else's rights, and so on.

From a legal perspective, the Google Web Service APIs TOS does not replace the normal TOS you agree to as a Google user. In other words, you should expect to comply with both TOS. You can read the terms of the normal user TOS at `www.google.com/intl/en/terms_of_service.html`.

Investigating infrastructure limitations

Google insists on setting some contractual limitations on using the Google APIs (see "Complying with the Terms of Service"). In addition, there are some infrastructure limitations when you use the Google APIs. The most significant of these are

- Each developer is limited to conducting 1,000 searches a day.
- Any results past the 1,000th for any given query are inaccessible.
- The maximum number of results you can retrieve per query is ten.

The heart of most applications that use the Google APIs is searching with Google (see Chapters 16–18 for some examples). And the heart of searching is coming up with the right query strings for your application. You don't have to waste any of your 1,000 searches per day on finding the right search strings for your code. Instead, you can do that using Google manually by using Google's Web search. When you've found the right search string using manual searches, you can add it your code, saving your 1,000 daily searches for running and debugging your software.

Querying with the APIs

The three APIs (or methods) that comprise the Google Web Service APIs are shown in Table 13-2. Grasping programming structures in the abstract is never easy. The information in this section shows you the names of the three Google APIs and how they are structured.

Chapters 16–18 put the APIs through their programming paces, showing you how to implement the APIs in program code.

It's good practice to name methods — such as the Google APIs — using a verb ("do") followed by a description of what the method does. For example, "do" + "GoogleSearch" equals doGoogleSearch, get it?

Table 13-2	Google Web Service APIs
API	*Purpose*
doGetCachedPage	Returns a page from the Google cache
doGoogleSearch	Runs a query using the Google search engine
doSpellingSuggestion	Returns a spelling suggestion (if any)

Each of these APIs expects a Google developer key as its first argument. I explain the other arguments (and the return value) of the three APIs in the following sections, "Getting a page from the cache," "Requesting a search," and "Doing a spelling request."

Getting a page from the cache

In addition to the developer key, the doGetCachedPage API accepts as its argument a string value containing a URL (the page you want to retrieve the cached version of). Not surprisingly, a call to doGetCachedPage returns the cached page corresponding to the URL, as an array of bytes. For an example of using doGetCachedPage to calculate the size of a page stored in the Google cache, see Chapter 16.

Requesting a search

To request a search, you use the doGoogleSearch API. This is far and away the most important of the APIs. In addition to your developer key, doGoogleSearch expects you to include a specific search query. The search query consists of keywords and operators for the most part like the ones you use in a manual search query (as explained in Chapters 4 and 5).

You can use just about any keyword or operator with this API that you can use in a manual Google query. However, a few operators, such as the Google phonebook: operators I explain in Chapter 5, cannot be used in an automated query.

For the full details of which operators can go into an automated query, see the Google Web APIs Reference, which is part of the SDK download, available at www.google.com/apis/reference.html.

The syntax of a call to doGoogleSearch looks more or less like this:

```
result = doGoogleSearch(key, query, start, maxResults,
    filter, restrict, safesearch, lr, ie, oe)
```

Table 13-3 shows what these doGoogleSearch arguments mean.

Table 13-3	doGoogleSearch Arguments
Argument	*Explanation*
key	The developer key.
query	Google search string (obviously, the most important parameter).
start	Zero-based integer value specifying the offset (where to start counting) when results are returned. If you want to see results starting with the first one, this value should be 0.
maxResults	Number of results to return, integer value 1 through 10.
filter	Boolean (true or false) value that determines whether close results (multiple results from the same Web site that are omitted by default in a manual search) are filtered out.
restrict	Usually left blank (with empty quotes, " "); used to restrict searchs to one of Google's four topics or to a country (see the API reference documentation for details).
safesearch	A Boolean (true or false) value that determines whether results are filtered for adult content.
lr	Stands for *language restrict;* can be used to control the languages that are included in search result matches.
ie	Stands for *input encoding;* not used anymore, so all results are returned in UTF-8, and whatever you put in this argument is ignored, so you can just leave it blank with empty quotes (" ").
oe	Stands for *output encoding;* as with ie, all results are returned in UTF-8, and this argument is ignored, so you can just leave it blank with empty quotes (" ").

Understanding search request return values

The return value from the doGoogleSearch API, which I call *result* in "Requesting a search," is of type GoogleSearchResult. Each GoogleSearchResult contains a number of members, the most important of which is an array called ResultElement.

If you'd like to learn more about programming concepts such as *return value, type, member,* and *array,* please pick up a copy of my book *Learn How to Program with Any Web Browser* (Apress). It assumes no previous programming background.

Each element of the `ResultElement` array returned from an automated search provides values that correspond to an individual search result:

- ✔ summary
- ✔ URL
- ✔ snippet
- ✔ title
- ✔ cached size
- ✔ whether or not the related query is supported for the URL
- ✔ the host name if multiple results from the same host are filtered out using the doGoogleSearch `filter` parameter
- ✔ the directory category in the Open Directory Project (ODP) (See Chapter 7 for more information about the Open Directory Project and its relationship with Google)
- ✔ the directory title (the ODP title for the result, if one exists)

The Google Web APIs Reference is the best place to see a full list of the members of GoogleSearchResult, and an explanation of what these values mean.

Doing a spelling request

To request a spelling suggestion, you use the doSpellingSuggestion API. In addition to your developer key, include a string as an argument (which is the text you want checked for spelling suggestions). The request returns a spelling suggestion if the Google search engine makes one, and an empty string if it does not.

To see what Google means by a spelling suggestion, try entering something badly misspelled, and see what Google suggests.

For example, if you enter the phrase *caint spall two good,* Google comes back with the suggestion *cannot spall two good* — not perfect, but an improvement!

Chapter 14

Downloading a Developer Key

· ·

In This Chapter

▶ Signing up for a developer key

▶ Receiving your key

▶ Why you should get a key even if you are not a developer

▶ Replacing a lost key

▶ Downloading the SDK

· ·

*T*he Google software development kit — or, as it is often called, the Google SDK — is a downloadable set of files containing the tools, examples, and documentation necessary for building applications using the Google APIs. (To find out more about what you can, and cannot, build using the Google APIs, see Chapter 13.) But before you can use the Google SDK, you need to sign up for your very own Google account.

By opening a Google account, you can get a Google *developer key,* sometimes called a *Google Web APIs license key,* a long unique string of many types of characters including letters and numerals. By whichever name you call it, your developer key and your account give you access to a number of important services — such as the ability to post questions to Google Answers, explained in Chapter 6, and to participate in Google Groups, described in Chapter 7 — in addition to the ability to build (and use) tools with the Google APIs.

In this chapter, I explain the mechanics of signing up for a Google account and receiving a Google developer key — and how to replace your key if you misplace it. I also explain what the developer key is used for (besides building Google APIs applications). Finally, I show you how to download the Google SDK and briefly explain what's in it. (You can find a detailed explanation of the files that are contained in the SDK, and what they are for, in Appendix A.)

Opening a Google account and downloading your own developer key are two of the easiest and most useful steps you can take towards building your own Google research tools, and using the tools Google and others have provided more effectively. So, what are you waiting for?

Getting Your Key

A Google developer key is the same thing as a Google Web APIs license key. You have instant access to the key when you open a Google account. This section explains how.

In any case, you need a developer key to successfully call the Google APIs in your programs.

Registering for a Google account

To register for a Google account and obtain your developer key, open the Google home page, www.google.com, in your Web browser, and follow these steps:

1. **Click the <u>More</u> link on the Google home page to open the Google Services and Tools page shown in Figure 14-1.**

2. **Scroll down until you see the Web APIs icon and link.**

   The Web APIs icon and link are the last items in the Google Tools section.

Figure 14-1: Open the Google Services and Tools page to start the process of obtaining your developer key.

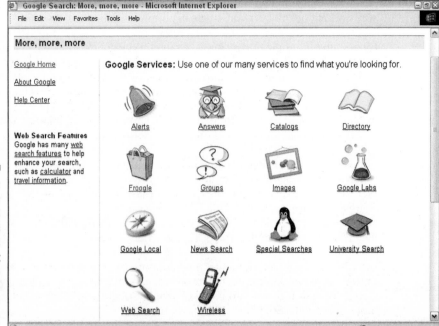

3. **Click the <u>Web APIs</u> link.**

   The Google Web APIs page, shown in Figure 14-2, opens.

4. **Click the <u>Create a Google Account</u> link.**

   The <u>Create a Google Account</u> link can be found in the text of the second step on the Google Web APIs page shown in Figure 14-2.

5. **Enter your e-mail address, a password, a password confirmation, and the text of the letters required for verification, as shown in Figure 14-3.**

6. **Click the Create My Account button to agree to the Google TOS and create your account.**

   The Google Terms of Service (or TOS) describe the rules you need to follow when using the Google APIs, and as a Google user. See Chapter 13 for more information about the Google APIs TOS.

These steps get you through the first part of the process of creating a Google account (and getting your developer key). Next, Google will e-mail you to confirm the validity of your e-mail address.

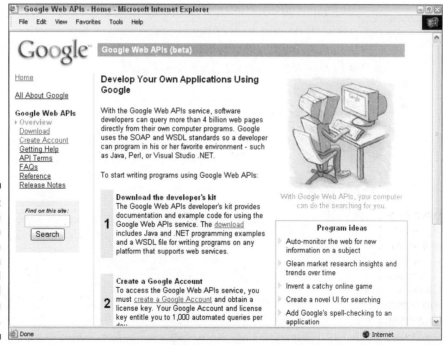

Figure 14-2: From the Google Web APIs page you can download the SDK and open an account.

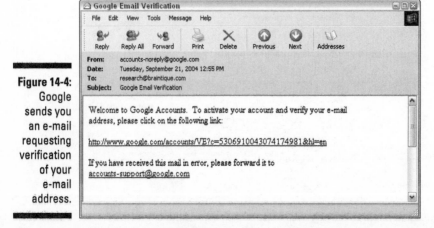

Figure 14-3:
Fill in this
info to get
the key sent
to you.

Getting the key by e-mail

Always assuming that you provide a valid e-mail address during the sign-up process (see "Registering for a Google account"), the next thing that happens is that you receive an e-mail from Google requesting verification of your e-mail address. One such e-mail is shown in Figure 14-4.

Figure 14-4:
Google
sends you
an e-mail
requesting
verification
of your
e-mail
address.

Click the link provided to verify your address. Your account now becomes magically activated, as shown in Figure 14-5.

Figure 14-5:
When you click the verification link, your account is activated.

If you click the <u>Click here to continue</u> link shown in Figure 14-5, your developer key is generated, as shown in Figure 14-6.

Figure 14-6:
With your account activated, a developer key is generated.

Next, your developer key will be e-mailed to you. Figure 14-7 shows a generated developer key that has been e-mailed to the corresponding Google account holder.

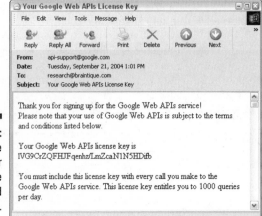

Figure 14-7: Your Google developer key will be e-mailed to you.

As you can see in Figure 14-7, the developer key is a long string of text including numerals, both lowercase and uppercase letters, and some special characters. This string is not something you can easily memorize (with good reason — it's hard for a hacker to crack), so you probably won't find yourself wanting to manually type it when you need it. I suggest that you hang on to the e-mail so that you can copy and paste the developer key when you need to. Keep the e-mail containing your key where you can find it — preferably on the computer that you will be using to build tools with the Google APIs. You can find out what your key is if you do end up losing it. See "Replacing a Lost Key," later in this chapter.

Your Google developer key is valuable; you should not share it with others.

If you're like me, you probably have a lot of e-mails floating around. The best way to keep track of important information such as your Google key is to create a folder for it, called something like *Google key,* within your e-mail program. I have just such a folder in Outlook, which contains all my Google APIs-related e-mail.

Why You Should Get a Key

You don't *need* a Google developer key to create applications, automate research queries, and build research tools with the Google APIs, but you do need it if you want to run those programs and have them function properly. I explain more about how to create applications with the APIs in the rest of Part IV.

A next step for Google accounts?

Here's something else to bear in mind: I can't read Google's mind, but it certainly seems like Google has plans for Google accounts (and the associated developer key). Google says that "in the future" these keys will be used for access to all Google services, including AdWords (a program for those who want to advertise with Google by purchasing links on pages that respond to specific word queries), Google stores, and more. I'm not making a tremendous jump to think that the Google account could become a kinder, gentler version of the Microsoft Passport, which is intended as general user authentication tool. But compared to Passport, getting a Google developer key is not onerous: You don't have to provide any personal information besides a valid e-mail address.

The Google developer key is required each time you call one of the Google APIs in code, so you cannot run an application without one.

Even if you're not up to coding your own applications using the Google APIs, I can think of a few other good reasons for opening a Google account and obtaining a developer key. These reasons include

✔ You can use other Google applications that require an account.

✔ You can use third-party applications using your developer key.

The following sections give you the lowdown on using the developer key to take your Google research up a notch.

Google applications that need an account

The Google services that currently require a verified Google account — besides the ability to use the Google Web APIs — include

✔ **Google Answers:** A service through which you post questions to be answered for a fee. As I explain in Chapter 6, Google Answers is a valuable resource for researchers.

✔ **Google Groups:** Discussion groups in which you post and read messages. (You can read messages without an account, but the only way to participate in the discussion is with an account.) I provide overview information about Google Groups, which may provide some kinds of information that is useful to researchers, in Chapter 7.

✔ **Google in Your Language:** A project that uses volunteers to translate Google's site into "all the languages scattered upon the face of the earth."

Third-party applications that use a key

As I explain in Chapter 13, the Google TOS limits each user of a Google developer key to 1,000 queries per day. As a result of this limitation, third-party developers who have built tools or services using the Google APIs often either encourage or require users to use their own developer key when using the tool or service.

For instance, to use many of the applications I describe in Chapter 20, you need your own developer key. At the very least, common politeness says that you should provide your own key if you have one (if the developer of the third-party tool gives you that choice and doesn't simply insist!).

You need a Google developer key to take advantage of the Google APIs functionality built in to a number of popular third-party products. For example, if you plan to host a Web log (or *blog*) using the popular Movable Type program (see www.movabletype.org), you need to enter your developer key when you configure your blog so that you can conduct Google searches on your blog pages.

Replacing a Lost Key

What if you lose your developer key? You can easily delete an e-mail by mistake, or simply lose an e-mail in the mass of electronic correspondence you send and receive every day.

Lost key, no problemo! The only thing you really have to remember is the e-mail address you used to create your Google account. If you've forgotten the password associated with your account, simply click the <u>Forgot your password?</u> link on the Google sign-in page; Google promptly e-mails the password to you.

You can find the Google sign-in page by opening the URL https://www.google.com/accounts/ in your Web browser.

With your e-mail address and password in hand, if you are already logged in, simply sign in again. Google will e-mail you a copy of your license key. (If you are not logged on, click the <u>Sign in Here</u> link.)

Downloading the SDK

After you create an account and have a developer key, downloading the SDK (software development kit) is only a click away. Here's how to download the SDK:

1. **Return to the Google Web APIs page.**

   The URL is `www.google.com/apis/`. Refer to Figure 14-2.

2. **Click the <u>Download</u> link found in the Download the Developer's Kit section.**

   A page appears that very briefly explains what is contained in the SDK. This page also includes extensive "Terms and Conditions" for using the APIs.

3. **Check the box to signify that you have read and agree with the Google Web APIs terms and click the Download Now button.**

   As expected, the file begins the download process. You are prompted to either Save or Open the file from its source. You should choose to Save the file.

4. **Specify where you want the SDK file to be saved on your computer, such as the folder you use for downloads, and click the Save button.**

   The SDK file, `googleapi.zip`, is a compressed archive file. After the download is complete, you'll need to *unzip* (or decompress) it.

   The easiest way to unzip a file under Windows is to use the WinZip utility, available from `www.winzip.com`.

   If you are using Unix or Linux, you can unzip the file by entering

   ```
   unzip -a googleapi.zip
   ```

   at the command line from the directory in which you saved the file.

You can find an extensive description of the contents of the SDK in Appendix A. For now, if you are interested in building tools with the APIs, you should know that it contains

✔ **Documentation** that provides release notes, licenses terms, and information about the specific APIs that make up the Google Web Service APIs.

My opinion is that you won't find this brief and obscure documentation of the APIs very helpful; but, of course, you should know that it is there. Here's the good news: Everything you need to know is available from this book.

✔ **License files** that explain the terms under which you can use portions of the Java Google Web APIs samples.

✔ **WSDL (Web Services Description Language) files** for use with any language and platform that support Web services (see Chapter 15 for information about the Google WSDL file and its uses).

✔ **Sample applications** that use the Google APIs with .NET, written in both Visual Basic and C# (see Chapter 16 for information about the sample C# application, and Appendix B for information about creating Google APIs application using VB).

✔ **A Java library** that provides a wrapper around the Google Web APIs SOAP implementation (see Appendix C for information about creating and deploying a Google APIs application using Java).

Chapter 15

Understanding WSDL and Web Services

*I*f you're like me as a programmer, you have some interest in understanding *why* things work, but mainly you want to know *how* to do things. This chapter shines that practical spotlight on the WSDL (Web Services Description Language) file associated with the Google Web APIs service. This file is called `GoogleSearch.wsdl`, and is probably the most important part of the Google software development kit (SDK).

The WSDL (usually pronounced "whiz-dull") file is written in XML (eXtensible Markup Language) and is a "contract" that specifies the *methods* (and the method signatures) that comprise a Web service. The Web service provider *publishes* a particular Web service by making a WSDL file (and corresponding actual methods) available. A programmer *consumes* the Web service by calling the methods specified in the WSDL file over the Internet.

Web services can be published using HTTP *form mechanisms* — HTTP GET — or using SOAP (Simple Object Access Protocol), or both. I explain the advantages and disadvantages to both publication protocols in this chapter. Although the Google Web APIs service is SOAP-based (and not intended for use with HTTP form mechanisms), I show you a work-around so that you can get a quick-and-dirty response from the Web service using HTTP.

This chapter is chock-full of useful information that you need to program with the Google Web APIs service and the Google WSDL file. So, get ready to "WSDL while you work!"

Understanding XML Basics

If you've already worked with XML — eXtensible Markup Language — you can probably safely skip this section. If you aren't familiar with XML, this section won't make you an expert. But it will give you enough information to go on, and enough information to work with the GoogleSearch WSDL file.

Since emerging a few years ago, XML has had a great impact on the interoperability of applications and data because XML

- ✔ Is easy to understand and to use
- ✔ Can be read by both humans and machines
- ✔ Is very flexible

Don't hate XML just because it's easy! As you get to know your way around XML, you'll see that it is also an immensely powerful tool.

As you probably know, HTML and XML are related markup languages; both HTML and XML documents are made up of

- ✔ *Tags,* which describe the content in the context of a document (for example, in an HTML document, all top-level headings are marked with an ⟨h1⟩ tag).
- ✔ The actual content (or data) inside open and close tags (for example, in an HTML document title like this ⟨title⟩My Page⟨/title⟩ the content is "My Page").

That's about where the similarity ends. Table 15-1 shows some of the differences between HTML and XML. I describe these differences in the following sections.

Table 15-1	Differences between HTML and XML	
	HTML	*XML*
What tags do	Tags have predefined meaning in each version of HTML. ***Example:*** ⟨h1⟩. . . ⟨/h1⟩ tags denote a level one heading.	Meaning of tags depends on specific XML schema. ***Example:*** ⟨employee_id⟩. . . ⟨/employee-id⟩ XML tags might denote an employee ID.
What tags describe	Tags primarily describe formatting. ***Example:*** Headings, page titles, and so on.	Tags describe all sorts of data, including(but by no means limited to) product IDs, employee IDs, and so on.

Getting more eXtensibility for your buck

In contrast to HTML, which is fairly limited, XML tags can be customized (that's what makes them *extensible* in nature), meaning that they can be specially defined depending on the nature of the data they are used with. Here are some of the customizations you should know about:

- ✔ **Tags describe content, not form:** XML tags are used to describe any kind of data itself (rather than describing the formatting of one kind of data, the elements of a Web page, as HTML does).

    For example, an XML tag such as `<address></address>` could mean a street address, and an XML tag `<phone></phone>` might mean a telephone number.

- ✔ **You can write your own tags:** XML tags can be used for anything that you might logically use when structuring data. You can invent your own XML tags and use them to mark data as you'd like.

    The meaning of an XML tag is really up to you — or whoever invents a flavor of XML: The meaning of an XML tag is not fixed for all users the way an HTML tag is. For example, in one flavor of XML a `<name>` tag might identify a first name, and in another flavor of XML the `<name>` tag might mean first, middle, and last names.

    There's no single flavor of XML; instead, lots of different versions of XML are already floating around, each an agreed-upon standard for communicating data.

You may have heard of XHTML (eXtensible Hypertext Markup Language), which is a reformulation of HTML so that it complies with the XML specification. If you want, you can write your Web pages in XHTML, which is itself a kind of XML.

So long as you mark your data as elements following a specific schema, humans who are familiar with the schema and computers programmed to understand the schema will know what you are talking about (at least that's the idea behind XML).

You can think of XML as a formal mechanism for describing a hierarchy (or taxonomy). See Chapter 10 for more information about hierarchies and taxonomies.

Describing XML with schemas

Essentially, any kind of data can be described using XML. A *schema* (which is itself an XML document) specifies the structure of other XML documents so that they can be standardized and validated. It says what kinds of elements can be in XML documents that comply with the schema, and what types of values the elements can have (for example, string, Boolean, and so on).

With all the extensibility I discuss in the previous section, "Getting more eXtensibility for your buck," comes the danger that with so much freedom to go your own way no one else will be able to follow you — and what's the good of describing data if no one else knows what you are talking about? In order that other users (whether human or machine) of a specific XML flavor know what each other is talking about, the smart people who developed XML also developed schemas. For example, you might have one computer in New York transmitting data over the Internet to a computer in Los Angeles. The New York computer could mark the data using a particular set of tags that the programmers in both cities previously agreed on (that's the schema). When the data arrives at the Los Angeles computer, the Los Angeles computer knows what the data means because it's used the schema as a guide. Say that the New York computer is transmitting the addresses of customers. If it uses an `<address>` tag, the receiving computer must be programmed to know that the data that follows is a customer address, offered in a specified format.

The word *schema* comes from database technology, where it means the structure of the tables within a relational database. Interestingly — and usefully — XML schemas and relational database schemas can be converted to and from each other.

For the most part, XML schemas are created by business communities or others who have an interest in standardizing communication. For example, WSDL is based on an XML schema developed to standardize Web services. The schema for WSDL, which you can view at `http://schemas.xmlsoap.org/wsdl/`, primarily provides a common mechanism for defining programmatic types, or kinds of values that can be communicated. For more information about the technical specifications that are the foundations for WSDL, see `www.w3.org/2002/ws/desc/`.

Schemas specify XML elements and their attributes, and, as I've mentioned, the types of values associated with them. For example, an XML schema might specify a product element that contained a product name, description, identification number, and so on.

You can check your XML document against the schema that goes with it to make sure that you've done it right (all the elements that are supposed to be there are there, they are of the right type, and so on). This is the process called *validating,* and it's usually done via a computer program (not a human).

Most XML schemas today are called XSD (XML Schema Data) documents. These documents are XML files saved with a `.xsd` file extension. XSD is a standard specified by the W3C (World Wide Web Consortium). You can learn more about XSD schemas on the W3C site, `www.w3c.org/TR/xmlschema-2/`.

(You may also come across some older XML schema types, which are not used so much anymore: DTD, or Document Type Definition, and XDR, a proprietary Microsoft schema specification.)

If you have XML data, you can convert it into HTML using an XSLT (eXtensible Stylesheet Language Transformation). The purpose of XSLT is to convert the form or structure of an XML document to another format or structure. Here's the W3C specification for XSLT: `www.w3.org/TR/xslt`. You can also learn more about this technology and its uses on the Web by typing **XSLT** into the Google search box and checking out the results.

Working with the Google WSDL File

Generally, a WSDL file — and in particular the Google WSDL file — is a text file written in XML following a schema and rules specified by the W3C organization. (See `www.w3.org/2002/ws/desc/` for more information about the W3C WSDL specification.)

The WSDL file is used to tell programmers (and programs) what methods can be used to access a Web service across the Internet. Besides the methods themselves, the WSDL file specifies the type of values that are returned by the methods, and the arguments these methods require.

The XML elements in the WSDL file correspond to the programmatic methods that can be used to access a Web service.

The bottom line is that if you — or a research program you've written — have access to the Google WSDL file, then you (or the program) can figure out how to use the Google Web service.

Using the Google WSDL file with Visual Studio .NET

This section explains the basics of working with the Google WSDL file and Visual Studio .NET as a beginning to creating great research applications.

You can use the Google WSDL file to call the Google Web APIs from .NET programs written in C# (pronounced *c-sharp*) and Visual Basic. (For more information about creating research applications using C#, see Chapters 16 through 18; for help with VB .NET research programs, see Appendix B.)

In C# .NET (as in VB .NET) there are two ways to work with a WSDL file to programmatically interact with a Web service. You can either:

✔ Use the WSDL utility to create a *proxy* file (a class that intermediates between the Google Web service and your code). Another way of putting this is that the WSL utility takes the Google WSDL file and uses it to build a class whose methods call the Web service APIs.

✔ Use the tools in the development environment to add a Web reference to your project.

To use the WSDL utility that is part of Visual Studio .NET, follow these steps:

1. **Open the Visual Studio .NET Command Prompt window.**

   Choose Microsoft Visual Studio .NET⇨Visual Studio Tools⇨Visual Studio Command Prompt from the Windows Start menu.

2. **Enter** wsdl **in the command line, followed by your language choice (CS for C# and VB for Visual Basic), followed by the URL of the Web service. At the end of all this, type** ?WSDL.

   For example, to use the WSDL to create a C# proxy for the Google Web service, you could enter a command like this (all on one line):

   ```
   wsdl /language:CS http://api.google.com/GoogleSearch.
       wsdl?WSDL
   ```

   The proxy file generated by the WSDL utility contains classes with the code needed to use the Google APIs in your project.

To use the classes in the proxy file, you'll need to manually add the proxy file to your project. Adding a Web reference to your project within Visual Studio .NET using the Visual tool included in the development environment is really easy. I show you how to add Web references to your Visual Studio projects in Chapter 16. All you need to know is the address on the Web of the WSDL file for the Web service (http://api.google.com/GoogleSearch.wsdl for the Google APIs Web service). Adding the Web reference causes a proxy file to be created, which — just as if you'd used the WSDL utility — provides the class methods you need to call the Google Web service APIs.

Adding the Web reference also automatically adds the proxy file to your project, so you don't need to do this as a separate step.

Either way you go about using the tools provided by Visual Studio to generate a proxy file, after the classes you need have been generated in a proxy file, from within your Visual Studio .NET project the methods of the Web service are called just like methods that are members of any other class. The classes in the .NET Framework supply the mechanisms that you need just to use the methods in your code.

I've chosen to use C# and Visual Studio .NET to demonstrate programming with the Google APIs Web service in Chapters 16, 17, and 18. My reason for this is because Visual Studio .NET lets you concentrate on the programming without having to worry much about the underlying mechanism. If you're using some other programming language, such as Java, you should be able to translate the examples in these chapters to Java (see Appendix C for information about using the Java library file provided by Google to create research applications).

Calling a Web service in Visual Studio .NET using Visual Basic rather than C# works in almost exactly the same way, with minor differences of syntax. See Appendix B for information about using Visual Basic and Visual Studio .NET to build research tools with the Google APIs.

Using the WSDL file in other languages

Besides the .NET languages — C# and VB .NET — you can use the Google Web APIs service from almost any programming language that is currently popular, particularly any language used to create Web service applications. These programming languages may require special SOAP libraries to work with SOAP-based Web services.

You either use a local copy of the GoogleSearch WSDL file to generate the right intermediate code for accessing the Google APIs, or you access the copy on Google's servers at `http://api.google.com/GoogleSearch.wsdl`, depending on the mechanism that works best with the language you're using to write the program.

Languages that can be easily used to program the Google APIs Web service include

- ✔ Java (see Appendix C for information about creating Java applications that use the Google APIs)
- ✔ PERL
- ✔ PHP
- ✔ Python

For example, you can run a PERL script against the Google APIs Web service if you have the SOAP::Lite library installed. (For more information about SOAP::Lite, see `www.soaplite.com`.) With SOAP::Lite installed, you can create a proxy for the Google APIs Web service using the GoogleSearch WSDL file with just a couple of lines of code.

A great way to find more information about using the GoogleSearch WSDL file to create a mechanism for calling the Google APIs in a particular language is to search for the language followed by *GoogleSearch*. For example, search for *Python GoogleSearch* and see what kinds of results you end up with.

Finding Web services with UDDI

UDDI (Universal Description Discovery and Integration protocol) specifies a standardized way to maintain directories of Web services. You can learn more about UDDI from the OASIS UDDI Web site, www.uddi.org. (OASIS is the standards group that promotes, promulgates, and maintains UDDI.)

Part of the idea behind UDDI is to make Web services interoperable. Therefore, UDDI directories (also called *registries*) are searchable both by people and by software tools. (An example of software-driven UDDI searching is included in Microsoft Visual Studio .NET, which provides an easy way to search UDDI directories as part of its Web services mechanism.)

If you are a Web services publisher, listing in a UDDI directory is a way to get consumers to find your Web service.

There are currently three UDDI registries. These registries are run by IBM, Microsoft, and SAP. The flavor of this list should give you a hint about the expected users of UDDI — large enterprises — although there is nothing to stop little old you or me from listing or looking up a Web service.

Don't worry about which registry you use. All three contain all of the entries from the other registries (in other words, the three UDDI directories are practically identical). It's free to use the UDDI directories, but you will have to register.

Here are the Web addresses for the three UDDI directories:

- **IBM:** https://uddi.ibm.com/ubr/registry.html
- **Microsoft:** http://uddi.microsoft.com/default.aspx
- **SAP:** http://uddi.sap.com/

As you can see in the figure, the UDDI directories are a great way to look for a Web service.

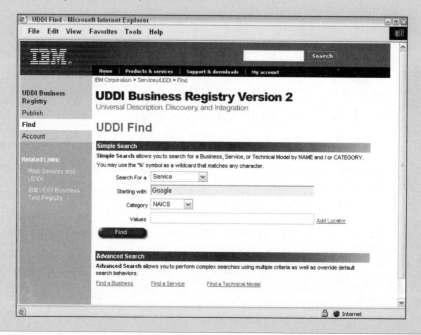

If you find a Web service you are interested in, the UDDI directory tells you the Web location of the WSDL file that defines the Web service — so you're pretty much ready to go ahead and use the Web service you've found.

As I show you in Chapter 16, Microsoft's UDDI directory has been integrated with Visual Studio .NET — so you can use UDDI to search for a Web service and its corresponding WSDL file without ever leaving the comfort of your friendly development environment.

To HTTP or to SOAP?

When a client computer talks over the Internet to a computer offering a Web service (such as the Google Web service), the two computers must communicate with each other, transferring data between them. The method they use for transferring data is called a *protocol*.

Web services, specified by a WSDL file, can be published using a SOAP — Simple Object Access Protocol — mechanism or using HTTP (Hypertext Transfer Protocol, the protocol used by Web servers and browsers), or both.

I bet your mama never said to you, "I'll wash your HTTP out with SOAP!" Joking aside, there's no real need to go into the ins and outs of SOAP in order for you to build research tools with the Google APIs. But you should know a *little bit* about SOAP. In particular, you need to understand how SOAP functions differently than HTTP as a Web services transfer mechanism.

Introducing the SOAP Standard

Generally, the SOAP standard defines three parts used for communication between Web service publishers and consumers:

- ✔ An *envelope* that defines a framework for describing what is in a message.

- ✔ Encoding and decoding rules for types of data used in the message.

- ✔ A way of expressing remote calls to methods (also called remote procedure calls, or RPC) and the method response.

You can find out more about SOAP by typing **define:SOAP** into the Google search box and following some of the resulting links (those that do not have to with cleaning products). Also, if you are interested, check out the W3C specifications: www.w3.org/TR/SOAP/.

The Google Web APIs service — specified by `GoogleSearch.wsdl` — is a Web service only available via SOAP. You can't very easily run an ad-hoc query against a SOAP Web service (as you can with an HTTP Web service by simply entering the URL in a Web browser).

As I show you in the upcoming section, "Calling the Google Web Methods with HTTP," some programmers have missed HTTP discovery of the Google Web service badly enough to write their own programmatic wrapper. The wrapper enables you to use HTTP even though the program itself communicates with the Google Web service via SOAP.

Calling the Google Web Methods with HTTP

From the practical programmer's perspective, a major difference between a Web service published using SOAP and one published using HTTP is that you cannot call (or *invoke*) a SOAP Web service directly using a Web address, or URL (Uniform Resource Locator). In contrast, when you call a Web service published using HTTP by entering its URL in a browser, a test page response is generated. This response page returns the XML generated by the Web service based on your request. In other words, HTTP lets you try out the methods associated with the Web service. Often, you can manually enter arguments (if the Web method accepts values) and see what the response is.

The ability to simply enter a URL and get back an XML test page with information and/or access to all the methods of a Web service makes it easier to get instant feedback with HTTP. This means that you can get to know the methods that are part of HTTP-based Web services more easily than you can get to know their SOAP equivalents.

There's no way to directly send an HTTP request via a URL to the Google Web service (because it is SOAP-based). However, a number of clever programmers have written HTTP wrappers that translate the Google SOAP Web service into an HTTP Web service. Here's how it works:

1. You call the translation wrapper via HTTP.

2. The translation wrapper calls Google using SOAP.

3. The wrapper receives a SOAP response.

4. The wrapper translates the SOAP response to an HTML test response page.

5. The test response page is returned to you.

   See Figure 15-1.

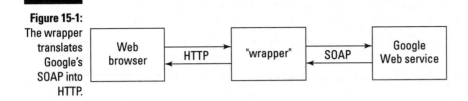

Figure 15-1:
The wrapper translates Google's SOAP into HTTP.

Using XooMLe to have it both ways

One of the best of these wrappers is XooMLe. You can find out more information about XooMLe at www.dentedreality.com.au/xoomle/. Using the XooMLe site, you can run HTTP queries against Google and get XML responses back.

Things really do start to get fun (and useful) when you use XooMLe to run queries against the Google Web APIs service using a URL and HTTP!

Essentially, any query you can run using the Google APIs, you can run against XooMLe using HTTP. Of course, by using an intermediary you are adding processing overhead to any query.

You need to have your Google developer key in hand to query Google via XooMLe using HTTP.

Here's how you can use XooMLe to run the doGoogleSearch Google API using HTTP:

1. **Open a URL of the following format in your Web browser:**

   ```
   http://xoomle.dentedreality.com.au/search/?key=Google
           DeveloperKey&q=searchString
   ```

   Insert the long code of letters, numbers, and other characters in place of *GoogleDeveloperKey*.

   There should be no line break when you type this code string.

   The URL is composed of your developer key and your query string.

2. **You can also tack on any of the other doGoogleSearch arguments after the search string if you'd like; for example, to return only the first result for a given search query, type**

   ```
   ...&q=searchString&maxResults=1
   ```

Comparable XooMLe addresses are available for the other two Google APIs.

If the call to the Google API is successful, your results page is returned in XML format. If there are problems, a detailed error page is returned instead.

Dealing with nonalphanumeric snafus

One significant wrinkle to the easy process of using XooMLe is that you need to make sure that your developer key, the query string, and any other arguments contain only characters that can be transmitted through HTTP. Some nonalphanumeric characters, for example a plus sign (+) in the developer key, need to be URL encoded so they can go through HTTP.

In a nutshell, URL encoding of a character consists of a "%" symbol, followed by the two-digit hexadecimal representation (case-insensitive) of the ISO-Latin character code for the letter. You can learn more about this by conducting a Google search for *URL encoding*.

You may need to experiment via trial and error to find out exactly which characters need to be URL encoded, and which don't. Say you want to call the XooMLe doGoogleSearch with the following developer key and search string:

Developer key: `wlCj3+cTSgCKTJH/amit56sKWOKtk9`

Search string: *braintique writing*

Using these values, your URL would look like this:

```
http://xoomle.dentedreality.com.au/search/?key=wlCj3+cTSgCKTJ
    H/amit56sKWOKtk9&q=braintique+writing
```

Opening this URL in a browser returns an error message stating that the developer key isn't valid. The problem is with the + in the developer key (although for some reason the plus sign that separates search terms doesn't cause a problem).

If you're running Windows, the easiest way to find the character code for a character that needs to be encoded is to use the Character Map dialog box:

1. From the Windows Start menu, choose All Programs⊏>Accessories⊏> System Tools⊏>Character Map.

The Character Map dialog box opens.

2. **Locate the symbol that you suspect HTTP won't accept and click it.**

   See Figure 15-2.

3. **Run your mouse across the thumbnail of the symbol to see its Unicode equivalent.**

   The Unicode equivalent also appears in the lower-left corner of the dialog box. In this case, the URL encoded replacement for the plus sign is %2B (the Unicode number shown is +002B, which is the same as 2B, which is %2B when URL-encoded).

4. **Close the dialog box when you're done.**

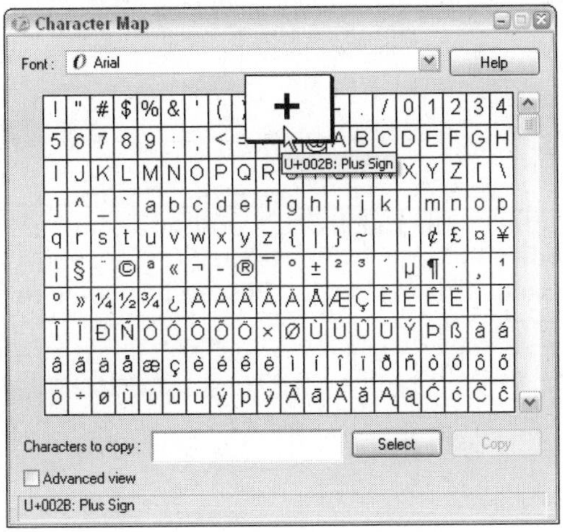

Figure 15-2:
You can find the character code to use for URL encoding from the Character Map.

The revised URL looks something like this (note the %2B rather than the plus sign):

```
http://xoomle.dentedreality.com.au/search/?key=wlCj3%2BcTSgCK
        TJH/amit56sKWOKtk9&q=braintique+writing
```

The URL in this set of steps includes a Google developer key that is not real. You won't be able to run a search against the Google APIs using this (or any other) technique with your real developer key. When you open the URL in your browser, you get a set of ten results, snippets and all, in XML format, as shown in Figure 15-3.

If you use the XooMLe service as an intermediary between your application and Google, you should take note of the fact that (essentially) you are depending on the kindness of strangers (meaning XooMLe, which is a free service put online by programming enthusiasts). Don't rely on the XooMLe service staying put, or staying online.

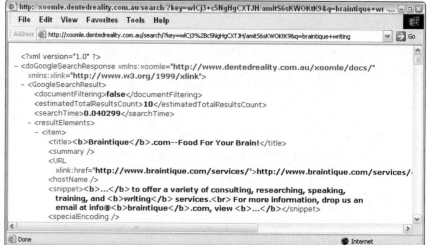

```
<?xml version="1.0" ?>
- <doGoogleSearchResponse xmlns:xoomle="http://www.dentedreality.com.au/xoomle/docs/"
    xmlns:xlink="http://www.w3.org/1999/xlink">
  - <GoogleSearchResult>
      <documentFiltering>false</documentFiltering>
      <estimatedTotalResultsCount>10</estimatedTotalResultsCount>
      <searchTime>0.040299</searchTime>
    - <resultElements>
      - <item>
          <title><b>Braintique</b>.com--Food For Your Brain!</title>
          <summary />
          <URL
            xlink:href="http://www.braintique.com/services/">http://www.braintique.com/services/<
          <hostName />
          <snippet><b>...</b> to offer a variety of consulting, researching, speaking,
            training, and <b>writing</b> services.<br> For more information, drop us an
            email at info@<b>braintique</b>.com, view <b>...</b></snippet>
          <specialEncoding />
```

Figure 15-3:
XooMLe returns the search results using XML.

Although XooMLe is a little on the rough-and-ready side, and it may take a little effort to URL-encode your strings if necessary, it gives you a great way to test what the return value from a Google API search is going to be without having to write program code.

Chapter 16

Building a C# Google Application

. . . .

In This Chapter

▶ Calling the Google APIs Web service

▶ Understanding the Visual Studio .NET project structure

▶ Using the Google Web APIs to make a spelling suggestion

▶ Returning the first result URL and title

▶ Understanding the SDK sample application

. . . .

You can call the Google APIs from any programming language capable of working with Web services and WSDL files — which, today, is almost every programming language. (I go into WSDL, or Web Services Development Language, in Chapter 15.)

I've chosen to focus the code construction examples in this book on C# in the Visual Studio .NET development environment. The popular Visual Studio .NET has a lot of scaffolding built in, so I can concentrate on showing you how to create applications.

If you prefer to work in another language (or use another development tool), you should be able to translate fairly easily the C# examples to your programming tool of choice. Appendix B explains how to use Visual Basic to build Google APIs applications, and Appendix C shows you how to put together Java applications that use the Google APIs. For an explanation of the APIs themselves, see Chapter 13.

In this chapter you learn how to create both Web (ASP.NET) and Windows applications that use the Google APIs. My small examples show you everything you need to know to create real-world programs. I also explain the purpose of the C# sample application that is part of the Google SDK.

If you'd like to download the source code for the projects in this chapter, go to www.braintique.com/research/.

Creating an Application and Adding a Web Reference

In the following sections, I show you how to add a Web reference to ASP.NET applications (.NET Web applications) and Windows applications. *Web references* are the mechanisms inside Visual Studio .NET that allow programs to call the methods associated with a Web service.

Creating an ASP.NET application

To add the Web reference to the Google APIs Web service, start by creating an ASP.NET Web application (you need to have an application to which to add the reference, after all). Here's how:

1. **On the Visual Studio .NET Start page, click the New Project button.**

   Alternatively, choose File⇨New⇨Project.

   The New Project window opens.

2. **In the Project Types pane, choose the Visual C# Projects folder.**

3. **Choose ASP.NET Web Application in the Templates pane.**

   This is your project type.

4. **Provide a path for the project relative to your Web server.**

   The URL for the Web server will be `http://localhost/` if you're using your desktop computer to host your ASP.NET application.

5. **Click OK to create the project.**

   Visual Studio .NET creates the default files for an ASP.NET Web application, which opens in the Visual Studio development environment.

Making sure IIS is running

If you have problems running your ASP.NET Web project in the Visual Studio environment, you should check that IIS (Internet Information Services) is running on your computer. IIS is Microsoft's Web server. You can verify that IIS has been started by opening the Services applet (accessible from the Administrative Tools portion of the Windows Control Panel). In the Services applet, scroll down to IIS Admin, and check that its status is Started. If IIS has not been started, you can start it by right-clicking in the Services applet and choosing Start from the context menu.

To create ASP.NET Web applications with Visual Studio .NET, you must use the Professional version of the Windows XP operating system (Windows XP Home Edition will not do).

You can find out how the virtual path `http://localhost/` translates into an actual file path on your computer by viewing the properties of the default Web site in the IIS administrative utility. By default, the actual path on your computer that corresponds to the virtual path is `Inetpub\wwwroot`, and it's where you'll find the folder created for your ASP.NET project.

Adding a Web reference to an ASP.NET application

With your ASP.NET project created (see "Creating an ASP.NET application"), you can add a Web reference so that you can use the application with the Google Web APIs:

1. **Choose Add Web Reference from the Visual Studio .NET project menu.**

   An Add Web Reference window appears (see Figure 16-1). In this window you see a URL box.

2. **Enter the address for the Google APIs Web service WSDL file,** `http://api.google.com/GoogleSearch.wsdl.`

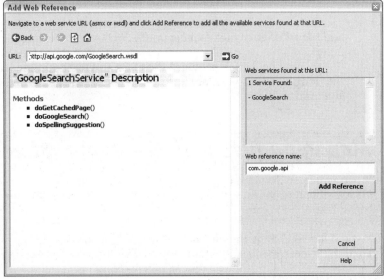

Figure 16-1:
Add the URL for the Google APIs Web service WSDL file in the Add Web Reference window.

3. **Click the Go button.**

   Visual Studio .NET searches for the Google APIs Web service and lists it in the Web Service Found at This URL box. The default Web Reference name, com.api.google, is also shown (you can change this name if you'd like, now or later).

4. **Click Add Reference to add the Web reference to the Google APIs Web service to your project.**

5. **Open Solution Explorer by choosing Solution Explorer from the View menu.**

   You see the Web reference (shown in Figure 16-2).

Show All Files button

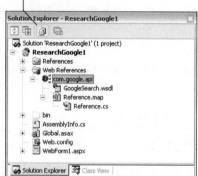

Figure 16-2:
Solution
Explorer
shows the
Web
reference
files.

You see a bunch of files making up the Web reference, including the GoogleSearch.wsdl file. The most important of these files is Reference.cs, which provides the class and methods needed to call the Google APIs as I explain in "Understanding the generated code and classes."

Managing files with Solution Explorer

When you open Solution Explorer, you may not see all the files in Figure 16-2. To see all of these files, you may need to click the Show All Files button at the top of Solution Explorer.

If you'd like to change the internal name used for the Google Web service to something more manageable than com.api.google — for example, to

`Google` — you can right-click on the file and select Properties from the menu that appears. The Properties window, shown in Figure 16-3, opens.

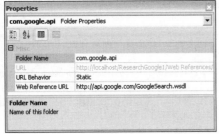

In the Properties window, change the Folder name from `com.google.api` to `Google`.

You're now good to go to program in your ASP.NET Web application using the Google APIs Web service.

Adding a Web reference to a Windows application

In order to use an application with the Google APIs, you have to add a Web reference. Adding a Web reference to a Windows application works in just the same way as adding the reference to a Web application.

Follow these steps to create an application and add a Web reference to it:

1. **On the Visual Studio .NET Start page, click the New Project button.**

   Alternatively, choose File➪New➪Project.

   The New Project window opens.

2. **In the Templates pane, choose Windows Application.**

3. **Choose Visual C# Project from the Project Types pane.**

4. **Provide an application name and location for the application.**

5. **Click OK.**

6. **To add the Web reference to the project, choose Add Web Reference from the Project menu.**

The Add Web Reference window appears.

7. **In the URL box, enter the address for the Google APIs Web service WSDL file,** `http://api.google.com/GoolgeSearch.wsdl`, **and click Go.**

Visual Studio .NET searches for the Web service and lists it when it's found.

8. **When the Web service has been found, click Add Reference.**

You should change the name of the Google Web service from the default (`com.google.api`) to something easy to work with in code, for example, `Google`. Check out "Managing files with Solution Explorer," earlier in this chapter, for information about doing this.

Working with UDDI from within Visual Studio .NET

In the previous sections, I show you how to enter the address for the Google WSDL file in the Add Web Reference window of Visual Studio .NET. This is simple stuff — just click Go and then add the Web reference to your project. This method works easily when you happen to know the address for the Google Web APIs service for which you want to create a Web reference.

But if you don't know the address for a particular Web service, or if you want to find a Web service with some special functionality, you're out of luck.

Well, not totally out of luck. Visual Studio .NET provides a number of Web search features built into the Add Web Reference window that use UDDI (*Universal Description Discovery and Integration*) protocol. For more information about UDDI, see Chapter 15.

If you don't have all the address information you need to create your Web reference, you can get help by clicking the UDDI Directory link in the Start Browsing for Web Services pane that is part of the Add Web Reference window in Visual Studio .NET. (To open the Add Web Reference window, choose Project➪Add Web Reference.)

A search screen opens that lets you search for Web services in a number of different ways:

- ✔ Web service name
- ✔ Web service provider name
- ✔ Industry categorization scheme

Figure 16-4 shows the results of one UDDI Web service lookup (the Web service shown is an enhanced zip code lookup called GeoPlaces).

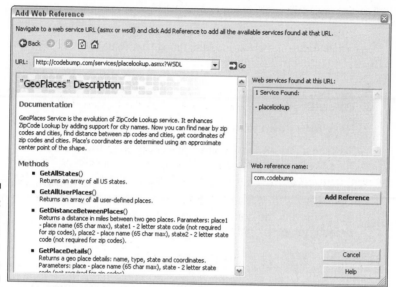

Figure 16-4:
Using UDDI
to search
for a Web
service.

Understanding the generated code and classes

When you add a Web reference, like the reference to the Google APIs Web service, Visual Studio .NET generates code so that you can immediately use the Web service and its methods in your own projects. Like everything in Visual Studio .NET, this code takes the form of a *class*. The class sits between your C# project and the Google APIs, which are called over the Internet. This relationship is shown in Figure 16-5.

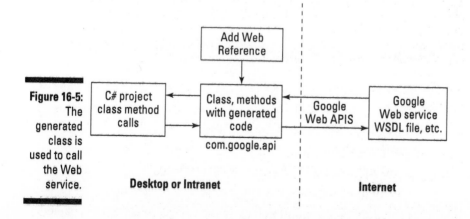

Figure 16-5:
The
generated
class is
used to call
the Web
service.

TIP

The generated class code sits in a file named `Reference.cs`.

You can examine the created class using the Visual Studio .NET Object Browser. Follow these steps:

1. **To open the Visual Studio .NET Object Browser, choose View⇨ Object Browser.**

2. **Next, drill down with the Object Browser.**

   You see a namespace in your project that contains a class (`GoogleSearchService`).

   In Figure 16-6, the namespace is called `Google`. When you look at the Object Browser, however, the namespace may be called `com.google. api`, which is the default name for the Web reference. (To change the default name, see "Managing Files with Solution Explorer.")

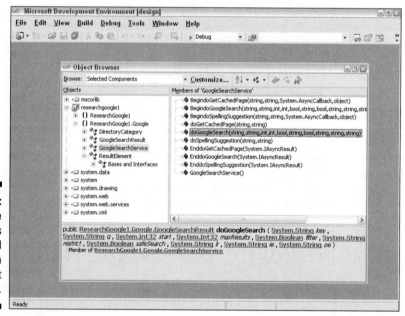

Figure 16-6: The Google APIs class and methods in Object Browser.

Within the `GoogleSearchService` class, you can see three methods that correspond to the Google APIs explained in Chapter 13. They are

- **doGetCachedPage:** Returns a cached page

- **doGoogleSearch:** Runs a query against Google

- **doSpellingSuggestion:** Returns a spelling suggestion

These methods correspond exactly to the Google APIs (and are named the same way).

3. To use the Google APIs, you must call these methods with appropriate arguments in your code.

Figure 16-6 shows some additional methods. These methods implement the asynchronous forms of the underlying Web service methods. For more information, see "Asynchronous method calls."

Chapter 13 contains information about the type of value each Google API expects for its arguments (and the method return type). The Object Browser also provides information about arguments and type, as does Visual Studio Class View.

Figure 16-7 shows the Google API Web service-generated class and members in Class View.

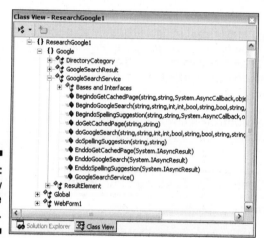

Figure 16-7:
Class View shows the APIs.

Programming with the Google APIs

When you've added a Web reference and understand how Web reference code works, you're probably ready to get practical and *do something* with the Google APIs!

There are lots of cool things you can do with the Google APIs. For example, you can

✓ Perform a spell check operation.

✓ Get a Web page from the Google cache.

✓ Let users perform customized searches.

> ✔ Use Google's operators (explained in Chapters 4 and 5) to create special-ized searches — such as finding all the pages that are linked to a given page, or are similar to the page.
>
> ✔ Track the number of search results you get for a particular keyword over time.
>
> ✔ Lots, lots more — the only limiting factors are your research needs and your imagination!

Making a spelling suggestion

If you want to help bad spellers use your Web applications, adding a Google-generated spelling suggestion box to an ASP.NET Web application might be right up your alley.

Start with your ASP.NET Web application, with the Web reference to the Google Web service (if you haven't created an application and a Web refer-ence, see the earlier sections of this chapter that show you how to do so), and use the Visual Studio Toolbox to add some Web form controls to the application's Web form.

You need to include the controls shown (along with their programmatic names) in Table 16-1 in order for the spelling check application to function.

Table 16-1	Controls for Spelling Suggestion Application	
Control	*Programmatic Name*	*Purpose*
TextBox	`txtDevKey`	User enters Google developer key
TextBox	`txtCheck`	User enters text to check
Label	`lblSuggest`	Displays spelling suggestion (if any)
Button	`btnSpell`	Clicking the button checks the spelling

Here's what you do:

1. **With the controls for the user interface added to the Web form, double-click the Button control to open the Code Editor and create a click event procedure for the Button control:**

   ```
   private void btnSpell_Click(object sender,
       System.EventArgs e)
       {
   ...
   }
   ```

2. Within the click event procedure, create an object that is an instance of the GoogleSearchService **class:**

```
Google.GoogleSearchService s = new
    Google.GoogleSearchService();
```

3. Call the doSpellingSuggestion API, passing it the developer key and the text to be checked:

```
String suggestion =
    s.doSpellingSuggestion (txtDevKey.Text,
        txtCheck.Text);
```

The return results of the API are saved in a variable named suggestion. If suggestion has a non-null value, display it, and otherwise display an appropriate message for the null value:

```
if (suggestion == null)
    lblSuggest.Text = "Can't help you with this!";
else
    lblSuggest.Text = suggestion;
```

Listing 16-1 shows the complete code for the button click event procedure with the call to the Google API.

Listing 16-1:   Button Click Event Procedure for Spelling Suggestion

```
private void btnSpell_Click(object sender,
    System.EventArgs e)
    {
    // Create a Google Search object
    Google.GoogleSearchService s = new
        Google.GoogleSearchService();
    try
        {
        // Ask for spelling suggestion
        String suggestion =
            s.doSpellingSuggestion
            (txtDevKey.Text, txtCheck.Text);
        // Display the suggestion, if any
        if (suggestion == null)
            lblSuggest.Text = "Can't help you with this!";
        else
            lblSuggest.Text = suggestion;
        }
    catch (System.Web.Services.Protocols.SoapException ex)
        {
        lblSuggest.Text = ex.Message;
        }
    }
```

The code in Listing 16-1 adds some structured exception handling for the sake of good programming practice. The structured exception handling technique places the program code within a `try` block, and execution of this code is attempted. If an exception, or error condition, is encountered, the code within the `catch` block is processed. All programs should be created using structured exception handling, but it is particularly important when your program uses a Web service like the Google APIs. If there is a problem connecting to the APIs (for example, the developer key is not valid), the message passed back to the user by the exception-handling code in the `catch` block gives the user some idea about the nature of the problem and how to fix it.

If you run the spell checking program and enter a phrase to search, depending on the phrase, Google may give you some good spelling suggestions, as you can see in Figure 16-8. If the phrase or name is relatively well known, Google supplies good suggestions. If your phrase is more obscure, you might not get good results. (By the way, the developer key in this figure isn't real. Never give your key out to other people.)

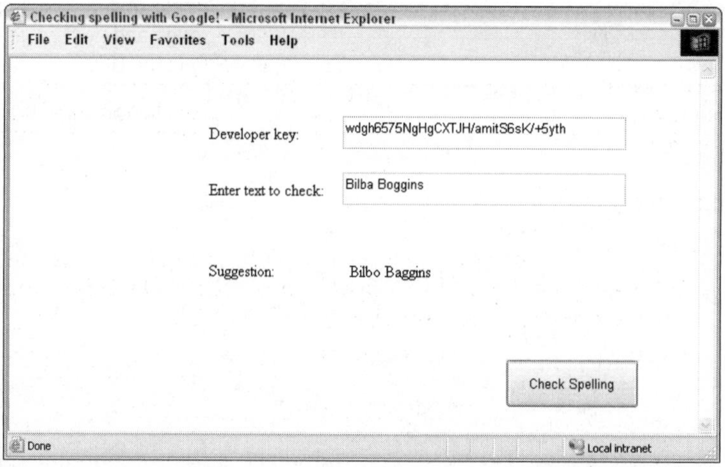

Figure 16-8:
Google suggests a better way to spell.

> Checking spelling with Google! - Microsoft Internet Explorer
>
> File   Edit   View   Favorites   Tools   Help
>
> Developer key: wdgh6575NgHgCXTJH/amitS6sK/+5yth
>
> Enter text to check: Bilba Boggins
>
> Suggestion: Bilbo Baggins
>
> [Check Spelling]
>
> Done   Local intranet

Depending on how IIS is configured on your computer, you may need to run the program by choosing the Start without Debugging option from the Debug menu.

Returning a "lucky" result URL and snippet

Far and away the most important of the three Google APIs is doGoogleSearch, which runs a query against Google and returns an array of the resulting values.

The example in this section shows you how to return the snippet and URL of the first result for a search in a Windows application. This example provides results that are a bit like clicking the I'm Feeling Lucky button in the main Google Web search window — which opens the first search result Web page in your browser.

Starting with a C# application with a Web reference to the Google Web service (in my example, the Web reference is named `Google`), add the controls shown in Table 16-2.

Table 16-2	Controls for Lucky Search Application	
Control	*Programmatic Name*	*Purpose*
TextBox	`txtDevKey`	User enters Google developer key
TextBox	`txtSearchTerm`	User enters search term(s)
Label	`lblSnippet`	Displays resulting snippet
LinkLabel	`lblURL`	Displays resulting URL, allows user to click through and open page corresponding to the URL
Button	`btnSearch`	Clicking the button starts the search

Follow these steps:

1. **With the controls for the user interface added to the Web form, double-click the Button control to open the Code Editor and create a click event procedure for the Button control:**

```
private void btnSearch_Click(object sender,
    System.EventArgs e)
    {
...
}
```

2. **Within the click event procedure, create an object that is an instance of the** `GoogleSearchService` **class:**

```
Google.GoogleSearchService s = new
    Google.GoogleSearchService();
```

3. **Using the** `GoogleSearchClass` **object, call the doGoogleSearch API, passing it:**

   • The developer key.

   • The search term.

- The search offset (because 0 is passed, the return result count starts with the first result).

- The maximum number of results to be returned (because you only want the first result, 1).

  - Filtering (false to run it off), restrict ("" to leave blank), SafeSearch (false to not restrict adult content), lr ("" not to restrict language), and "" for the ie and oe arguments. (See Chapter 13 for more information about these arguments.)

The results of the query are stored in a GoogleSearchResult object named r:

```
Google.GoogleSearchResult r = s.doGoogleSearch
    (txtDevKey.Text, txtSearchTerm.Text,
    0, 1, false, "", false, "", "", "");
```

4. **Check to make sure that some results were actually returned by checking the length of the** resultElements **array:**

```
if (r.resultElements.Length > 0)
```

5. **If there were some return results, display the value of the snippet property for the first element in the** resultElements **array returned in the** GoogleSearchResult **object:**

```
lblSnippet.Text = r.resultElements[0].snippet;
```

6. **Display the value of the URL property for the first element in the** resultElements **array returned in the** GoogleSearchResult **object using a** LinkLabel **so that it is clickable:**

```
lblURL.Text = r.resultElements[0].URL;
```

7. **If there were no return results (because there were no matches for the Google search), display a message to the user:**

```
else
    lblSnippet.Text =
        "No results! Please try another search.";
```

Listing 16-2 shows the complete code for the button click event procedure with the call to the Google API with some structured exception handling added.

Listing 16-2:   Button Click Event Procedure for Lucky Search

```
private void btnSearch_Click(object sender,
    System.EventArgs e)
    {
    // Create a Google Search object
    Google.GoogleSearchService s = new
        Google.GoogleSearchService();
    try
```

```
        {
        // Invoke the search method
        Google.GoogleSearchResult r =
            s.doGoogleSearch(txtDevKey.Text, txtSearchTerm.Text,
            0, 1, false, "", false, "", "", "");
        if (r.resultElements.Length > 0)
            {
            lblSnippet.Text = r.resultElements[0].snippet;
            lblURL.Text = r.resultElements[0].URL;
            }
        else
            lblSnippet.Text =
                "No results! Please try another search.";
        }
    catch (System.Web.Services.Protocols.SoapException ex)
        {
        MessageBox.Show(ex.Message);
        }
    }
```

To test the program, run it. Enter your Google developer key. Enter a search term, such as *ambidextrous scallywags*. Click Search. If everything works, the first result snippet and URL appears, as shown in Figure 16-9.

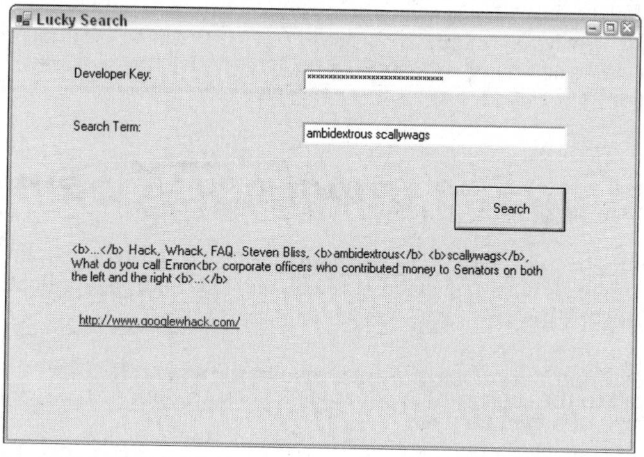

Figure 16-9:
The first
result URL
and title.

> **Lucky Search**
>
> Developer Key: ****************************
>
> Search Term: ambidextrous scallywags
>
> [Search]
>
> \<b>...\</b> Hack, Whack, FAQ. Steven Bliss. \<b>ambidextrous\</b> \<b>scallywags\</b>.
> What do you call Enron\
 corporate officers who contributed money to Senators on both
> the left and the right \<b>...\</b>
>
> http://www.googlewhack.com/

The result snippet that's returned is formatted in HTML, primarily meaning that it uses \<b> \</b> to mark words in the search term found in the result. You can easily use the excellent string-handling capabilities provided by C# and .NET to strip these HTML tags out of the result snippet if you'd like.

In a Windows application, you can easily use the .NET Regular Expression classes to strip out the HTML for display purposes — or you can write code that does something with the information about which words in the search result were also in the search terms.

Asynchronous method calls

The calls to the Google Web methods using the methods in the class auto-generated by Visual Studio .NET in this chapter are *synchronous*. When you call a method synchronously, the program waits for the method to complete before it continues and executes subsequent code.

In contrast, an *asynchronous* method call does not block a program from continuing. Instead, processing continues, and the asynchronous method sends a message when it is done. Your program can then respond to that message in whatever way is appropriate.

Programming with asynchronous methods is a little more complicated than programming synchronously. The reason for using asynchronous method calls is you don't want to hold everything up if you think the call to the method may take time.

Google makes a point of showing off its ability to respond to queries incredibly rapidly, so there's usually no real need to call the Google Web service APIs asynchronously. (An exception might be if you expect your programs to call Google over a very slow connection.)

If you do need to call the Google APIs asynchronously, you should know that the class generated for the Google Web service contains asynchronous methods as well as the synchronous methods that I show you in this chapter. For example, the synchronous method do-GoogleSearch sends a query to Google. The related asynchronous methods are Begindo-GoogleSearch and EnddoGoogleSearch.

I've posted a code example using asynchronous method calls to access the Google APIs on www.braintique.com/research/.

Understanding the Google SDK Sample

As part of the Google SDK, or software development kit, you can find a sample C# .NET Google APIs Web service application. This sample application, shown in Figure 16-10, shows

▶ The estimated number of return results for a search

▶ The size of a cached page

▶ Google's spelling suggestion based on the phrase entered

See Chapter 14 and Appendix A for information about the SDK.

You can use the sample application as a model for your own Google API applications — and to better understand how to program with the APIs.

Figure 16-10:
The SDK
sample
application.

I won't bother showing you the spelling suggestion code because it's pretty close to the application I show you earlier in this chapter. But you may find having a look at the estimated number of returns for a search result, and the size of a cached page, worthwhile.

You can look at code in the sample project in the SDK after you download it, so to keep things simple I've omitted some details here.

For both applications, start by creating a `GoogleSearchService` object:

```
Google.GoogleSearchService s = new
    Google.GoogleSearchService();
```

Estimating return results

With the `GoogleSearchService` object, call doGoogleSearch, passing it a developer key and a search term:

```
Google.GoogleSearchResult r = s.doGoogleSearch(keyBox.Text,
    searchBox.Text, 0, 1, false, "", false, "", "", "");
```

Here's how to use the `GoogleSearchResult` object to display the estimated result count:

```
int estResults = r.estimatedTotalResultsCount;
searchResultLabel.Text = Convert.ToString(estResults);
```

Finding the size of a cached page

To find the size of a cached page, use the GoogleSearchService object to call doGetCachedPage, passing it a developer key and a URL:

```
System.Byte[] bytes = s.doGetCachedPage(keyBox.Text,
    cacheBox.Text);
```

The sample application is written so that the user enters a URL, such as www.google.com, in the TextBox named cacheBox.

The cached page is returned as an array of bytes. The size of the page is the length of the array. You can display size of the page using code like this:

```
cacheResultLabel.Text = Convert.ToString(bytes.Length);
```

Chapter 17

Creating Your Own Search Window with the Google APIs

. . . .

In This Chapter

▶ Creating an advanced search window

▶ Putting together a query string

▶ Returning a window of results

▶ Cycling through multiple results sets

. . . .

*Y*ou can't beat the simplicity of the main Google Web search interface. The Google Advanced Search page also works pretty well. But just suppose that you think you can do better than Google for your own special purposes. Alternatively, you simply want to add Google search functionality to a Windows application. This chapter shows you how to create your own search window using the Google APIs for either of these purposes.

An application with a custom search uses one Google API — doGoogleSearch. (See Chapter 13 and Chapter 16 for more information about the doGoogleSearch method of the Google APIs Web service.)

As I show you in Chapter 16, there's nothing particularly difficult about running a simple Google search using the doGoogleSearch API in a Windows application. However, putting together the query string that the doGoogleSearch API uses can be tricky because you have to have a clear understanding of the Google operators (see Chapter 4 and Chapter 5) to understand how to create a Google query.

The complete project source code is available at `www.braintique.com/ research/`. You can modify it to suit your needs (or add a search feature to a Windows application of your own, using it more or less as it is).

Constructing the Advanced Search Program

Creating a search window with advanced functions means replicating the functionality of Google's own Advanced Search window to some degree (I explain how Google's Advanced Search window works in Chapter 4).

Although it works just fine, some users find the Google Advanced Search window design a little confusing. My search application (called Harold's Google Search) contrasts with the Google Advanced Search window because you enter queries by describing the operators instead of describing the results you want. A few examples of this shift are shown in Table 17-1.

Table 17-1	Changing the Emphasis of a Search
Google Advanced Search	*Harold's Google Search*
With the exact phrase	Literal (quoted) term or phrase
Without the words	Term excluded

Whether you think my way of putting things is better than Google's or not is not really the point (it probably depends on how you think, and, as they say, beauty is in the eye of the beholder). The point is that you *can* change the way an advanced search works by creating your own advanced search window using the APIs.

A real problem with both the regular Google Web search and the Google Advanced Web Search is that there are some operators you simple cannot use without entering them "in code" in the search window. For example, in order to get Google Advanced Web Search to look for synonyms, you have to use the synonym operator (~).

Harold's Google Search window doesn't claim to provide ways to enter all the Google operators, but it does create queries without the user having to enter the operators — because the programmer knows all the operators, the user doesn't have to know them and can just check or uncheck boxes, or select from a list.

You can also use code to provide constraints, making sure that a user's search string follows Google rules. For example, an `allin:` occurrence operator must start a search string, and the search string that begins with an `allin:` operator cannot contain another operator. There's nothing to stop a user from violating this rule when you use Google's Web search (or the Google Advanced Search), with Google perhaps literally searching for the second operator (not the result you intended).

In Harold's Google Search window, users will be hard-pressed to find a way to construct a search that violates the rule against having an operator in a search that began with an `allin:` occurrence operator.

There are three programmatic parts to creating your own Advanced Search window using the Google APIs:

1. **Constructing the query string.**

   The query string is at the heart of a search; it is constructed using the operators and techniques I explain in Chapters 4 and 5.

2. **Calling the doGoogleSearch API.**

   I explain the mechanics of working with the doGoogleSearch API in Chapter 17.

3. **Displaying the search results.**

   There's more to this part of the program than you might think because it involves keeping track of index values of the `resultElement` being displaying. Tracking index values is one of the most error-prone tasks in programming.

Creating an Advanced Search Window

Table 17-2 shows the controls used in Harold's Google Search window and their purpose, more or less in the order they are used (from top to bottom).

Table 17-2	**Controls Used in Harold's Google Search Window**	
Control	*Control Name*	*Purpose*
TextBox	`txtDevKey`	User enters Google developer key (see Chapter 14)
TextBox	`txtTerm`	User enters raw search term
RadioButtons	`rdoUnquote`, `rdoQuoted`	User clicks to choose to search all terms or exact phrase
CheckBox	`chkGlobal`	User clicks to choose whether or not to apply global operator
ListBox	`lstGlobalOps`	User chooses a global operator (one of the `allin:` operators) from drop-down menu

(continued)

Table 17-2 *(continued)*

Control	Control Name	Purpose
CheckBox	`chkApplyOp`	User clicks to choose whether or not to apply operator to single term
ListBox	`lstTermOps`	User chooses an operator to apply to a term from drop-down menu
RadioButtons	`rdoInclude, rdoExclude`	User clicks to determine whether the term is inclusive or exclusive
RadioButtons	`rdoAnd, rdoOr`	User clicks to determine whether words in search phrase are connected with an AND (the default) or an OR
Button	`btnAddTerm`	User clicks to add term to search string
TextBox	`txtSearchString`	User adds terms to this TextBox, which is used for the Google query when the search is launched
Button	`btnClear`	User clicks to clear the search string
Button	`btnSearch`	User clicks to launch the Google search using `txtSearchString`

To add the operators themselves to the ListBox controls used to select an operator, I used the Visual Studio Properties window and String Collection Editor, shown in Figure 17-1.

Figure 17-1: Adding the `allin:` operators to a ListBox control.

Alternatively, you can add the text corresponding to `ListBox` items in code, using methods of the Items collection associated with each `ListBox` control.

Here's how Harold's Google Search window works:

1. **Enter your Google developer key in the text box at the top of the window (see Chapter 14).**

2. **In the Create Your Search section, enter a "raw" search term or phrase.**

   A raw search term is just a word or phrase (such as *ambidextrous scallywags*) without any operators included.

3. **To search exactly for the phrase you have entered, select the Literal (Quoted) Term or Phrase radio button.**

   This searches for an exact phrase such as *ambidextrous scallywags.* Instead, if you want to search for both terms with the `AND` operator assumed, select the Unquoted Term or Phrase radio button.

4. **Select the Global Operator check box if you want to add a global operator to the beginning of your search.**

   You can only select this option for the first search term that you enter. For example, *allinurl:research braintique.*

5. **Select the Apply Operator to Term or Phrase check box if you want to add an individual operator to a search term.**

   For example, *~desert.*

6. **In the Term Included or Excluded area, select the Inclusion radio button to include the term in your search.**

   Alternately, if you want to exclude the term from your search, choose the Exclusion radio button.

7. **In the Terms Connected With area, select the AND radio button to use the default `AND` operator to use with this search term.**

   Instead, if want to use the `OR` operator, select the OR radio button.

8. **Click Add Term.**

   The term and the operator(s) you chose appear in the Generated Search String text box at the bottom of Harold's Google Search window.

9. **Repeat Steps 2 through 8 to add another term or phrase to your search.**

   You can add as many terms or phrases as you like up to Google's limit for working with the Google APIs (see Chapter 13).

10. **Click Search.**

    Google searches using the terms and operators that you specified.

If you decide that you want to start a new search, click Clear. Your developer key is not erased, so you don't have to enter that again!

Figure 17-2 shows Harold's Google Search window ready for searching, with a search string created using two modified terms:

```
intitle:enron -inurl:enron
```

The terms are *enron*, entered twice. The first time it is modified using the `intitle:` operator. The second time it is modified by exclusion (`-`) and the `inurl:` operator. In other words, this search finds results that include *enron* in a page title, but that do not have the term *enron* in the page URL. (See Chapter 5 for an explanation of the utility of this particular search pattern.)

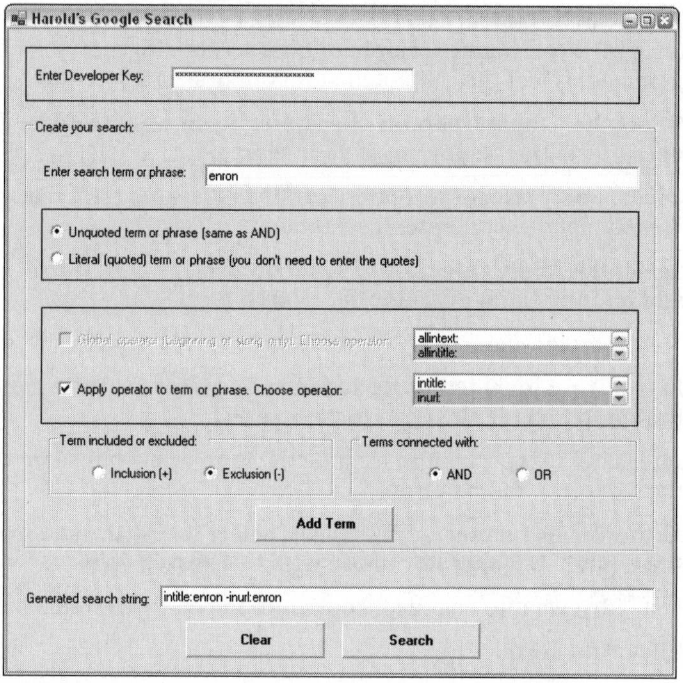

Figure 17-2:
Harold's
Google
Search
window.

Using Code to Create Your Search String

Putting together a search string, or *query*, means adding successive search terms. The first programmatic step towards making the search window functional is to implement the code that adds a search term (the mechanism for creating the search string, when all the search terms have been added).

If you know how to build a search string in code, you are probably 90 percent of the way towards understanding how to build applications with the Google APIs.

To start with, add a click event procedure to `btnAddTerm` (refer to Table 17-2 for information about the controls used to create the Harold's Google Search user interface):

```
private void btnAddTerm_Click(object sender,
    System.EventArgs e)
{
    try
    {
        ...
    }
    catch (Exception excep)
    {
        MessageBox.Show (excep.Message);
    }
}
```

This is where the code will go that adds a term to the search string depending on the user's input.

As a matter of good programming practice, I've added some minimal structured exception handling to the click event.

Here's how to write the code that adds the term to the search string that goes within the try block:

1. **Declare an empty string to hold the new term:**

   ```
   String buildTerm = "";
   ```

2. **Add code to let the user decide whether the term should be quoted.**

   If the term should have quotes, add the contents of the `txtTerm` TextBox with quotes, and if the term should not have quotes, add the text without quotes, like this:

   ```
   if (rdoUnquote.Checked == true)
       buildTerm = txtTerm.Text;
   else
       buildTerm = "\"" + txtTerm.Text + "\"";
   ```

`\"` is an *escape sequence*, which uses the \ control character to mean a double quote.

3. **Add code to let the user decide whether a global occurrence operator should be inserted:**

```
if (chkGlobal.Checked == true && txtSearchString.Text ==
    "")
    buildTerm = lstGlobalOps.SelectedItem.ToString() +
    buildTerm;
```

You can only add a global occurrence operator at the beginning of a search string, so you need to make sure that the program checks to make sure that the string is empty before adding the global occurrence operator.

4. **Add code to let the user select individual operators:**

```
if (chkApplyOp.Checked == true)
{
    if (lstTermOps.SelectedIndex == 0 )
        buildTerm = "~" + buildTerm;
    else
        buildTerm = lstTermOps.SelectedItem.ToString() +
            buildTerm;
}
```

Your code must specially check for the synonym operator, and add a ~ if it has been selected, because the operator is written out — *synonym(~)* — for better comprehension in the ListBox. The rest of the operators appear in the ListBox just as they're used in a search string, so nothing special needs to be done with them.

5. **To let the user select an exclusion operator (-), add the following code:**

```
if (rdoExclude.Checked == true)
    buildTerm = "-" + buildTerm;
```

6. **Add code to let the user select the OR connector:**

```
if (txtSearchString.Text != "")
    if (rdoOr.Checked == true)
        buildTerm = " OR " + buildTerm;
    else
        buildTerm = " " + buildTerm;
```

This code adds the OR connector before the search term, provided that it is not the first term.

7. **Add code to let the user enter another search term:**

```
if (txtTerm.Text != "")
{
    txtSearchString.Text += buildTerm;
    buildTerm = "";
    txtTerm.Text = "";
    chkGlobal.Enabled = false;
}
```

This code checks to make sure the term is not empty, and then adds the term to the search string. In addition, it clears the variable and TextBox holding the term so that another term can be entered. Finally, it disables the chkGlobal CheckBox control so that a global operator cannot now be applied to the search string.

Because a search term has been added to the search string, the user can now add a subsequent term to the search string containing a global operator. This constraint is accomplished by disabling the chkGlobal CheckBox control both when a term is added to a string, and in the CheckChanged event of the CheckBox control:

```csharp
private void chkGlobal_CheckedChanged(object sender,
    System.EventArgs e)
{
    if (chkGlobal.Checked == true
        && txtSearchString.Text == "")
    {
        chkApplyOp.Enabled = false;
        rdoAnd.Enabled = false;
        rdoOr.Enabled = false;
    }
    else
    {
        chkApplyOp.Enabled = true;
        rdoAnd.Enabled = true;
        rdoOr.Enabled = true;
    }
}
```

Figure 17-3 shows how this looks to a user.

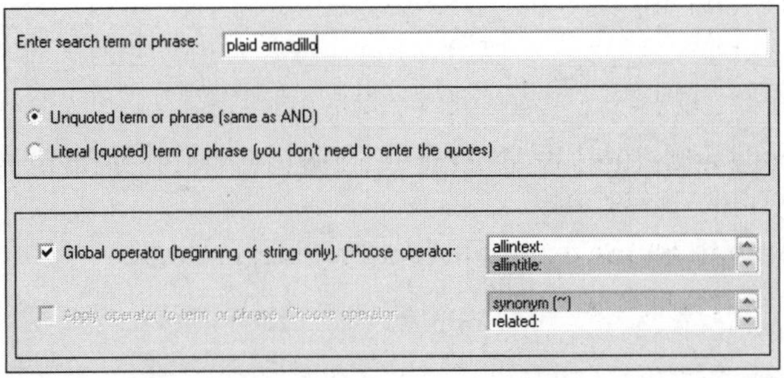

Figure 17-3:
If an
allin:
operator is
selected,
the in:
operators
can't be
added to
the query.

Enter search term or phrase:	plaid armadillo

- Unquoted term or phrase (same as AND)
- Literal (quoted) term or phrase (you don't need to enter the quotes)

- ☑ Global operator (beginning of string only). Choose operator:
  - allintext:
  - allintitle:
- ☐ Apply operator to term or phrase. Choose operator:
  - synonym (~)
  - related:

Listing 17-1 shows the complete click event code for adding a term to the search string.

Listing 17-1:   Adding a Term to a Search String

```csharp
private void btnAddTerm_Click(object sender,
   System.EventArgs e)
{
   try
   {
   // see if it should be quoted
   if (rdoUnquote.Checked == true)
      buildTerm = txtTerm.Text;
   else
      buildTerm = "\"" + txtTerm.Text + "\"";
   //check to add an allin term
   if (chkGlobal.Checked == true &&
      txtSearchString.Text == "")
      buildTerm = lstGlobalOps.SelectedItem.ToString()
         + buildTerm;
   //check for a term operator
   if (chkApplyOp.Checked == true)
   {
      if (lstTermOps.SelectedIndex == 0 )
         buildTerm = "~" + buildTerm;
      else
         buildTerm = lstTermOps.SelectedItem.ToString()
         + buildTerm;
   }
   // check for exclusion
   if (rdoExclude.Checked == true)
      buildTerm = "-" + buildTerm;
   // see if it is an OR (not the first term)
   if (txtSearchString.Text != "")
      if (rdoOr.Checked == true)
         buildTerm = " OR " + buildTerm;
      else
         buildTerm = " " + buildTerm;
   if (txtTerm.Text != "")
   {
      txtSearchString.Text += buildTerm;
      buildTerm = "";
      txtTerm.Text = "";
      chkGlobal.Enabled = false;
   }
   }
   catch (Exception excep)
   {
      MessageBox.Show (excep.Message);
   }
}
```

Calling the Google APIs

After you create a search string by adding one or more terms, you need to do the following:

1. Create an instance of the Google APIs Web service.

2. Call the doGoogleSearch Web method (or API).

I explain the mechanics of this process in Chapter 16.

In Harold's Google Search, I decided to separate the creation of the Web service instance from calling and displaying the results set. I did this so that I can reuse the code that calls the doGoogleSearch API and displays the results generally — and not just for the first results set of a search.

The code that is processed when the user clicks the btnSearch Button creates the instance of the Web service and calls the ShowResults generalized procedure, passing it a value for the starting return result, the developer key, and the search string (also called a query or query string) that the user has created:

```
public Google.GoogleSearchService s;
public int beginResultPage = 0;
public string q;
...
private void btnSearch_Click(object sender,
    System.EventArgs e)
{
    try
    {
        // Create a Google Search object
        s = new Google.GoogleSearchService();
        q = this.txtSearchString.Text;
        showResults(this.beginResultPage,
            this.txtDevKey.Text, q);
    }
    catch (Exception excep)
    {
        MessageBox.Show (excep.Message);
    }
}
```

TECHNICAL STUFF

Class communications

The variables used to store the Google Web service (s), the starting return value (begin ResultPage), and the query string (q) are all declared at the form class level as Public variables. This means that these variables

✔ Are accessible from any procedure within the class because of the declaration at the form class level

✔ Are also accessible, provided the code knows the instance of the form class, from other classes besides the form class because of the Public access control keyword

✔ Can be used to communicate information between instances of the form class and instances of other classes

An alternative approach to communicating information between instances of classes is to use Property procedures. From the viewpoint of sound code construction, this is the best approach because Property procedures allow the programmer to control access so that information can't be inappropriately modified. Using Property procedures adds a layer of complexity, and there's no real need to perform validation in Harold's Google search, so I've opted here for the simpler approach of using public variables to hold information that will be used for communication between class instances.

You can find more information about the best ways to engineer inter-form class communications in C# at www.braintique.com/csharp/.

Displaying a Results Set

To display the results set, you need:

  ✔ A form that displays the results (ResultsForm)
  ✔ The code that calls the doGoogleSearch API
  ✔ The code that populates the ResultsForm

The following sections tell you what you need to know to create the ResultsForm, call the doGoogleSearch API, and display the results of the search to the user.

Creating the form

To create the form for displaying the results, add a new form to the project and change its name to ResultsForm.

Next, add a RichTextBox control for displaying the search results. You also need to add Prev, Save, and Next buttons. (I show you how to add code to the

Save button in "Saving search results" and how to implement navigation through search results sets using the Next and Prev buttons in "Cycling through Multiple Results.")

The results window, based on the `ResultsForm` form, with an initial set of search returns, is shown in Figure 17-4.

Your application won't produce results like those shown in Figure 17-4 until you add the code that calls the doGoogleSearch API and displays the results. The doGoogleSearch API returns a maximum of ten of the results for a search each time it is called.

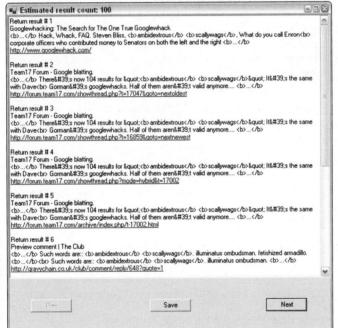

Figure 17-4:
The first
ten results
returned are
displayed.

Calling the doGoogleSearch API

As a preliminary activity, with the `ResultsForm` class, you should create two variables. I've named one variable `SearchForm` and the other `elementCount`. Here's what they do:

- ✔ `SearchForm` is a reference to Harold's Google Search window form so that its variables and methods can be used from the `ResultsForm` class.

- ✔ `elementCount` stores the actual number of returned results (members of the `resultElement` array).

Here are the declarations in `ResultsForm` for these two variables:

```
public Form1 SearchForm;
public int elementCount = 0;
```

Here's the framework for the `ShowResults` method in the `Form1` class (it takes the starting return result, a developer key, and the query string as arguments):

```
public void showResults(int beginResultPage, string
          DeveloperKey, string q)
{
   try
   {
      ...
   }
   catch (System.Web.Services.Protocols.SoapException ex)
   {
      MessageBox.Show(ex.Message);
   }
   catch (Exception ex)
   {
      MessageBox.Show (ex.Message);
   }
}
```

In the preceding code, I have made a point of catching any SOAP exceptions separately in the structured exception processing. This way, if there is a problem with calling the doGoogleSearch API, the user knows it right away.

Here's calling the doGoogleSearch API within that framework:

```
Google.GoogleSearchResult r = s.doGoogleSearch (DeveloperKey,
     q, beginResultPage, 10 , false, "", false, "", "", "");
```

See Chapter 16 for an explanation of the mechanics of calling the doGoogle-Search API.

Displaying search results

To display the first set of search results, create an instance of `ResultsForm`:

```
ResultsForm X = new ResultsForm();
```

Save a reference to the current form in the new form instance:

```
X.SearchForm = this;
```

Display the estimated total results for the search in the caption bar of the `ResultsForm` instance (using the return value of the doGoogleSearch API):

```
X.Text = "Estimated result count: " +
    r.estimatedTotalResultsCount.ToString();
```

Find out how many results have been returned for display, using the Length property of the `resultElements` array returned by the doGoogleSearch API, and store the value in the `elementCount` variable of the `ResultsForm` instance:

```
int j = r.resultElements.Length;
X.elementCount = j;
```

If there are no results to be displayed, you need to make sure that your application sends the `ResultsForm` instance an appropriate message to be displayed to the user:

```
if (j == 0 )
{
    X.richTextBox1.Text += "Harold's Google search sez:" +
        "\r";
    X.richTextBox1.Text +=
        "Sorry, no search results to display!";
}
```

If there are no search results to return, the preceding code generates a message for users like the one shown in Figure 17-5.

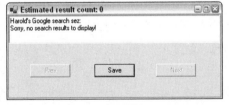

Figure 17-5:
There are
no matches
for this
search.

On the other hand, if there are results to be displayed, then the program needs to cycle through the `resultsElements` array and display the number of each element, and its properties, using the title, snippet, and URL properties of each element. Here's the code that does that:

```
for (int i = 0; i < j; i++)
{
    if (r.resultElements[i] != null)
    {
        X.richTextBox1.Text += "Return result # " +
            (beginResultPage + i + 1).ToString() + "\r";
        X.richTextBox1.Text +=
            r.resultElements[i].title + "\r";
        X.richTextBox1.Text +=
```

```
            r.resultElements[i].snippet + "\r";
        X.richTextBox1.Text += r.resultElements[i].URL
            + "\r\r";
    }
}
```

The return result number of each element is the starting result for the set, plus the number in the array for the element plus 1. The 1 offset is needed because the `returnElements` array is zero-based (meaning it goes from 0 to its length minus 1).

The `\r` symbol is a special control character that means carriage return.

Finally, to show the instance of the `ResultsForm`, call the `Show` method of the results form instance:

```
X.Show();
```

Listing 17-2 shows the complete code for displaying a results set.

Listing 17-2: Displaying a Search Results Set

```
public void showResults(int beginResultPage, string
        DeveloperKey, string q)
{
    try
    {
        Google.GoogleSearchResult r =
            s.doGoogleSearch(DeveloperKey, q,
            beginResultPage, 10 , false, "", false, "", "", "");
        ResultsForm X = new ResultsForm();
        X.SearchForm = this;
        X.Text = "Estimated result count: " +
            r.estimatedTotalResultsCount.ToString();
        int j = r.resultElements.Length;
        X.elementCount = j;
        if (j == 0 )
        {
            X.richTextBox1.Text += "Harold's Google search sez:"
                + "\r";
            X.richTextBox1.Text += "Sorry, no search results to
                display!";
        }
        else
        {
            for (int i = 0; i < j; i++)
            {
                if (r.resultElements[i] != null)
                {
                    X.richTextBox1.Text += "Return result # " +
                        (beginResultPage + i + 1).ToString() +
```

```
                              "\r";
                 X.richTextBox1.Text +=
                     r.resultElements[i].title + "\r";
                 X.richTextBox1.Text +=
                     r.resultElements[i].snippet + "\r";
                 X.richTextBox1.Text += r.resultElements[i].URL
                     + "\r\r";
             }
         }
     }
     X.Show();
 }
 catch (System.Web.Services.Protocols.SoapException ex)
 {
     MessageBox.Show(ex.Message);
 }
 catch (Exception ex)
 {
     MessageBox.Show (ex.Message);
 }
}
```

Saving search results

A nifty feature to add to any research tool is an easy way to save search results. I've implemented this in the ResultsForm for Harold's Google Search by using the functionality built into the RichTextBox control. I've also added a SaveFileDialog common dialog control to the ResultsForm.

This code manually saves a results set as a rich text file (RTF file).

Here's the code I added to the ResultsForm Save button's click event in Harold's Google Search that lets the user save a results set:

```
private void btnSave_Click(object sender, System.EventArgs e)
{
    saveFileDialog1.InitialDirectory =
        Application.ExecutablePath;
    saveFileDialog1.DefaultExt = ".rtf";
    saveFileDialog1.FileName = "harold";
    saveFileDialog1.Filter =
      "Rich Text Files (*.rtf) | *.rtf|All files (*.*) | *.*";
    saveFileDialog1.ShowDialog()
    richTextBox1.SaveFile(saveFileDialog1.FileName);
}
```

When the user clicks the Save button on the results form, the standard common dialog box for choosing a filename and location appears (see Figure 17-6).

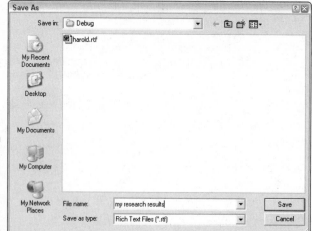

Figure 17-6:
You can
save your
research
results.

By clicking the Save button, a file containing the results set information is saved in the location designated by the user.

Cycling through Multiple Results

There are some programmatic issues involved in cycling through Google search results because these results are returned ten at a time (up to the Google API maximum of 1,000 results per day). In order to display the right results set, you need to keep track of what results have already been returned and displayed.

The generalized `DisplayResults` method shows the first ten results, but can easily be used to display any ten results for a given Google search (for example, search results 991–1,000).

In Harold's Google Search, the click event procedures associated with the Next and Prev buttons on the `ResultsForm` are used to move through results sets.

Here's the code to display the next ten results of a search:

```
private void btnNext_Click(object sender, System.EventArgs e)
{
    SearchForm.beginResultPage += 10;
    int newPageStart = SearchForm.beginResultPage;
    SearchForm.showResults(newPageStart,
        SearchForm.txtDevKey.Text, SearchForm.q);
    this.Hide();
}
```

The starting search element is upped by ten (because ten results are returned per call to the doGoogleSearch API, and displayed using a ResultsForm window). The showResults method is called, and passed the new starting value, along with the developer key and the query. Finally, the current instance of the ResultsForm is hidden (so that only one instance of the form is displayed at a time).

Going backwards through the search results works in the same way, except that ten is subtracted rather than added:

```
private void btnPrev_Click(object sender, System.EventArgs e)
{
    SearchForm.beginResultPage -= 10;
    int newPageStart = SearchForm.beginResultPage;
    SearchForm.showResults(newPageStart,
        SearchForm.txtDevKey.Text, SearchForm.q);
    this.Hide();
}
```

You should disable the Next button when there are no more results to display (as shown in Figure 17-7).

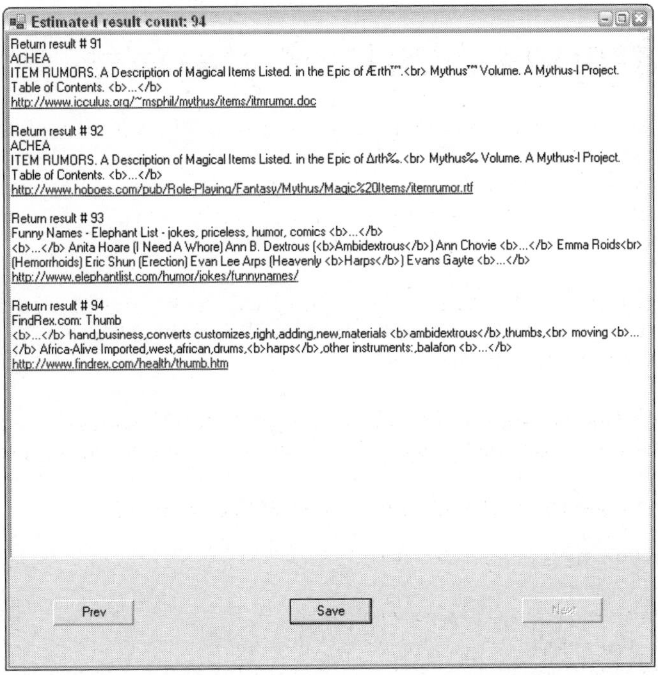

Figure 17-7:
If there are no more search results, the Next button is disabled.

Similarly, you should disable the Prev button when the first results set — the zero element of the `resultsElement` array — is displayed.

The code that disables the Next and Prev buttons is placed in the `ResultsForm` instance's `Activated` event:

```
private void ResultsForm_Activated(object sender,
    System.EventArgs e)
{
    if (SearchForm.beginResultPage >= 10)
        btnPrev.Enabled = true;
    else
        btnPrev.Enabled = false;
    if (this.elementCount >= 10)
        btnNext.Enabled = true;
    else
        btnNext.Enabled = false;
}
```

Chapter 18

Understanding and Following Trends

Webmasters and others — for example, people involved in marketing and product development — are interested in the sheer number of results for keyword (and phrase) searches. These search results provide information on how important keywords (and the topics they represent) are within Google's index servers. (I explain in Chapter 11 how index servers are used within Google's technology as a whole.) The reality is that the estimated number of hits for popular keywords varies with time; sometimes the number varies a great deal in surprisingly short amounts of time. This information can tell you whether a topic (represented by the keyword) is waxing or waning in popularity, as well as how important the topic is.

This chapter explains how to use the doGoogleSearch API to get an estimated hit count for one or more keywords. I also show you how to track changing keyword-hit values over time.

Following the Spirit of the Times

Google makes available a great deal of information about interesting user trends on its Zeitgeist — Zeitgeist means roughly "spirit of the times" — page, located at `www.google.com/press/zeitgeist.html` and shown in Figure 18-1.

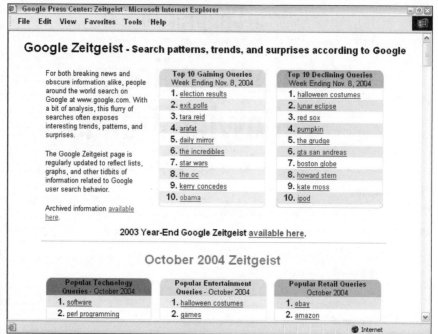

Figure 18-1:
The Google
"spirit of the
times" page.

The Zeitgeist page shows ranking by user actions; for example, it shows how popular searches for *Julia Roberts* were. It does not provide hit information (the number of times *Julia Roberts* appears in Web pages), and it doesn't actually list the number of times the phrase *Julia Roberts* was searched.

If you want up-to-date information, you won't find it on the Zeitgeist page. Information is typically two or three weeks old before it is posted. You never know what you're going to find on the Zeitgeist page. For example, at year's end you might find an interactive timeline for the year created in Macromedia Flash.

The information on the Zeitgeist page is fascinating. It's also idiosyncratic, dated, and incomplete. It's an interesting factoid (from October, 2004) that dragons are the second-most popular animals searched for using Google (after dogs), but dragons may be of no particular interest to you, your Web site, or your research.

Say you've been asked to follow the popularity of a specific television program as part of your research. If you need to have up-to-the-moment information about topics not covered on the Zeitgeist page, you may have to craft your own application using the Google APIs.

This application is particularly useful for topics that are popular enough to generate many hits. If you're researching something relatively obscure, you might not get much data.

To create a Zeitgeist-like application, you can pretty much assume that the number of search results (or *hits*) from Google's indexing of the Web is representative of the entire Web. This is more or less true, but as I discuss in Chapters 10 and 11, some research information can't be found in Google.

The Zeitgeist page bases its assessment of popularity primarily on the number of times users enter a particular keyword or term in the Google Web search box. This kind of comparative popularity of search terms is valuable information to Webmasters because it helps them relatively rank the importance of topics and to plan Web sites that will draw traffic.

A related measurement, the number of search results — or *hits* — for a keyword or phrase, is also important to trend watchers, people involved in marketing and market research, and those responsible for new product development. Essentially, a hit equals a Web page (that contains the keyword). Roughly, the more Web pages that have been put up with a given keyword, the more important the topic represented by that keyword is to people. This is particularly true with trendy topics, relating to popular culture, news events, or the mass psyche.

Using the APIs, you can fairly easily create a research application that tracks changing hit values over time.

TIP

Trend-tracking resources on the Web

If your research leads you to track popular trends, you may find these trend-tracking Web resources useful:

- BlogPulse (www.blogpulse.com) provides automated tools for tracking trends within the world of blogging.

- DailyCandy (www.dailycandy.com) is an e-mail newsletter focusing on fashion and food trends, with an emphasis on "hipness." DailyCandy comes in a national edition and several regional editions.

- Daypop (www.daypop.com/top) provides lists of the hottest blogging topics.

- Trendcentral (www.trendcentral.com) is a Web site and e-mail newsletter aimed

at tracking, er, trends. It focuses on lifestyles, technology, and entertainment, and it primarily covers youth markets.

- Trendwatching.com (www.trendwatching.com) is a site and e-mail newsletter primarily focused on international business trends; it is aimed at business executives and others involved in marketing.

- Yahoo! Buzz (http://buzz.yahoo.com) provides information about (and some analysis of) the top Yahoo! searches.

- MSN Search (www.imagine-msn.com/insider/) provides a flashy and fun display of what people are looking for on MSN.

Creating a User Interface to Track Results

To create an application that tracks hits on a per-keyword basis, start up Visual Studio .NET and create a new Windows Application project; in this chapter I have chosen the C# language, although you are free to rewrite the code in Visual Basic .NET if you prefer. You can use the default Windows form to create a user interface.

Figure 18-2 shows the controls added to the form in its designer. Table 18-1 shows the controls added to the form and used to track search result hits, in order from top to bottom (as they are encountered by the user).

Figure 18-2:
The controls used for tracking hits positioned on the form in design mode.

Table 18-1	Controls Used for Tracking Hits		
Type of Control	*Control Name*	*Purpose*	*Default Value*
TextBox	txtDevKey	Stores developer key	Your developer key
TextBox	txtKeywords	User enters keywords	n/a

Type of Control	Control Name	Purpose	Default Value
TextBox	`txtInterval`	User enters timer interval in minutes	10 minutes
Button	`btnStart`	Starts the keyword lookup	n/a
Button	`btnStop`	Stops time-based keyword lookup	n/a
Button	`btnClear`	Clears the results box, and sets internal structures to null	n/a
TextBox	`txtResults`	Shows hit count results	n/a

Returning the Estimated Hits for a Keyword

Before you can return the estimated hit counts for a keyword, you need to add a Web reference to the Google APIs Web service to your application. I explain the mechanics of this process in Chapter 16.

After you've added a Web reference to the Google APIs Web service, I recommend that you change the name of the class created by Visual Studio .NET and used to communicate with the Web service to `Google` (as I explain in Chapter 16).

In the Code Editor, at the form class level — right after the main function's closing brace so they're available throughout the class as class-member variables — declare variables for the Google Web service class and for the doGoogleSearch Web API (also called a Web method):

```
private Google.GoogleSearchService s;
private Google.GoogleSearchResult r;
```

Next, with the Google APIs Web service added to your project and form-level variables declared, double-click the `btnStart` control to create a click event procedure for the Button control:

```
private void btnStart_Click(object sender,
    System.EventArgs e)
{
    ...
}
```

You will be inserting lines of code into this procedure, as shown in Listing 18-1. Within the procedure, create an instance of the Web service class:

```
s = new Google.GoogleSearchService();
```

Follow this line with a call to the doGoogleSearch method, passing it the developer key, the search term, and just looking for one actual result:

```
Google.GoogleSearchResult r = s.doGoogleSearch
    (txtDevKey.Text, txtKeywords.Text, 0, 1 , false, "",
    false, "", "", "");
```

You can find more information on using the doGoogleSearch API in Chapters 13, 16, and 17.

Next, write code that shows a message box displaying the estimated result count from the keyword search (if you run this code after having entered a keyword, a message like that shown in Figure 18-3 displays):

```
MessageBox.Show("Estimated Results: " +
    r.estimatedTotalResultsCount.ToString(),
    this.Text,System.Windows.Forms.MessageBoxButtons.OK,
    System.Windows.Forms.MessageBoxIcon.Information);
```

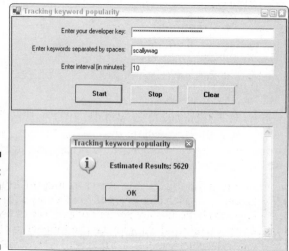

Figure 18-3:
Search
results for
a single
keyword.

As a matter of good practice, you should add some exception handling to your code. Listing 18-1 shows you what the procedure looks like with all your additions, including some exception handling.

Listing 18-1: Getting Estimated Hits for a Keyword

```
private void btnStart_Click(object sender,
    System.EventArgs e)
{
    try
    {
        s = new Google.GoogleSearchService();
        Google.GoogleSearchResult r = s.doGoogleSearch
            (txtDevKey.Text, txtKeywords.Text, 0, 1 , false, "",
            false, "", "", "");
        MessageBox.Show("Estimated Results: " +
            r.estimatedTotalResultsCount.ToString(),
            this.Text,System.Windows.Forms.MessageBoxButtons.OK,
            System.Windows.Forms.MessageBoxIcon.Information);
    }
    catch (System.Web.Services.Protocols.SoapException ex)
    {
        MessageBox.Show(ex.Message);
    }

    catch (Exception excep)
    {
        MessageBox.Show (excep.Message);
    }
}
```

Getting Multiple Results

Getting the hit count on multiple keywords takes a little more work because you have to parse out the individual keywords — and run the doGoogleSearch method multiple times.

First, declare a string array at the class level to store, one per element, the search terms:

```
string [] strTerms;
```

I've used the Split method of the .NET string object to split the input string into separate keywords, using a space character as the delimiter for the separating. Each separate keyword becomes an element of an array of keywords, strTerms. A doGoogleSearch method can then be run for each element in the strTerms array, beginning with the first (zero-based) element of the array, and using the length property of the array to end at its upper bound.

Here's the code that goes inside the try block of the click event procedure to display multiple search results in the `txtResults` TextBox:

```
string [] strTerms;
char delimiter = ' ';
strTerms = txtKeywords.Text.Split(delimiter);
for (int i = 0; i < strTerms.Length; i++)
{
    Google.GoogleSearchResult r = s.doGoogleSearch
        (txtDevKey.Text, strTerms[i], 0, 1 , false, "", false,
        "", "", "");
    txtResults.Text += strTerms[i] + " : " +
        r.estimatedTotalResultsCount.ToString() + "\r\n";
}
```

The special characters, \r\n, placed at the end of each result as it is displayed, represent a carriage return and line feed, so each result is on a line by itself.

As you can see from Figure 18-4, *Julia Roberts* gets considerably more hits than *Jude Law,* and *eBay* is better represented on the Web than *Reality TV.*

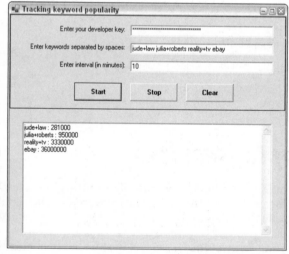

Figure 18-4: Search results with multiple keywords.

Because a space is used as the delimiter to separate terms, if you want to track hits for multiple words, you have to use a plus sign (+) between the words. For example, you enter the search term **Julia+Roberts**. To Google, this represents the default conjunction, and is no different in a typical search for *Julia Roberts* using the Google Search box.

Tracking Results over Time

As Ingrid Bergman said in the movie *Casablanca,* "Play it again, Sam!" In other words, search results are more meaningful, as the song has it, "as time goes by."

If you track results over time, you can understand trends, not just where things stand at a given moment in time. For example, you might be asked to research the popularity of various celebrities for possible product placements. The interesting thing is not how popular the celebrities are today — because there is always a time delay in creating and placing product campaigns — but predicting how popular the celebrity is likely to be in a couple of months. To provide a "guesstimate" about this, you should understand the trend of each celebrity's popularity.

To track results over time, the first step is to add a Timer component to your form as shown in Figure 18-5.

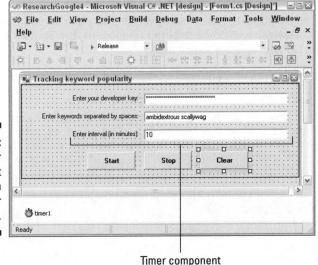

Figure 18-5: The timer component on the Form Designer tray.

Timer component

When the Timer component is added, it appears on the tray below the form rather on the form itself (and never appears visibly to the user of an application).

Choose View⇨Properties Window to open the Properties window. In the Properties window, set the Enabled property of the Timer to false by selecting Enabled in the left-hand column and choosing false from the drop-down menu in the right-hand column. Now the code in the Tick event of the Timer won't be executed until the program is ready for it, when your program changes the Enabled property to true.

Set the Interval property of the Timer to 60000. Because the Timer Interval property is expressed in milliseconds, 60000 is equal to 10 minutes and corresponds to the default value in the txtInterval control.

If you are going to the trouble of storing values over time, I recommend also finding a way to somehow keep those values. I've created a class, TimeValue Trio, which I use to store hit, time, and date information for each keyword.

Class instances get added to an ArrayList structure, which you can loop through to get to all keyword, time, and hit information.

The logic of the process is that the structures are created, and initial hit information added, the first time the user clicks the Start button. After this happens, the code enables the timer component by setting its Enabled property to true, and setting its Interval property to the value entered into the txtInterval control. Each time the interval elapses, the Timer's Tick event fires, and the Google APIs are called again.

This code is shown in Listing 18-2.

Listing 18-2:   Storing Hit Results over Time

```
private Google.GoogleSearchService s;
private Google.GoogleSearchResult r;
string [] strTerms;
private ArrayList al;

public class TimeValueTrio
{
    public string keyWord;
    public string resultCount;
    public string dateStr;
    public string timeStr;
}
...
private void btnStart_Click(object sender,
    System.EventArgs e)
{
    try
    {
        s = new Google.GoogleSearchService();
        char delimiter = ' ';
        strTerms = txtKeywords.Text.Split(delimiter);
```

```
        al = new ArrayList();
        for (int i = 0; i < strTerms.Length; i++)
        {
            r  = s.doGoogleSearch(txtDevKey.Text, strTerms[i],
                0, 1 , false, "", false, "", "", "");
            TimeValueTrio tvt = new TimeValueTrio();
            tvt.resultCount =
                r.estimatedTotalResultsCount.ToString();
            tvt.timeStr = DateTime.Now.ToShortTimeString();
            tvt.dateStr = DateTime.Now.ToShortDateString();
            tvt.keyWord = strTerms[i];
            al.Add (tvt);
            txtResults.Text += tvt.keyWord + " " +
                tvt.resultCount + " " + tvt.dateStr+ " " +
                tvt.timeStr + "\r\n";
        }
        timer1.Interval = Convert.ToInt16 (txtInterval.Text)
            * 60000; //convert to minutes
        timer1.Enabled = true;
    }
    catch (System.Web.Services.Protocols.SoapException ex)
    {
        MessageBox.Show(ex.Message);
    }
        catch (Exception excep)
    {
        MessageBox.Show (excep.Message);
    }
}

private void timer1_Tick(object sender, System.EventArgs e)
{
    try
    {
        for (int i = 0; i < strTerms.Length; i++)
        {
            r  = s.doGoogleSearch(txtDevKey.Text, strTerms[i],
                0, 1 , false, "", false, "", "", "");
            TimeValueTrio tvt = new TimeValueTrio();
            tvt.resultCount =
                r.estimatedTotalResultsCount.ToString();
            tvt.timeStr = DateTime.Now.ToShortTimeString();
            tvt.dateStr = DateTime.Now.ToShortDateString();
            tvt.keyWord = strTerms[i];
            al.Add (tvt);
            txtResults.Text += tvt.keyWord + " " +
                tvt.resultCount + " " + tvt.dateStr+ " " +
                tvt.timeStr + "\r\n";
        }
    }
    catch (System.Web.Services.Protocols.SoapException ex)
    {
```

(continued)

Listing 18-2 *(continued)*

```
        MessageBox.Show(ex.Message);
    }
    catch (Exception excep)
    {
        MessageBox.Show (excep.Message);
    }
}
```

You can't have that Timer running forever! The Enabled property of the Timer component needs to be set to false in the btnStop click event:

```
private void btnStop_Click(object sender, System.EventArgs e)
{
    timer1.Enabled = false;
}
```

Here's the code that clears the TextBox controls and resets the structures used for storing times and values, placed in the click event procedure associated with the btnClear Button:

```
private void btnClear_Click(object sender,
    System.EventArgs e)
{
    timer1.Enabled = false;
    txtResults.Text = "";
    txtInterval.Text = "10";
    txtKeywords.Text = "";
    al = null;
    strTerms = null;
}
```

Displaying Results

The code examples in "Tracking Results over Time" display hit values with a time stamp as these values were generated, but because this information is stored in code, displaying the results in real time isn't necessary.

You could, instead, simply loop through the ArrayList structure, and display the values of each of the elements, with code like this:

```
foreach (TimeValueTrio tvt in al)
{
    txtResults.Text += tvt.keyWord + " " + tvt.resultCount +
    " " + tvt.dateStr+ " " + tvt.timeStr + "\r\n";
}
```

Using either the real-time display or this kind of display procedure, running the program, entering some search terms, and letting it do its thing is pretty easy. Your results look a little something like those shown in Figure 18-6.

Tracking keyword popularity

Enter your developer key: ******************************

Enter keywords separated by spaces: julia+roberts jude+law reality+tv ebay

Enter interval (in minutes): 10

[Start]   [Stop]   [Clear]

```
julia+roberts 946000 11/30/2004 12:30 PM
jude+law 277000 11/30/2004 12:30 PM
reality+tv 3350000 11/30/2004 12:30 PM
ebay 35900000 11/30/2004 12:30 PM
julia+roberts 947000 11/30/2004 12:40 PM
jude+law 281000 11/30/2004 12:40 PM
reality+tv 3330000 11/30/2004 12:40 PM
ebay 36000000 11/30/2004 12:40 PM
julia+roberts 950000 11/30/2004 12:50 PM
jude+law 282000 11/30/2004 12:50 PM
reality+tv 3330000 11/30/2004 12:50 PM
ebay 36000000 11/30/2004 12:50 PM
julia+roberts 950000 11/30/2004 1:00 PM
jude+law 281000 11/30/2004 1:00 PM
```

Figure 18-6: Set up the application to display shifting results over time.

If you let the program track results over time (or if you take a close look at Figure 18-6), eventually you'll come to some conclusions:

- ✔ This kind of application makes it easy to use up the 1,000 searches a day you get with your developer key.

- ✔ Mostly, you need to use a pretty big time interval to see variations in hit results because it takes people even in the statistical aggregate time to take down and put up Web pages.

- ✔ With popular search terms, you can see some surprisingly big variations even in five- or ten-minute intervals.

- ✔ To get a solid sense of trends, you need to run this program for several days, months, or even years.

If tracking search hits over time is central to your research, the best way to get the most out of the information is to add the generated data to a database. You can update the database periodically and use its contents for further analysis.

To learn more about working with databases in Visual Studio .NET, choose Help⇨Search and look up the topic *Database Development and Visual Database Tools.*

If you opt to use a spreadsheet application, such as Microsoft Excel, to analyze and manipulate the data, you can find more information about how to integrate Microsoft Excel with a .NET Windows application that uses the Google APIs by choosing Help⇨Search and looking up the topic *Excel.*

Part V
The Part of Tens

The 5th Wave   By Rich Tennant

"This is amazing. You can stop looking for Derek. According to a Google search I did, he's hiding behind the dryer in the basement."

In this part . . .

This part contains two chapters, each listing ten things that are useful, fun, or even scary! (I'm just kidding about the scary part, of course.)

Chapter 19 tells you about Web sites that help you navigate the resources of Google or just plain become a more effective researcher. You'll find most of these sites really useful — but I have thrown in one or two that are gosh-darn silly and fun.

In Chapter 20, you can find information about tools that have been built using the Google Web APIs. Of course, I've included the Web addresses of these tools so that you can try them out for yourself. You may find some of these tools useful (I certainly have!) You'll find all of them inspirational. The software I tell you about in Chapter 20 shows you what can be done with the APIs — and may give you ideas about creating your own great research tools!

Chapter 19

Ten (Mostly Really Useful) Google Research Resources

· ·

In This Chapter

▶ CrossRef Search

▶ Enterprise Search Center

▶ Everything Google

▶ Google Zeitgeist

▶ Googlefight

▶ Googlewhack

▶ Open Directory Project Help Central

▶ PageRank Explained

▶ ResearchBuzz!

▶ TouchGraph GoogleBrowser

· ·

*E*xperienced researchers know that you can never have too much knowledge and understanding — particularly when it comes to something like Google. So this chapter points you to resources on the Web that help you use Google better for research, become a better researcher . . . or simply have fun with Google!

CrossRef Search

CrossRef Search, `www.iop.org/EJ/search_crossref`, harnesses the power of the Google search engine in cooperation with content from 29 peer-reviewed scholarly publications. You can find a list of the participating publishers at `www.crossref.org/crossrefsearch.html`.

This is a pilot program, with the hope of eventually extending it to include the more than 650 academic and scholarly publishers and societies that are the members of the not-for-profit CrossRef organization. CrossRef's goal is to create a scholarly citation and linking mechanism that can be generalized to work with all scholarly and academic content.

The CrossRef program provides the underlying taxonomy and content used by Google Scholar, an academic and scholarly search feature currently offered by Google (see Chapter 1).

Here's how it works. You visit the CrossRef site and conduct a Google-powered search using the CrossRef Search box. You are never bothered with a lot of Internet junk because only the academic and scholarly publications participating in the pilot program are included in the results. The result links are to academic and scholarly literature.

Enterprise Search Center

Enterprise Search Center, `www.enterprisesearchcenter.com/default.asp`, is an information repository focused — as the name implies — on enterprise searches, particularly the needs and concerns of information technology professionals.

Content categories provided by the Enterprise Search Center include

- ✔ News about search, such as news about search engine companies
- ✔ Enterprise search case studies, for example, information about how the FBI conducts searches
- ✔ Search technology analysis, for example, information about how to create a dynamic (or changing) taxonomy
- ✔ Tips and expert opinions related to searching, for example, analysis of natural language search tools and their effectiveness

The Enterprise Search Center provides a treasure trove of content related to enterprise searches, searching, and search technology.

Everything Google

Everything Google, `http://googlefan.com/modules/Everything/`, is a great page of links that can help you quickly find the Google resources you need. You can think of this as a kind of a non-Google-sponsored site map of Google info and resources. Link categories include Google:

> ✔ Searching
>
> ✔ The Company
>
> ✔ Fun
>
> ✔ Customization
>
> ✔ Tools
>
> ✔ For Webmasters
>
> ✔ Search Engine Optimization (SEO)

Google Zeitgeist

The Google Zeitgeist page, www.google.com/press/zeitgeist.html, is maintained by Google and updated weekly based on Google users' search behavior.

Zeitgeist uses graphs, lists, and tidbits of information to shed light on interesting (and sometimes surprising) search trends and patterns.

You can view archived Google Zeitgeist information week-by-week, going back to 2001 when Google started the page. Google Zeitgeist also compiles interesting — and fun — year-end results as well.

Zeitgeist is great fun and provides insights and impressions about the changing times. For more information about Zeitgeist, and to learn how to use the Google APIs to create your own Google trend analysis, see Chapter 18.

Googlefight

Googlefight, www.googlefight.com/, lets you compare the relative number of results for two Google search terms. Although it's a fun game, you can make some interesting observations about Google's behavior if you play with Googlefight. For example, it may be a comment on human psychology that *darth vader* wins a Googlefight against *luke skywalker* and that *evil* triumphs over *good*. This site is also a reminder that the Web, and Google search results, tend to look towards sensationalism, er, the dark side.

Googlefight is constructed using client-side scripting, explained in Chapter 5 and Chapter 13.

Googlewhack

A *googlewhack* is a Google search that produces exactly one result (remember, most searches result in millions of listings). Googlewhack, `www.google whack.com/`, is a site devoted to googlewhacks and googlewhacking. The site has some rules: Most significantly, you cannot use a quoted search term because it is just too easy to googlewhack with a literal phrase.

In addition, terms used in a googlewhack must exist in the dictionary; specifically, they must be linked by Google to Answers.com in the search results. See `www.googlewhack.com/rules.htm` for the complete rules of googlewhacking.

Some of the all-time great googlewhacks are

- *ambidextrous scallywags*
- *illuminatus ombudsman*
- *nigritude ultramarine*
- *squirreling dervishes*
- *assonant octosyllable*
- *fetishized armadillo*

As one of my friends puts it, "Googlewhacking is addictive, and a great way to waste time spent at the office." In addition, googlewhacking has become a cultural phenomenon, with artists exhibiting works all of whose titles are googlewhacks, media coverage of googlewhacks, theatrical productions based on googlewhacking, and more.

The most compelling googlewhacks don't retain their googlewhack status for long because of their celebrity status. One-time googlewhacks, like *ambidextrous scallywags,* for example, now get hundreds of Google hits because of their popularity as googlewhacks — an illustration of how quickly Google, and the Web that it indexes, change in response to the actions of its users.

Open Directory Project Help Central

The Open Directory Project (ODP), `http://dmoz.org`, provides the content and taxonomy used in the Google Directory (see Chapter 7 for information about using the Google Directory and Chapter 11 for more about taxonomies).

The ODP is probably the best single source of information on the Web. Its content is classified and vetted by human editors, and ODP aims to be the brains of the Web.

But understanding (and navigating) ODP can be a challenge. A good place to start is the Open Directory Project Help Central, `http://dmoz.org/help/helpmain.html`.

PageRank Explained

PageRank Explained, `www.webworkshop.net/pagerank.html`, provides everything you always wanted to know but were afraid to ask about the Google PageRank algorithm.

In addition to a highly technical explanation of PageRank, which may interest you geeks (you know who you are!) who want to know how Google does its thing, PageRank Explained also provides useful information about maximizing the PageRank of Web pages. This is useful even to researchers who don't maintain Web sites, because it helps to explain the ordering of Google search results.

PageRank also offers tips and examples of various linking scenarios. The PageRank calculator on the site is also fun and useful.

ResearchBuzz!

ResearchBuzz!, `www.researchbuzz.com/`, provides news and information about search engines and research topics.

Written and edited by search engine and research guru and author Tara Calishain, ResearchBuzz is a must-stop for anyone interested in the world of Internet research.

You can also sign up for a daily ResearchBuzz! e-mail newsletter in both free and paid subscription versions.

Tara says that ResearchBuzz! gives frequent updates on search engines and related technologies, providing information about information repositories and Web directories; basically, the site offers information about anything and everything that a reference librarian would find useful to know about research on the Web.

TouchGraph GoogleBrowser

The TouchGraph GoogleBrowser, www.touchgraph.com/TGGoogleBrowser.html, uses the Google APIs to show a visual representation of the links between Web pages and sites. For example, in Figure 19-1, you can see some of the connections between the PayPal and eBay sites, and the various inbound and outbound links to and from these sites.

Oh, what a tangled Web we weave! Understanding the interrelationships between Web pages and Web sites can be difficult, but the TouchGraph GoogleBrowser can make grasping these relationships quickly a little bit easier. Aside from their educational value, some of these graphs are beautiful. If I didn't have to spend my time writing this book, I could open up the TouchGraph GoogleBrowser and spend hours looking at the pictures!

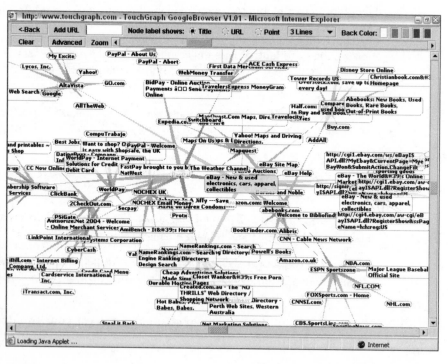

Figure 19-1: PayPal and eBay shown in the TouchGraph Google Browser.

Chapter 20

Ten Tools That Use the Google APIs

This chapter is inspirational and informative. (Yeah! If I do say so myself!) By finding out about ten great applications written using the Google Web APIs, you'll discover some great tools that you can use in your research. Maybe you can even use some of these tools to help build your own research tools. The breadth of what can be done with the Google APIs may take your breath away.

Some of the sites in this section require that you use your own Google developer key (see Chapter 14 for information on how to get one).

Amoebacode

Amoebacode, www.amoebacode.com/index/, is a demonstration project built with the Google Web APIs; it creates an alphabetized index of the text of a Web site. The index creation is automatic after you specify the search terms to use.

The program generates an XML file for all the terms selected for the index and adds search results to the document as they are returned from the Google service. It then builds a set of categories for the index terms (also created in XML format), and creates an HTML page for each of the terms and categories.

The demonstration on the Amoebacode site shows a single alphabetic index of the text of the columns of Bill Simmons (The Sports Guy) on ESPN.com. You can click any hyperlinked letter (say the letter *D*) to see which names and topics appear under the letter D. Want to know what Bill Simmons has to say about Dunkin Donuts?

You can apply this functionality to a variety of research projects and reports. For example, suppose you need an easy way to cross-reference a great deal of material. (Pretrial discovery is one place this comes up often.) If the material has been uploaded to the Web, Amoebacode provides an easy way to create a concordance of important terms.

You can download the complete Java source code for the demonstration project from the Amoebacode site.

Anacubis

Anacubis, `www.anacubis.com/googledemo/google/index.asp`, is a visual search tool powered by the Google Web APIs.

Anacubis shows links between sites (such as a link between PayPal and eBay), or lists similar sites together (such as BN.com and Amazon), or both. It's usually more interesting to try Anacubis on more obscure sites. For example, a site with information about antique typewriters, such as Mechanista, `www.mechanista.com`, is likely to be linked (and similar) to other sites about old machinery. If you are researching antique mechanical collections, you can use Anacubis to find out at a glance (using the first site as the starting place) which other sites are likely to be productive (for example, the Virtual Antique Typewriter Museum, `www.typewritermuseum.org`).

Under the covers, the `related:` operator (explained in Chapter 5) is used to determine which sites are similar.

The primary point of Anacubis is to use a visual display to help you see relationships that might not otherwise be clear. Certainly, I've found some surprisingly similar sites that I might not have paid any attention to otherwise when using this tool. At its simplest level, this tool allows you to easily see which sites are linked together even if there are some degrees of separation. You can see Anacubis in action in Figure 20-1.

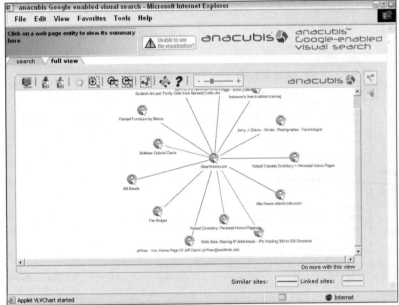

Figure 20-1:
Anacubis
lets you see
linked and
similar sites
visually.

CapeMail

CapeScience has used the Google APIs to create an e-mail interface with the
Google search engine. You can read about it at `http://capescience.`
`capeclear.com/google/`, but CapeMail is really very simple to use:

1. Send an e-mail message to the address `google@capeclear.com`.

2. Put your Google search query in the subject of the e-mail.

3. Pick up the Google response in your e-mail Inbox.

The CapeMail response to the Google query *ambidextrous scallywags* is
shown in Figure 20-2. CapeMail responds to inquiries quite quickly, and is
potentially useful in situations where you have access to e-mail but not the
Web (for example, using a device like a Blackberry).

Flash Search with Google

You can easily use the Google APIs with Macromedia Flash. The advantage of
using the APIs within Flash is that you can add the resulting Flash object inline
to any HTML Web page — such as a blog page. There's no need for additional
programming or server-side access, so long as you have the Flash object.

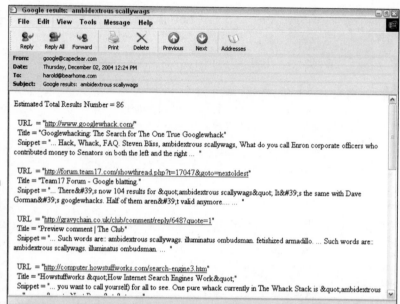

Figure 20-2:
CapeMail
lets you
search
Google
using
e-mail.

To learn more about combining Flash with the Google APIs Web service, see `www.flash-db.com/Google/`. This site provides a nice demo of searching Google using Flash (search results from the demo are shown in Flash in Figure 20-3) and the source code for programming Flash (in the PHP programming language).

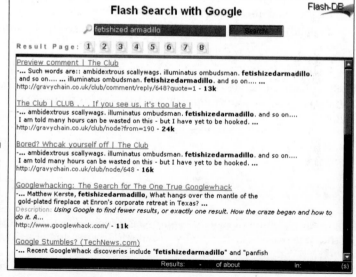

Figure 20-3:
Search
Google
within a
Flash object
using the
APIs.

GARBO, GAPS, and GAWSH

Find *GARBO* — Google API Relation Browsing Outliner — at www.stagger
nation.com/garbo/. GARBO uses the Google APIs to search for pages that
are similar to a given page (used the related: operator) or linked to a page.
You can then follow the relationship by using GARBO to see what pages the
related page has a relationship with, and so on.

At the same location as GARBO, you find two other oddly named browsing
tools that use the Google Web APIs:

- **GAPS:** *Google API Proximity Search,* uses the wildcard operator (*) to
  find results that have words within a specified proximity of one another.
  For example, you can search for words that are four words apart.

- **GAWSH:** *Google API Web Search by Host,* returns the Web hosts, or top-
  level URLs, in the results of a Google search. For example, a search for
  Harold Davis might return the specific home pages where my name
  appears (including www.bearhome.com and www.braintique.com).
  You can then individually expand the Web host to see all the pages
  on a particular site that include your search string, for example, www.
  bearhome.com, www.bearhome.com/harold_davis/, and so on.

Google Alert

Google Alert, www.googlealert.com/, is an alert service that tracks the Web
for topics you've specified and sends you updated results via daily e-mail.

As an individual user, you can use Google Alert without charge, although
Google Alert does market customized information alert services to institutional users.

Unaffiliated with Google, Google Alert is based upon a version of the Google
APIs (Google has made available to Google Alerts a high-traffic version of
the APIs that is not limited to 1,000 queries per day).

Mangle

Too much time on your hands? Want to imitate the random Web surfer that
is one of the theoretical underpinnings of the Google PageRank algorithm?
Try Mangle.

Mangle, www.mangle.ca/, uses the Google Web APIs to open a random Web page. The default random search chooses three words more or less out of thin air and opens the first Web page that results when the three words are combined as a Google query term.

You can customize various aspects of this randomness by changing the number of words, adding a specific word to the random terms, or by limiting the geographic search area.

My favorite feature — or, should I say, my favorite waste of time — is the random home page generator, which shows a different random home page each time. Boy, some of the families in these random home pages look geeky, as long as you're not talking about my family!

Mangle's worth a look because it shows you how much you can do with the Google APIs — although you may be inclined to use the technology to benefit your research rather than random surfing!

MetaLib

The MetaLib portal provided by Ex Libris is a research portal tool — or *meta-search engine* — primarily intended for reference librarians. (Chapter 10 has more information about meta-search engines.)

MetaLib lets users search a wide body of aggregated information in one fell swoop, including Google. Google access is provided under the covers using the Google Web APIs.

Most access to MetaLib is through an institutional subscription. Ex Libris does provide individual end-user access on an evaluation basis, but you need to be approved for access by Ex Libris.

You can find out more about MetaLib at www.exlibrisgroup.com/metalib. htm. You can start the process of gaining access to MetaLib at www.exlibris group.com/metalib_resources.htm.

I've included information about MetaLib even though it is intended for insti-tutional rather than individual access because it is a good example of a very serious research tool built using (in part) the Google APIs.

Speegle

Speegle, www.speegle.co.uk/, uses the Google APIs to play your choice of the Descriptions, Titles, and URLs of the results of your Google search.

You will, of course, need speakers or a headset on your computer for Speegle to work.

Although you can choose the gender of the voice that is used to read the Google results, you can't choose the accent: It is Scottish, Scottish, Scottish. I guess that's the prerogative of this Scottish software company, because they have done something so cool with Google.

Joking aside, this is a wonderful tool that gives Google search access to people who have visual difficulties with their computer screens. It wouldn't be possible without the Google APIs.

XooMLe

Dented Reality's XooMLe translates the SOAP-based Google APIs Web service to HTTP. This service provides a convenience for developers, as I explain in Chapter 15.

You can download a version of XooMLe to run on your development Web server, or invoke XooMLe directly on the Web (see Chapter 15 for details).

Learn more about XooMLe from the Dented Reality Web site, `www.dented reality.com.au/xoomle/`.

Part VI

Appendixes

"Do you remember which military Web site you downloaded your Bot software from?"

In this part...

Appendix A explains what is in the Google APIs software development kit (SDK).

Appendix B shows you how to use the Google APIs with Visual Basic .NET and Visual Studio. I show you a sample Visual Basic application in this appendix that searches for similar sites and displays links to these sites. You can use this application to understand what you need to do to create your own Visual Basic applications.

Appendix C tells you what you need to know to use the Google APIs with the Java class library included with the SDK. I show you a sample Java application in this appendix that returns the snippet of text associated with the first result of a search. You can use this application to understand what you need to do to create your own Java applications.

Appendix A

Using the SDK

● ●

*T*he Google APIs SDK (software development kit) provides information about the Google APIs and samples that use the APIs. If you are interested in building research applications with the Google APIs, you'll want to download and unzip the SDK.

This appendix tells what you find in the SDK.

Downloading and Unzipping the SDK

To download the SDK, just follow these simple steps:

1. **Open the URL in your browser.**

   The Download the Google APIs Developer's Kit page appears.

2. **Click to put a check mark in the box to indicate your agreement with the Google Web APIs license terms.**

   The license terms are also sometimes called the Google APIs Terms of Service, or TOS.

3. **Click the Download Now button.**

4. **When the File Download window opens, click the Save button.**

5. **Choose a location on your computer to save the Zip archive containing the SDK.**

After you download the Zip archive file to your computer, *unzip* — or expand — the archive file. Specify where on your computer you'd like to place the files contained in the archive file.

The easiest way to unzip a file on Windows is to use the WinZip utility. You can download WinZip from `www.winzip.com`. A free evaluation version of WinZip is available.

You don't need a Google developer key to download, unzip, and inspect the SDK. But you do need a key to use any of the sample applications that the SDK includes. For more information, see Chapter 14.

Understanding the SDK Contents

When you download, unzip, and save the contents of the SDK to your computer, the files are organized in a structure with a folder named `googleapi` at the highest level. The contents of the SDK are shown in Table A-1.

Table A-1	Contents of the SDK	
Folder	**Filename**	**What It Is**
`googleapi`	`APIs_Reference.html`	API reference document (also available on the Web)
`googleapi`	`googleapi.jar`	Executable Jar (Java) file that you can use to run the Java APIs demo
`googleapi`	`GoogleAPIDemo`	Java source code file
`googleapi`	`GoogleSearch.wsdl`	The Google APIs Web service WSDL file (see Chapter 15 for more information)
`googleapi`	`License.txt`	Google APIs TOS
`googleapi`	`Readme.txt`	Brief description of how to use the examples and a manifest of the contents of the SDK
`googleapi\dotnet`	`CSharp Example.exe`	Compiled C# sample application; requires .NET Framework

Folder	Filename	What It Is
googleapi\dotnet	VB Example.exe	Compiled Visual Basic sample application; requires .NET Framework
googleapi\ dotnet\CSharp	Various files	Source code and .NET project files for sample C# application (see Chapter 16 for more information)
googleapi\ dotnet\ VisualBasic	Various files	Source code and .NET project files for sample Visual Basic application (see Appendix B for more information and building Google APIs applications in Visual Basic .NET)
googleapi\javadoc	Various files	HTML documentation for the Java classes used to create the sample Java application
googleapi\ licenses	Various files	Text of licenses from the Apache Organization and Sun Microsystems covering some of the Java code used in the googleapi.jar file
googleapi\ soap-samples	Various files	Sample SOAP messages and responses in XML for invoking the GoogleSearch WSDL file

The most important parts of the SDK are the sample applications, which you can use as the starting place for your own applications.

The documentation portions of the SDK are sketchy (at best) — which may be why you'll find this book helpful if you'd like to build research applications based upon the Google Web APIs.

Table A-2 shows where to go in this book for more information about using the contents of the SDK (including the code samples).

Table A-2	Information in This Book about Using the SDK
You'd Like to Know More About . . .	**Where to Go . . .**
The specifics of the Google APIs	Chapter 13
Downloading a developer key	Chapter 14
Working with WSDL files	Chapter 15
Using the C# sample application	Chapter 16
Building C# Google APIs applications	Chapters 17 and 18
Using the Visual Basic sample, building VB Google API applications	Appendix B
Using the Java sample, building Java Google API applications	Appendix C

Appendix B

Building a Research Application with Visual Basic .NET

$\bullet$

You can easily create Windows and ASP.NET Web applications that use the Google APIs with Visual Basic .NET in Visual Studio. These steps are involved:

1. **Add a Web reference to the Google WSDL file (see Chapter 15 for information about WSDL files).**

    This action creates and adds a proxy class, which is used to call the Google APIs, to your project.

2. **Change the name of the proxy class to** `Google`.

    This step is not required, but changing the name of the class helps to keep your program simple and clear.

3. **In code, create an instance of the** `Google` **class.**

4. **Use one or more of the Web methods (Google APIs) associated with the** `Google` **class.**

5. **Do something with the return values from the Web methods (such as displaying a page of results).**

In this appendix I cover each of these points in detail.

Creating an application that uses the Google APIs in Visual Basic is exactly like creating one in C#, except that the syntax of the language used is a little different (after all, Visual Basic is a different language than C#). You can follow the general directions for creating applications with the Google APIs using C# in Chapter 16, and these mechanics work similarly with Visual Basic, although of course the language is different.

Adding a Web Reference

To add a Web reference to the Google APIs Web service to your Visual Basic project, follow these steps:

1. **Choose Add Web Reference from the Project menu.**

   The Add Web Reference window opens.

2. **In the URL text box, enter the Web address for the Google WSDL file,** `http://api.google.com/GoogleSearch.wsdl`.

3. **Click the Go button.**

   When the Google WSDL file is found on the Web, the Google Web service and its Web methods display, as shown in Figure B-1.

4. **Click Add Reference.**

   The Web reference is added to your project.

The three Web methods shown in Figure B-1, such as `doGoogleSearch`, are the three Google APIs that collectively make up the Google Web service. See Chapter 13 for more information about each of the three APIs.

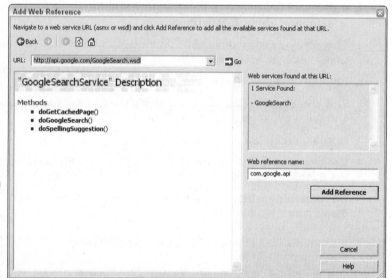

Figure B-1:
Adding a Web reference to the Google APIs.

Changing the Name of the Proxy Class

I recommend changing the default name given the Web service proxy class that is created when you add the reference to the Google Web service.

The default name for the proxy class is `api.google.com`, which is the location of the `GoogleSearch` WSDL file on the Web.

The reasons for changing this name are so that you can do the following:

- ✔ Write clearer code using a less complex name.
- ✔ Conform to the name used in Google's sample applications that are in the SDK (see Appendix A for more information about the contents of the SDK).

In the SDK sample applications, Google names the class `Google`. Simple and clear, right? So why not follow suit?

To change the default name for the Web reference:

1. **Open Solution Explorer by choosing View⇨Solution Explorer.**

   Solution Explorer opens.

2. **Expand Web References by clicking the plus icon (+) to the left of the Web Reference folder.**

   Keep expanding the folder until you see a listing for the Google Web service.

3. **Right-click the Google Web service folder.**

   Choose Properties from the context menu to open the Properties window.

4. **In the Properties window, change the Folder Name property from** `api.google.com` **to** `Google`.

   See Figure B-2.

In order to see the Google Web service in the Web References folder, you may need to click the Show All Files button, which is the second button from the left in the Solution Explorer toolbar shown in Figure B-2.

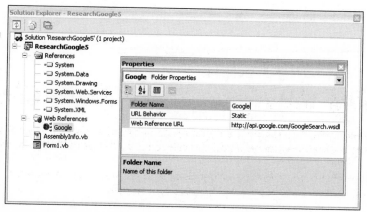

Figure B-2:
Use Solution Explorer and the Properties window to change the Web reference's name.

Creating an Instance of the Class

It's easy to create an instance of the proxy class that represents the Google Web service in code, like this:

```
Dim s As New Google.GoogleSearchService
```

To see this declaration and instantiation in context, have a look at Listing B-1.

Using the Web Methods (The APIs)

You need to use your Google developer key each time you call a Google Web method (the Google Web methods are the same thing as the Google APIs).

Downloading a Google developer key is pretty simple stuff. See Chapter 14 for more information about getting a Google developer key of your very own!

Before you start calling the Web methods in code, declare a string variable and assign your developer key to it:

```
Dim devKey As String = "xxxxxxxxxxxxxxxxxxxxxxxxxxxxx"
```

In your programs, you'll need to replace the blanks with your own developer key.

There are three Google Web methods:

- ✔ doGoogleSearch, used to search Google
- ✔ doGetCachedPage, used to retrieve a page from the Google cache (and/or information about the page)
- ✔ doSpellingSuggestions, which returns a Google spelling suggestion

Searching Google

As an example, suppose you want to create an application that searches for Web pages that are similar to a given page.

The user enters a URL into a TextBox named txtURL. The related keyword is then put in front of the text entered by the user and used for the search, like this:

```
Dim searchStr As String = "related:" & txtURL.Text
```

The `related:` operator is used in a Google search to find Web pages that are similar to a given Web page. See Chapter 5 for more information about how this and other search operators work in Google.

You can now declare a variable, `r`, to hold the search result, and use the instance of the Google proxy class to call the doGoogleSearch Web method:

```
Dim r As Google.GoogleSearchResult = _
    s.doGoogleSearch(devKey, searchStr, 0, 10, _
    False, "", False, "", "", "")
```

This code passes the doGoogleSearch Web method your developer key, the search string, the starting result number to return (0), and the number of results to return (10) as arguments. For information about the other arguments passed to the `doGoogleSearch` Web method, see Chapter 13.

In Visual Basic, the end of a line serves to mark the end of a statement. A special character sequence, space underscore (_) is used to indicate that a statement continues to the next line. When you put these two characters at the very end of the line (with nothing after them), the Visual Basic compiler treats the next line as a continuation of the current line.

Retrieving a page from the cache

You can let the user specify the page to retrieve from the Google cache in a TextBox named `txtCachePage`. To get the bytes that make up the page selected by the user, call the `doGetCachedPage` API with your developer key and the URL entered by the user:

```
Dim bytes() As System.Byte = _
    s.doGetCachedPage (devKey, txtCachePage.Text)
```

Getting a spelling suggestion

You can get a spelling suggestion from Google by using the `doSpelling Suggestion` API to pass it some text (along with your developer key, of course):

```
Dim suggestion As String = s.doSpellingSuggestion _
    (devKey, txtSpell.Text)
```

Displaying Results

How you display the results of a call to one of the Google Web methods depends on what information you need to display (and, of course, which Web method you're using). Here are some examples.

Showing search results

Earlier in this appendix, I show an example in which you can let a user search for similar sites by using the `related:` operator; you might want to display the results in a `LinkLabel` control. Adding the title of each resulting similar Web page to the `LinkLabel` control makes sense because you can associate the title with the actual URL of the Web page. When the user clicks the title, the similar Web page opens in the user's Web browser.

Figure B-3 shows the results of a search for similar pages to `www.google.com`. If the user clicks one of the titles shown in this figure, the corresponding Web page opens.

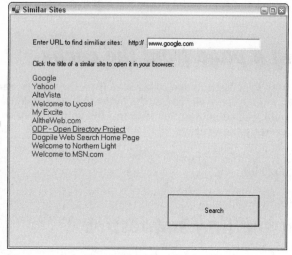

Figure B-3:
The addresses of the first ten similar sites are displayed.

To implement this functionality, you need to use the return results of the Google search, stored in the variable `r`.

You can use the `resultElements` array associated with `r` to assign each similar page title as part of the `LinkLabel` text and associate the URLs belonging to the similar pages with the title text:

```
Dim j As Integer = r.resultElements.Length - 1
Dim i As Integer
For i = 0 To j
    If (Not (r.resultElements(i) Is Nothing)) Then
        Dim labelLen As Integer = LinkLabel1.Text.Length
        LinkLabel1.Text += r.resultElements(i).title & _
            vbCrLf
        Dim titleLen As Integer = _
            r.resultElements(i).title.Length
        LinkLabel1.Links.Add(labelLen, titleLen, _
            r.resultElements(i).URL)
    End If
Next
```

The code that actually opens the URLs corresponding to the similar page title goes in the `LinkClicked` event of the `LinkLabel` control.

Listing B-1 shows the code for searching Google for similar sites, displaying the site titles, and opening the target URL when a similar site is selected by title.

Listing B-1:   Displaying and Providing Links for Similar Results

```
Dim devKey As String = "xxxxxxxxxxxxxxxxxxxxxxxxxxxxxxxx"

Private Sub btnSearch_Click(ByVal sender As System.Object, _
    ByVal e As System.EventArgs) Handles btnSearch.Click
    ' Create a Google Web service object
    Dim s As New Google.GoogleSearchService
    Try
        Me.Cursor = Cursors.WaitCursor
        Dim searchStr As String = "related:" & txtURL.Text
        Dim r As Google.GoogleSearchResult = _
            s.doGoogleSearch(devKey, searchStr, 0, 10, _
            False, "", False, "", "", "")
        Dim j As Integer = r.resultElements.Length - 1
        Dim i As Integer
        For i = 0 To j
            If (Not (r.resultElements(i) Is Nothing)) Then
                Dim labelLen As Integer = LinkLabel1.Text.Length
                LinkLabel1.Text += r.resultElements(i).title & _
                    vbCrLf
                Dim titleLen As Integer = _
                    r.resultElements(i).title.Length
                LinkLabel1.Links.Add(labelLen, titleLen, _
                    r.resultElements(i).URL)
            End If
        Next
    Catch ex As System.Web.Services.Protocols.SoapException
        MessageBox.Show(ex.Message, "SOAP Exception")
```

(continued)

Listing B-1 *(continued)*

```
    Catch excep As Exception
        MessageBox.Show(excep.Message, "Program Exception")
    Finally
        Me.Cursor = Cursors.Default
    End Try
End Sub

Private Sub LinkLabel1_LinkClicked(ByVal sender _
    As Object, ByVal e As _
    System.Windows.Forms.LinkLabelLinkClickedEventArgs) _
    Handles LinkLabel1.LinkClicked
    Dim target As String = CType(e.Link.LinkData, String)
    Diagnostics.Process.Start(target)
End Sub
```

Visit www.braintique.com/research/ to download the sample project. The source code enables you to search for similar sites and display the top-ten results as clickable links.

Showing the size of a page in the cache

If you use the doGetCachedPage API, the page that is retrieved from the cache is stored as an array of bytes. The length of this array is the size of the page in bytes. If the array is named bytes, you could display this information like this:

```
lblCacheResults.Text = CStr(bytes.Length)
```

Showing a spelling suggestion

The return value for a call to the doSpellingSuggestion API is a string. If the string is named suggestion, its value could be displayed like this:

```
If suggestion Is Nothing Then
    lblSpellResults.Text = "<no suggestion>"
Else
    lblSpellResults.Text = suggestion
End If
```

Appendix C

Using the Google APIs with Java

● ●

*T*he appendix tells you what you need to know to get started working with the Google APIs using the Java programming language and the tools provided in the SDK (software development kit). In this appendix, you'll find information about

- ✔ Where to go for more information about Java

- ✔ The tools you need to work with Java

- ✔ Running the test Java program that is part of the Google APIs SDK

- ✔ Building Java programs that use the Java library file included in the SDK

This book doesn't cover Java programming, the .NET Framework, or any other programming language. It assumes that you already have a background in programming.

Getting Your Java Ducks in a Row

As a first step in evaluating whether you want to write applications that use the Java programming language to access the Google APIs, you should consider the advantages and disadvantages of using Java as opposed to C# .NET or Visual Basic .NET.

Understanding issues with Java

There are differences of opinion about whether programmers should use Java instead of one of the .NET languages (such as C# or Visual Basic .NET) for creating applications that use Web services (such as the Google APIs).

Visual Studio .NET certainly provides tools that make using Web services (like the Google APIs) easier and more intuitive to use than using the same Web services from a Java program. However, Java programs can be run on almost any operating system that has the correct Java Virtual Machine running on it — you're not stuck with running programs that run only on Microsoft Windows.

Of course, coexistence seems to be the watchword of the day with large enterprise applications. Many shops use both Java and .NET, as appropriate for a given situation.

For more information about the Java versus .NET controversy, search Google for *Java versus .NET* and browse the interesting results you get for this search.

Java applications are run using a Java Virtual Machine (JVM). You should know that not all JVMs are identical; the way they work depends on the operating system and vendor. A notorious example is the Microsoft JVM, which is not identical to the Sun Microsystems JVM. In a much-publicized lawsuit, Sun (the creator of Java) forced Microsoft to stop distributing its version of the JVM.

From a programmer's perspective, the upshot is that you cannot be entirely sure which JVM users have installed on their systems, or even whether they have a JVM at all (some older versions of Windows XP were shipped without the JVM as a result of the Sun Microsystems lawsuit). This is a downside to distributing programs written in Java because you can't be entirely sure whether they will run on a given system unless the individual downloads and installs the version of the JVM that you used to write the Web service.

A good place to learn more about JVMs is `www.java-virtual-machine.net`.

Java compilers and editors

In order to compile programs written in Java, you need a Java compiler. You can download the current version (1.5.0) of the Java 2 Platform, Standard Edition (J2SE), which includes `javac.exe`, the Java compiler, from Sun Microsystems at `http://java.sun.com/j2se/1.5.0/download.html`.

Theoretically, you can create Java source code in a text editor (such as Windows Notepad or TextEdit on the Mac OS X). A little more realistically, to be productive creating Java applications you should have a decent programming environment. This environment should provide both a code editor with syntax help and a way to visually create user interfaces (as Visual Studio .NET does in the .NET world).

One possible programming environment you can use is the NetBeans IDE (Integrated Development Environment). You can download the NetBeans IDE from `www.netbeans.org`. You can also download NetBeans as part of a bundle from Sun Microsystems.

NetBeans has the (rather large in my mind) virtue of being completely free to use. It's got some decent tools for visual development. In fact, I used NetBeans to create the user interface for the application I outline in the section "Using the Google Library," later in this appendix.

Sun Microsystems also makes its rather more sophisticated development environment, Sun Java Studio, available in an evaluation edition. If you want to use Sun Java Studio beyond the evaluation period, you need to purchase a license.

You can download your evaluation copy of Sun Java Studio from `www.sun.com/software/sundev/jde/`.

You have a number of other appealing Java development environments to choose from. You might also want to consider:

✔ Eclipse, available for free download from `www.eclipse.org/`, an excellent development environment that can be used with a variety of languages, including Java.

✔ JBuilder, from Borland, a sophisticated cross-platform Java development environment. You can download an evaluation version of JBuilder from `www.borland.com/jbuilder/`.

✔ JCreator, which has some nice (read: easy to use) code editor features. You can download a freeware (or light) version of the product from `www.jcreator.com/download.htm`. (You can get a professional version of the product; however, the professional version requires a licensing fee after the 30-day evaluation period.)

If you're into one-stop shopping, you can download both JCreator and J2SE — this may be everything you need for Java development — from the JCreator site. However, if you're new to Java, I would recommend a visit to the Sun site. For example, if you would like to learn more about Java, a good place to start is the Sun Microsystems New to Java Center:

`http://java.sun.com/learning/new2java/index.html`

Running the Test

The Google APIs SDK provides a library file, `googleapi.jar`, which you can use to test, or demonstrate, that you can communicate with the Google APIs from your computer. (See Appendix A for more information about the contents of the SDK.)

You can also use the `googleapi.jar` file in your own applications that use the Google APIs. See the section, later in this appendix, "Using the Google Library," for more details.

The `googleapi.jar` file provides a method, `GoogleAPIDemo()`, especially made for the purpose of running tests. You call the method from the command line of your computer using the Java interpreter.

The `googlapi.jar` file contains a compiled version of the `GoogleAPIDemo` class, which is a demonstration provided by Google showing you how to use the Google API in a Java program.

To run the test, you need to know where `googleapi.jar` is located. This depends upon where you unzipped the SDK files. A likely location is `C:\googleapi`.

To run the test in Windows, follow these steps:

1. **Open a Command Prompt window.**

   The Command Prompt window can be opened from the Windows Start menu in All Programs➪Accessories➪Command Prompt.

2. **Using the actual location of the `googleapi.jar` file, type in a command like this all on one line:**

   ```
   java -cp c:\googleapi\googleapi.jar
       com.google.soap.search.GoogleAPIDemo
   ```

3. **When you are finished entering the code, press the Enter key.**

   When you don't provide any command-line parameters beyond the class name, you get back a quick response showing the three possible usages for the test of the APIs, corresponding to the three individual APIs described in Chapter 13 (search Google, return a cached page, do a spell check):

   ```
   Usage: java com.google.soap.search.GoogleAPIDemo <client-
       key>
     (search <query> | cached <url> | spell <phrase>)
   ```

This output tells you how to submit an actual query to the `googleapi.jar` Java library. You have to be a little careful (and not only about not making typos when you enter your developer key); enter searches exactly in the order specified.

For example, to search for the phrase *ambidextrous armadillo,* you could enter the following at the command prompt (replacing xxxxxxxxxxx in the command with your own developer key):

```
java -cp c:\googleapi\googleapi.jar
   com.google.soap.search.GoogleAPIDemo xxxxxxxxxxx
   search "ambidextrous armadillo" | More
```

The | More I put at the end of the command displays results one page at a time.

To avoid going stark-raving mad entering commands (including your developer key) over and over again, you can copy text in and out of the Command Prompt window by clicking the title bar and choosing Edit⇨Copy or Edit⇨Paste from the context menu.

When a command such as the search for the keywords *ambidextrous armadillo* is entered and run against the Java library file, the results are displayed in the Command Prompt window, as shown in Figure C-1.

Figure C-1: The results of the search are shown in the Command Prompt window.

```
Command Prompt                                                    _ □ x
Parameters:
Client key = xxxxxxxxxxxxxxxxxxxxxxxxxx
Directive   = search
Args        = ambidextrous armadillo
Google Search Results:
=======================
{
TM = 0.606741
Q = "ambidextrous armadillo"
CT = ""
TT = ""
CATs =
   {
   <EMPTY>
   }
Start Index = 1
End   Index = 10
Estimated Total Results Number = 689
Document Filtering = true
Estimate Correct = false
Rs =
   {
   [
   URL   = "http://www.talesfromthevault.com/archives/poem34.html"
   Title = "Serial Poem 34 - A Tale from the Vault"
   Snippet = "<b>...</b> <b>Armadillo</b> Eighteen wheeler Armajello: - Saila, <3
/19/98) <b>Armadillo</b> gaskin and<br> mangold-wurzel Pie for Mel de Hyde. - Sa
ila, <3/30/98) <b>Ambidextrous</b> Monkeys spank <b>...</b> "
   Directory Category = (SE="", FUN="")
   Directory Title = ""
   Summary = ""
   Cached Size = "12k"
   Related information present = true
   Host Name = ""
   ],
```

To see the code that is used in the demonstration program to call the Google APIs, you can open the source code file `GoogleAPIDemo.java` in your Java editor (or any text editor). Looking at this code can help you figure out how to call the APIs in your own programs.

Now that you know that you can speak to the Google APIs using Java, it's time to create your own Google API application in Java.

Using the Google Library

The Java library file that is part of the SDK — `googleapi.jar` — provides code that *encapsulates* (makes it easier to call) the Google APIs in your own programs. To access this functionality, you have to import the library `com.google.soap.search.*` (this includes the classes used to work with the Google APIs) into your application.

An easy way to understand the syntax used to call the APIs using this library is to browse the documentation in the `javadoc` folder of the SDK. Start with `index.html`. Click the `GoogleSearch` class in the frame on the left side of the screen. The methods of the `GoogleSearch` class — for example, `doGetCachedPage` — are displayed in the frame on the right side.

Building a Java application in NetBeans

I use the NetBeans Integrated Development Environment (IDE) to create Java applications that use the `googleapi.jar` library file. But, of course, you can use any Java development environment you'd like (see the section "Java compilers and editors," earlier in this appendix, for details).

To access the classes that you can use to call the Java APIs with NetBeans, you need to add the `googleapi.jar` file to your project. After you add this file to your project, you can view the classes (and class methods) that the library file contains in the Filesystems window, as shown in Figure C-2.

The classes and methods in the `googleapi.jar` library don't correspond exactly to Google APIs themselves (see Chapter 13) as defined in the Google WSDL file or to the .NET versions of the APIs (see Chapter 16).

Unlike the .NET proxy class, which is generated directly from the Google WSDL file (see Chapter 15 for more information about WSDL files), the classes within the `googleapi.jar` file were created by Google programmers to make calling the APIs easier. The functionality is identical to the APIs as defined in the WSDL file — and as they appear to .NET applications — but the syntax and names of the methods are a little bit different.

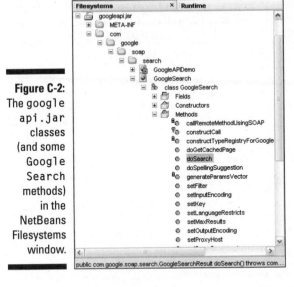

From a programmer's viewpoint, this means working with them is a little different than working with the Google APIs in .NET (see Chapters 16 through 18 for .NET examples).

To show you how to use the `googleapi.jar` library classes, I created an application that searches Google and displays the snippet associated with the first return result. Obviously, in your own research applications, you might want to perform more complex actions, but this application shows you the mechanics you need to use to get started.

Creating the visual interface

NetBeans provides facilities for creating a visual user interface using components supplied by the Java swing or AWT (Abstract Window Toolkit) libraries. Both libraries are part of the JFC (Java Foundation Classes). You can find more information about swing at

```
http://java.sun.com/products/jfc/index.jsp
```

and AWT at

```
http://java.sun.com/products/jdk/awt/
```

I added the swing components shown in Table C-1 to create the user interface for my application.

Table C-1	Components for the User Interface	
Component Type	*Name*	*What It Does*
JtextField	jTextDevKey	Google developer key
JtextField	jTextSearchTerm	Search term or phrase
Jbutton	jButtonSearch	Used to initiate Google search
JtextArea	jTextResult	Displays snippet

Using the NetBeans visual development environment, you can add support for a MouseClicked event, fired when the search button is clicked. The code that is executed when this event is processed will go in the jButtonSearchMouseClicked procedure.

The NetBeans development environment generates the code necessary to create an instance of these visual components, the form they are contained on, and to support the MouseClicked event. I omit the generated code in this section, but you can download the entire Java class that contains it from www.braintique.com/research/.

Coding the application

In code, first you need to import the classes from the googleapi.jar library file:

```
import com.google.soap.search.*;
```

The class that is used to create the form for the user interface is based on the swing JFrame class. Within the framework code that has been generated for this class, specifically, within the search button's MouseClicked event, you should add the code to perform the Google search.

This code needs to go within a try . . . catch block so that any error messages Google sends back can be captured and displayed. For example, suppose there's a problem with a search because the Google developer key has been incorrectly entered. The user of the application would certainly want to know why the search failed, so that the problem can be corrected. Here's the framework for the try . . . catch block:

```
try {
...
}
catch (GoogleSearchFault f) {
    jTextResult.setText("There has been a problem:   " + f);
}
```

The text of the `GoogleSearchFault f` argument passed to the catch block describes the error that occurred.

Within the try block, you need to create an instance of the GoogleSearch class:

```
GoogleSearch s = new GoogleSearch();
```

Set the developer key, the maximum number of results (in my case I set the max to one because I am only interested in the first snippet), and the search string:

```
s.setKey(jTextDevKey.getText());
s.setMaxResults(1);
s.setQueryString(jTextSearchTerm.getText());
```

I call the `doSearch` method of the `GoogleSearch` instance and store the result in a `GoogleSearchResult` variable:

```
GoogleSearchResult r = s.doSearch()
```

Using the `getSnippet` method of the first element in the `GetResultElements` array that is a member of the `GoogleSearchResult`, you then assign the text of the snippet to a `String` variable, `str`:

```
java.lang.String str = r.getResultElements()[0].getSnippet();
```

The snippets that Google returns tend to have nasty bits of HTML embedded in the text, such as `<b>` tags to mark the keywords that were found. You can easily get rid of these using Java's excellent string-handling capabilities (using the `replaceAll` method of the `String` class):

```
str = str.replaceAll ("<b>", "");
str = str.replaceAll ("</b>", "");
str = str.replaceAll ("<br>", "");
```

Finally, to display the cleaned-up snippet, enter the following code:

```
jTextResult.setText(str);
```

Listing C-1 shows the code for searching Google and returning the first snippet. This listing offers a pretty good idea of how to go about coding a Java application that calls the `googleapi.jar` Java classes to use the Google APIs.

In Listing C-1, I've omitted the generated code that NetBeans used to create the user interface for me. You can see the code, including the generated code omitted from the listing, by downloading the entire Java `formGoogleSearch` class from `www.braintique.com/research/`.

Listing C-1: Searching Google and Returning the First Snippet

```
import com.google.soap.search.*;
import javax.swing.JFrame;

public class formGoogleSearch extends JFrame {
    /** Creates new form formGoogleSearch */
    public formGoogleSearch() {
        initComponents();
    }
    // Generated form and component code omitted
    // ...

    private void jButtonSearchMouseClicked
        (java.awt.event.MouseEvent evt) {
        try {
            GoogleSearch s = new GoogleSearch();
            s.setKey(jTextDevKey.getText());
            s.setMaxResults(1);
            s.setQueryString(jTextSearchTerm.getText());
            GoogleSearchResult r = s.doSearch();
            java.lang.String str =
                r.getResultElements()[0].getSnippet();
            str = str.replaceAll ("<b>", "");
            str = str.replaceAll ("</b>", "");
            str = str.replaceAll ("<br>", "");
            jTextResult.setText(str);
        }
        catch (GoogleSearchFault f) {
            jTextResult.setText("There has been a problem:   "
                + f);
        }
    }

    /** Exit the Application */
    private void exitForm(java.awt.event.WindowEvent evt) {
        System.exit(0);
    }

    public static void main(java.lang.String[] args) {
        new formGoogleSearch().show();
    }
}
```

If you run this code to display the form, you must enter a Google developer key and a search term, and then click Search. The first snippet displays in the results box, as shown in Figure C-3.

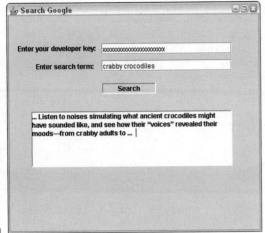

Figure C-3:
This Google
APIs Java
application
displays the
snippet
associated
with the
first search
result.

You can run the class containing the code to search Google from within the
NetBeans IDE by selecting Execute from the Build menu.

Moving on

As the example in this chapter demonstrates, you can use the Google APIs by
working with the classes in the `googleapi.jar` library file (supplied by Google
as part of the SDK).

As with any application that uses the Google APIs, the key issue is the query
string you use with your `GoogleSearch` class instance. (See Chapters 4 and 5
for information about constructing sophisticated query strings.)

So go to town, and use the power of Java to create great Google API research
applications that

✔ Perform customized searches.

✔ Remember and compare search results.

✔ Track changing results over time.

✔ Display search results in unusual and useful ways.

Index

• D •

• G •

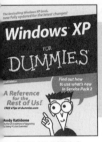

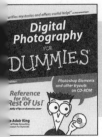

SPORTS, FITNESS, PARENTING, RELIGION & SPIRITUALITY

0-7645-5146-9

0-7645-5418-2

Also available:
- Adoption For Dummies
  0-7645-5488-3
- Basketball For Dummies
  0-7645-5248-1
- The Bible For Dummies
  0-7645-5296-1
- Buddhism For Dummies
  0-7645-5359-3
- Catholicism For Dummies
  0-7645-5391-7
- Hockey For Dummies
  0-7645-5228-7

- Judaism For Dummies
  0-7645-5299-6
- Martial Arts For Dummies
  0-7645-5358-5
- Pilates For Dummies
  0-7645-5397-6
- Religion For Dummies
  0-7645-5264-3
- Teaching Kids to Read For Dummies
  0-7645-4043-2
- Weight Training For Dummies
  0-7645-5168-X
- Yoga For Dummies
  0-7645-5117-5

TRAVEL

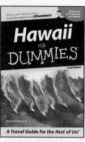

0-7645-5438-7

0-7645-5453-0

Also available:
- Alaska For Dummies
  0-7645-1761-9
- Arizona For Dummies
  0-7645-6938-4
- Cancún and the Yucatán For Dummies
  0-7645-2437-2
- Cruise Vacations For Dummies
  0-7645-6941-4
- Europe For Dummies
  0-7645-5456-5
- Ireland For Dummies
  0-7645-5455-7

- Las Vegas For Dummies
  0-7645-5448-4
- London For Dummies
  0-7645-4277-X
- New York City For Dummies
  0-7645-6945-7
- Paris For Dummies
  0-7645-5494-8
- RV Vacations For Dummies
  0-7645-5443-3
- Walt Disney World & Orlando For Dummi
  0-7645-6943-0

GRAPHICS, DESIGN & WEB DEVELOPMENT

0-7645-4345-8

0-7645-5589-8

Also available:
- Adobe Acrobat 6 PDF For Dummies
  0-7645-3760-1
- Building a Web Site For Dummies
  0-7645-7144-3
- Dreamweaver MX 2004 For Dummies
  0-7645-4342-3
- FrontPage 2003 For Dummies
  0-7645-3882-9
- HTML 4 For Dummies
  0-7645-1995-6
- Illustrator cs For Dummies
  0-7645-4084-X

- Macromedia Flash MX 2004 For Dumm
  0-7645-4358-X
- Photoshop 7 All-in-One Desk
  Reference For Dummies
  0-7645-1667-1
- Photoshop cs Timesaving Technique
  For Dummies
  0-7645-6782-9
- PHP 5 For Dummies
  0-7645-4166-8
- PowerPoint 2003 For Dummies
  0-7645-3908-6
- QuarkXPress 6 For Dummies
  0-7645-2593-X

NETWORKING, SECURITY, PROGRAMMING & DATABASES

0-7645-6852-3

0-7645-5784-X

Also available:
- A+ Certification For Dummies
  0-7645-4187-0
- Access 2003 All-in-One Desk
  Reference For Dummies
  0-7645-3988-4
- Beginning Programming For Dummies
  0-7645-4997-9
- C For Dummies
  0-7645-7068-4
- Firewalls For Dummies
  0-7645-4048-3
- Home Networking For Dummies
  0-7645-42796

- Network Security For Dummies
  0-7645-1679-5
- Networking For Dummies
  0-7645-1677-9
- TCP/IP For Dummies
  0-7645-1760-0
- VBA For Dummies
  0-7645-3989-2
- Wireless All In-One Desk Reference
  For Dummies
  0-7645-7496-5
- Wireless Home Networking For Dumm
  0-7645-3910-8